THE GERMAN REVOLUTIONS

CLASSIC EUROPEAN HISTORIANS

A SERIES EDITED BY LEONARD KRIEGER

Friedrich Engels

THE GERMAN
REVOLUTIONS

The Peasant War in Germany

and

Germany: Revolution and Counter-Revolution

Edited and with an Introduction
by Leonard Krieger

Phoenix Books

THE UNIVERSITY OF CHICAGO PRESS

CHICAGO & LONDON

THE UNIVERSITY OF CHICAGO PRESS

CHICAGO & LONDON

The University of Toronto Press, Toronto 5, Canada

© *1967 by The University of Chicago*
All rights reserved
Published 1967

First Phoenix Edition 1967

Printed in the United States of America

Series Editor's Preface

THIS volume is an entry in the University of Chicago Press series, "Classic European Historians." The series is designed to make readily available to American and English readers those works which have contributed markedly to our historical knowledge of the European continent and to the historical sense by which we know it. The reprinting of such works, then, is in the service of both history and historiography, for it should recall a decisive stage in both our understanding of definite historical eras and the development of the conceptual tools through which we understand all historical eras.

The canonization of a classic implies the sanctity of its text. This series consists, accordingly, in reprints rather than re-editions and is governed by the policy of cleaving as closely to the original as the requirements of English translation and a one-volume format permit. But the immortalization of literature is also itself a process, involving acknowledgment by men of varying persuasions and separate generations. Thus a classic, by definition, includes both an original work and that work's own history. This history in turn requires both the reconstruction of the author's meaning and the changes which this meaning has undergone as it has been socialized through human space and time. The history of the work in this sense is the business of the introduction which cradles each reprint in the series. In it a contemporary historian who combines an interest in historiography with a specialty in the field of the classic analyzes the author's approach to history, identifies the original contribution of the work toward history in general and its field of history in particular, and assesses its proportions of validity and anachronism for our own practice and knowledge of history.

The present volume brings together two classics of nineteenth-century Marxist historiography. That the economic interpretation of history, in the systematic form that Marx and Engels gave it, has been and continues to be a powerful force in modern attitudes toward history is patent. Not only has it entered prominently into the expansion of the scope of Western history from its traditional religious and political preoccupations, but it has also functioned as the conduit for the infusion of a Western-style historical sense into non-Western cultures. But if the substance and the extent of Marx's and Engels' contribution to history are unequivocal, the forms of it are ambiguous. Actually, it consists of three different forms—a philosophy of history, a sketch of general history, and some specific histories of definite movements in France and Germany, to list them in descending order of familiarity. This volume addresses itself to the last of these genres—to definite Marxist history as such.

The histories written by Marx and Engels pose special problems for the historiographer because they ambiguously commingle what is separate in other historians. Philosophers of history who have worked their principles out in general sketches of history are legion, but philosophers of history who, like Marx and Engels, also worked their principles out in the particularized arena of specific history are very few. Conversely, the historians who require for their understanding anything more articulate and systematic than a laconic and loosely (if at all) associated set of discrete assumptions are equally few. If, then, we take Marx and Engels simply as practitioners of history rather than as philosophers of history or even as patterners of universal history, we are confronted with a singular problem: the analysis of their historical writing in terms of presuppositions that were themselves a systematic theory designed for quite another level of history.

The illumination of the original Marxist approach to history, then, requires a discussion of the dual relationship between their history and their philosophy of history which made them at once separate and mutually dependent. This discussion furnishes one of the two main themes for the introduction that follows. The other theme, obviously related to the first, is the discrimination of Engels from Marx, with the purpose of showing how the former's distinctive attitude toward history and his own share in their joint philosophy of history make him the more appropriate subject for the origins of Marxist historiography.

Engels is the characteristic Marxist historian, not only because the troubled relationship between history and the philosophy of history that is implicit in Marxism became explicit in him, but also because he was the mediator between Marx and Marxism. The two works reproduced here in full are, in turn, the characteristic Engelsian histories. *The Peasant War in Germany*—the history of the Peasants' Revolt of 1525-26—is reprinted in the English translation of Engels' *Der deutsche Bauernkrieg* (1850) made by Moissaye J. Olgin for International Publishers in 1926, while *Germany: Revolution and Counter-Revolution* is the original English-language history of the Revolution of 1848 written by Engels for the *New York Tribune* in 1851-52. Together they represent *the* history of social revolution in Germany, for, as the Introduction shows, Engels conceived them to be continuous sections of this single theme, and they remain historiographically vital as complementary chapters in it.

The nonpartisan acclaim which *Germany: Revolution and Counter-Revolution* in particular has received may serve to remind us that of all the fields to which Marxists have applied themselves, Marxist history remains the most communicable and the most respectable to non-Marxists. By refreshing ourselves at the sources of Marxist historiography we equip ourselves for carrying on the dialogue so needed in our own time.

LEONARD KRIEGER

Editor's Introduction

THE team of Marx and Engels is indissolubly linked with the associated concepts of historical materialism and the economic interpretation of history. The first is the philosophical concept which defines ultimate reality as the incessant practical activity through which men engage nature to produce the changing material conditions of their lives. The second is the universal historical concept which explains the overt forms of man's movement through time as functions of the social relations produced by the successive stages of this basic material production. Together, these concepts constitute the most influential philosophy of history ever devised. So overpowering has the theory been that the excursions undertaken by Marx and Engels into history proper have often enough seemed more like the verifications of a scientific hypothesis than like authentic inquiries into the past. No less an authority than Engels himself characterized one of Marx's histories as an occasion for him to have "put his law to the test on these historical events," and he indicated that the limited sequences which were the subjects of their historical works represented an intermediate stage in the theoretical continuum between the abstract statement of universal law and the interpretation of the discrete political events of the present in terms of this law.[1]

From this point of view, the historical works of Marx and Engels have been immortalized as models for the application of Marxist categories to any concrete history whatsoever. They

---

[1] See Engels' introductions to Marx's *The Class Struggles in France 1848–1850* (1895 edition) and *The Eighteenth Brumaire of Louis Bonaparte,* in Karl Marx, *Selected Works* (London, 1942), II, 169–70, 315.

remain models in this way, moreover, to believers and non-believers alike. To the devout, they form part of the canon and provide literal lessons for the interpretation of history in terms of class struggles. To the uncommitted historian, their relevance has been archetypal, providing case studies in the use of economic and social structure as the secular rational unity behind the apparently fortuitous series of heterogeneous intellectual and political events.

But this is only one side of the position that the historical works of Marx and Engels hold in the history of history. Over and above the philosophy of history which they exemplify, they remain classics in their own right, landmarks in the interpretation of the specific aspects of the European past that is their subject matter. Without exception, their full-scale historical writings dealt with revolutions.[2] This focus indicates that Marx and Engels wrote history not simply to confirm their principles but to explain particular historical situations in which they were vitally interested. For to them, revolutions were the occasions for men to act directly upon the political and theoretical superstructure of their lives in the light of their economic basis, and they were the only occasions therefore on which political events and ideas were, both individually and in sequence, fundamentally meaningful. More, this historical course of revolutionary events and ideas had an independent rather than a derived meaning: the knowledge of its specific history was necessary to pinpoint the precise point of development reached by an economic process which yielded only general structural relations to direct analysis. Only when the empirical determination of what happened in particular was meshed

---

[2] Marx's *The Class Struggles in France, 1848–1850* (1850), *The Eighteenth Brumaire of Louis Bonaparte* (1852), *The Civil War in France* (1870–71)—all reprinted in full English translation in *ibid.*, II, 169–426, 446–527—and Engels' *Germany: Revolution and Counter-Revolution* (1851–52)—fully reprinted below—were contemporary histories of revolutions. Engels' *The Peasant War in Germany* (1850)—reprinted below in full English translation—and *The Origin of the Family, Private Property, and the State* (1884) (English translation; Chicago, 1902) dealt with social revolutions of the remote past.

with the rational analysis of the general situation in which it happened was the Marxist explanation complete. And so it was that Marx and Engels became historians as well as philosophers of history.[3]

Undoubtedly it was the integration of history and the philosophy of history which Marx and Engels achieved by logicizing history and historicizing philosophy that is their ecumenical contribution to historiography. So tight does the integration appear that it is often hard to find where the one leaves off and the other begins. Thus the two fullest statements of the philosophy of history, in the *German Ideology* of 1846 and the *Communist Manifesto* of 1848, have sketches of universal history built into them, while the empirical histories of particular revolutions refer to the philosophy of history continuously as their assumption and sporadically as their explicit explanation. The pattern of authorship, moreover, seems to offer external confirmation of the interpenetration, since Marx and Engels composed the standard works on their philosophy of history jointly and since both followed with specific histories in apparent application of it.

But if the history written by Marx and Engels seemed continuous with their philosophy of history by virtue of the homologous combinations of philosophy and history that they put into both kinds of works, this same history becomes discontinuous from the same philosophy of history by virtue of the problem which Marx and Engels confronted in combining philosophy and history. The intensity and persistence of this problem, which may be identified in Marx and Engels with the problem of relating the general and the particular levels of reality, not only infected both their philosophy of history and their history but, what is more important in this context, infected them in different ways. In their philosophy of history, Marx and Engels sought to relate general and particular reality from the point

---

[3] For a discussion of this relationship between history and the philosophy of history in Marx and Engels, considered as *joint* authors, see Leonard Krieger, "Marx and Engels as Historians, "in *Journal of the History of Ideas,* XIV (1953), 381–403.

of view of general reality; in their history, they sought to relate general and particular reality from the point of view of particular reality. When so considered, the movement from the subsumption of historical facts under dialectical law in the philosophy of history to the inference of social evolution from political and ideological events in the histories is not so much a specific application of a closed theory as a succession of equivalent attempts to solve an open problem. Even the external evidence that seems to confirm the general impression that Marx and Engels dovetailed their philosophy of history and their history turns out, upon closer inspection, to belie the appearance of indiscriminate authorship and to imply a differentiation in the respective approaches to the two fields. First, Marx and Engels were the joint authors of the works that developed their philosophy of history, but they wrote their histories separately. Second, Marx was predominant in the philosophical partnership that produced the first category of works, while Engels' own writings were the more genuinely empirical of the histories that composed the second.

Thus, whether we start from the general impressions of the works or from the external evidence of their authorship, the relationship of history and the philosophy of history in Marx and Engels points in two contrary directions: it indicates both their conjunction and their disjunction. But this same evidence also yields two inferences that open a path to the investigation of the problem. It shows, first, that the problematical relationship between the two fields may be profitably studied in terms of the intellectual relationship between the two men. It shows, second, that if the relationship between the fields is to be investigated from the side of history, it is Engels rather than Marx who should be our protagonist. Hence it is Engels' history that we reprint here, and in the following essay on its theoretical assumptions we shall attempt the delicate surgery of detaching Engels from Marx.

Friedrich Engels enjoys a unique place among the immortals of our culture. It is a place fixed by two different functions, whose juncture is inherently problematical and yet has been essential to Engels' apotheosis since neither was sufficiently creative by itself to account for it. Engels was both Karl Marx's collaborator in the formulation of the original system that bears their joint imprint and, as executor of that system, the founder of Marx*ism* as a doctrine stemming from the original system but assuming forms independent of it. When considered from the point of view of the original achievement—as it usually is—this anomaly is resolved pejoratively: since Engels is generally acknowledged to have been Marx's first disciple and himself freely admitted that the basic idea of the system "belongs solely and exclusively to Marx," the ancillary character of his early collaboration joins the derivative character of his later adaptations to bestow upon him a borrowed glory. But when considered from the point of view of the system's longevity, then Engels' two roles acquire a positive connection: he equipped the original system with the capacity for adaptation which permitted its development from theory into doctrine—that is, from Marx into Marxism. From this angle, Engels can be seen as having inserted at one end the thread that he ultimately drew out at the other.

What was the nature of this thread? What, in other words, did Engels bring into the joint philosophy of history that made it usable for his own brand of history?

Behind the most harmonious intellectual duet in the history of Western culture lay, obviously, a relevant set of fundamental attributes which Marx and Engels shared. The common features of their environment, training, and orientation were direct influences upon the initial convergence and ultimate accord of their ideas. By origin and early rearing, both were middle class, urban, non-Catholic, and Rhenish—circumstances which exposed them to the legally most advanced status and the socially most advanced movements in German life, to an appreciation of political power in the form of Prussian sovereignty, and to the resentments of a minority position vis-à-vis both province and state. Members of the same post-1815 generation, both grew to young manhood during the agitated years that followed on the revolutionary movement of 1830, and ran the usual gamut of the avant-garde from the defiant composition of bad poetry to the definitive appropriation of the radical form of the Hegelian heritage, with its demand for the systematic renovation of the world. Both grew up to be activist by disposition, communist by conviction, and revolutionary by policy. They even began with parallel filial rebellions of a kind that would be later stereotyped by Freud, although with Marx and Engels it seems to have been rather the effect than the cause of their alienation from respectable society.

But harmony is not unison; the importance of the qualities that Marx and Engels did share should not obscure either the existence or the intellectual effect of those they did not. The differences seemed indeed comparatively personal and superficial, and in the context of a basic concord they attracted rather than repelled. But this very attraction indicates the relationship of opposites which these differences could attain within their limited sphere. However superficial in origin, moreover, at least Engels' personal idiosyncrasies colored his understanding of the joint Marxist principles and infected his style of applying them to history.

Taken separately, the distinctive features in Engels' background, disposition, and interests seem inessential, but there was a consistency about them that made their cumulative impact highly relevant to his thought. Where Marx came from the liberal administrative city of Trier, Engels came from the more obscure and conservative industrial town of Barmen. Where Marx grew up in the free-wheeling atmosphere of the liberal professions and Enlightment rationalism, Engels grew up in a household dominated by the narrow values of the family enterprise and pietistic Lutheranism—environments which may well have contributed to Marx's taste for abstract ideas and indifference to religion and to Engels' conversion of these sentiments. Where Marx acquired his philosophical tools through six years of university study, emerging with a doctorate and the ambition to teach philosophy, Engels never went past secondary school and completed his self-education in direct communication with

the vital groups of whatever community his business appren-
ticeship, his military service, and his managerial career brought
him to. Where Marx tried his fancy on vague romantic poetiz-
ing, dedicated to love and disembodied ideals, Engels tried his
on pseudo-epics celebrating legendary national—and particularly the German—pasts. Where Marx came to Young Hegelian
politics through Hegelian philosophy, Engels came to Hegelian
philosophy through liberal politics in an ever widening circle
that carried him through the German Student Union movement
and the littérateurs of Young Germany before entering the
Hegelian orbit.[4] Where Marx found the circumstantial basis of
his conversion to socialism in the vicarious experience of French
revolutionary politics, Engels found his in the firsthand observation of the English working class. And when, in the spring of
1849, the revolution that was to trigger their writing of
history was in its death throes, Marx and Engels wound up
their joint career as active revolutionaries with a characteristic
parting: Marx went to Paris to agitate politically for the resurrection of the social revolution in France, and Engels went to
the Palatinate to participate in the last-ditch military insurrection for a democratic and united Germany.

The temperaments of the two friends varied directly with
these experiences that gave them their definitive form. Where
Marx was intense and sardonic, Engels was expansive and
witty. Where Marx was arrogant and mistrusted even within the
narrow circle of like-minded socialist intellectuals, Engels was
flexible and at ease even in the broad circle of Manchester
society. Where Engels acknowledged Marx to be the deeper,
Marx acknowledged Engels to be the quicker.

Their variant backgrounds and dispositions found intellectual
expression in the different channels they chose for the articula-
tion of their common faith after it had taken definite form with
the close of the revolutionary era in 1850. Where Marx focused
ever more sharply on the twin activities of scholarly economic

---

[4] For Engels' youthful development, see Auguste Cornu, *Karl Marx et
Friedrich Engels: leur vie et leur oeuvre* (Paris, 1955), I, 123–31, and
Horst Ullrich, *Der junge Engels* (Berlin, 1961), *passim.*

analysis and partisan political organization, Engels spread his
beliefs to cover a whole complex of academic and cultural
interests which his practical and restless mind found relevant to
the continuing validity of historical materialism or to the successful issue of the future communist revolution. He cultivated
the natural and life sciences, anthropology, military science,
languages of all shapes and kinds—ancient and modern, Germanic, Slavic, and Oriental—and history. Marx himself admired
the universality and pliability of Engels' knowledge, a judgment
which confirms the impression yielded by the list of his accom-
plishments. And yet both the judgment and the impression are
seriously misleading if they are not immediately qualified. For
Engels' was the more universal mind only if knowledge is taken
in the sense of information rather than understanding. It was
not only that his cosmopolitan collection of facts and tools for
getting facts was accompanied by a parochial preference for
things German, but more fundamentally that this preference
testified to the limited range of the universal principles he used
to organize the collection. Marx, whose universality was more
authentic, was perhaps dimly aware of this lack in his friend
when he complained that Engels spread himself thinly among
so many objects "for his own enjoyment." [5] In truth, the distinctive factors in Engels' experience and character illuminate the
peculiar distribution of his interests: his intimate affirmation of
life in all its concrete manifestations, his passion for all possible
facts, his appreciation of the infinite multiplicity of forms that
must be practically managed, all led him through and beyond
the inverted Hegelianism that Marx had provided to account
for a more disciplined vision of actuality. For Engels, historical
materialism replaced his original familial Pietism as his absolute
principle because it was designed to come more directly to
grips with the richly diversified existence which he would
appropriate, but in his hands the forms of existence that historical materialism did rationalize supplied an emotional

[5] Quoted in Gustav Mayer, *Friedrich Engels: eine Biographie* (The
Hague, 1934), II, 528.

certainty that supported his confident excursions among the forms that it could not rationalize.

The role of historical materialism in Engels offers the clue to the role of Engels in historical materialism. His role in the Marxist philosophy of history thus comprised two related functions: first, he intentionally extended and adapted it to make it account for as many real facts as possible; second, he unintentionally claimed that it accounted for particular circumstances for which it could not logically account. The combination of these two functions made Engels' work a model for the subsequent indiscriminate applications of Marxism as both a revised and an unrevised doctrine. The overt forms of Engels' relationship to the system manifest the first function, his own version of historical materialism the second.

The tangible contributions of Engels to the formation of historical materialism and to the elaboration of the theory after it had taken its definite form are of a piece: they emphasize the empirical and pragmatic bearing of the doctrine. The appearances in this respect—that is, the bare record of publications —are deceptive, for they seem to indicate a development of Engels from economics to philosophy that balances Marx's development from philosophy to economics. Engels' share in the principles of historical materialism that Marx and he worked out together during 1845 and 1846 was indeed to give to materialism a concrete economic substance. He brought to the partnership both the socialist critique of classical economic doctrine in terms of capitalistic realities that he had already published in article form during 1844 and the intimate acquaintance with the proletariat under conditions of industrial revolution that he had written up as *The Condition of the Working Class in England*.[6] But the shift in the field of Engels'

---

[6] Engels' "Outlines of a Critique of Political Economy" has been recently republished as an appendix in Dirk J. Struik (ed.), *The Economic and Philosophic Manuscripts of 1844 by Karl Marx* (English translation by Martin Milligan; New York, 1964). See too, W. O. Henderson and W. H. Chaloner (eds. and English translators), *Engels' The Condition of the Working Class in England* (Oxford, 1958), for best translation of the work from the original German edition of 1845.

main publications from economics to philosophy after 1850 did *not* bring, as one might expect it would, a shift from the concrete to the abstract. It is a common error, in the interpretation of Marxism, to identify concretion exclusively with economics and philosophy exclusively with ideology. In Engels' case the same emphasis on the practical and the actual that found an economic expression in his early career was applied to philosophical issues in his later years. This consistency is indicated both by the context of his other intellectual interests in these same years as they appear in his correspondence and his subordinate publications and by the general tendency of the major philosophical works themselves.

On the first count, the massive weight of unspectacular evidence demonstrates his overriding concern with extending Marxism in an empirical direction and adducing its relevance to all kinds of facts and conditions. The historical and anthropological studies that came to the surface in his *Origin of the Family, Private Property, and the State* of 1884, and the numerous prefaces that elaborated Marxism in the light of the changing social, political, and technological conditions of the latter nineteenth century are the best-known cases in point.

On the second count, the graduation of Engels' two late philosophical works into permanent monuments of Marxist philosophy has obscured the practical orientation that sponsored them. *Herr Eugen Dühring's Revolution in Science* of 1878 (better known as *Anti-Dühring* and best known in its abridged form as *Socialism: Utopian and Scientific*) and *Ludwig Feuerbach and the Outcome of Classical German Philosophy* of 1888 share three attributes that reveal a characteristically empirical orientation within the philosophical field they inhabit. First, they were, in their origins, occasional essays, designed like so many of Engels' social and political comments to apply Marxism to the newer circumstances of his day: only in this case the circumstances were the intellectual ones of a fashionable scientific materialism and an equally modish neo-Kantian idealism. Indeed, each volume was a re-edition in book form of what had originally been published in journals as extended review articles. Second, the whole point of Engels' philosophical analysis was to demonstrate the replacement of philosophy by the sciences. Third, the single tendency which runs through Engels' conception of nature—the central theme common to both works—is the emphasis upon its relative, particular, and transitory character, a character that he demonstrated by using Darwin and cognate recent developments in the sciences to historicize nature. Thus Engels extended Marxism into a philosophy of science by elevating the empirical and the historical over the lawful and the logical elements in the dialectic that he found common to both.

Obviously, the empirical emphasis through which Engels exalted science over philosophy and the historical emphasis through which he exalted the developmental over the absolute laws of nature produced a version of the Marxist philosophy of history that was more appropriate to an independent historical discipline than was the original. But Engels paid a price for this adaptation, for it meant that what in Marx was a problem of the relationship between a logical philosophy of history and an empirical history was carried by Engels into the very heart of the philosophy of history itself. Engels' appreciation of the empirical historical element in Marxism was so strong that it bore him, even in theory, beyond the point at which the Marxist logic could actively engage it. The gap which was thereby opened in his philosophy of history became manifest in Engels' growing tendency to think of philosophy of history in terms of the relations between nature and history once natural science replaced philosophy as the primary locus of a unified reality. However common he conceived the empirical foundations of natural and historical knowledge to be, Engels' own thought reveals that even he could not succeed in making the unity of nature the model for a unity in history. He returned to the subject time and again in his later philosophical works and his correspondence, where his simultaneous insistence on the necessity of a lawful explanation of all the facts and inability to see how a historical version of natural laws could explain all the facts testified dramatically to the problem that kept gnawing at him.

His aim was to make nature and history mutually convertible, but he foundered upon his recognition of a distinctive recalcitrant quality in human history. He had little difficulty in borrowing the movement from history which gave him his dialectical view of nature, but he implicitly confessed to a large difficulty in borrowing a lawfulness from nature which he now needed to give him a unified view of history. Where Marx grounded the unity of history in an overt philosophical logic appropriate to human activity, Engels had resort to a covert natural analogy antithetical to human activity. The covert quality is a matter not of our interpretation but of Engels' admission: although the interplay of "individual actions in the domain of history produces a state of affairs entirely analogous to that in the realm of unconscious nature," "the general laws of motion" which govern both realms are, in history alone, always "inner, hidden laws" which must be "discovered." [7] This acknowledgement of the gap between the event and the law which requires the latter to be "hidden" reveals the two basic and unreconciled factors in Engels' philosophy of history: his appreciation of the unique quality of the individual human act and his concomitant requirement of a unity to which it must somehow be referred. Hence the bizarre mixture of categories whereby individual acts were at once purposeful and accidental while the social results of those acts were at once blind and lawful. Both levels of human activity are "important . . . to historical investigation," and it is the function of historical law to connect them, if it is to hold sway, as it should, "both in history as a whole and at particular periods and in particular lands." [8]

There thus opened, in Engels, a gulf between nature and human history, and he could connect them only by appeal to the dialectical logic which he thought common to the under-

---

[7] Engels, *Ludwig Feuerbach and the Outcome of Classical German Philosophy*, in Marx, *Selected Works*, I, 457.

[8] *Ibid.*, I, 457, 459.

standing of both realms. But the link was ambiguous, for the dialectic was his only permitted remnant of philosophy, which he had derogated in general and which he subordinated even in this licit particular to the divergent facts of the respective realms. These fundamental terms of Engels' philosophy of history—nature, history, dialectic—set up the conflicting tendencies toward polarity and synthesis which is its main problem. For the way in which he worked out the problem we must turn to his philosophy of history itself.

Engels always held that the economic interpretation of history, devised jointly by Marx and himself, did provide a valid synthesis of the basic factors in human history. As he formulated it in terms of these basic factors, at each stage of history the mode of economic production established fundamental general conditions which acted as common "driving forces" upon the various "forms" of individual motivation to produce common historical effects, and the rationale of this process was historical law.[9] But this formula afforded an abstract solution only, and it tended, like the other expressions of Engels' philosophy of history, to decompose whenever he elaborated upon it. Under Engels' treatment, the economic interpretation broke down in two different ways.

First, Engels' thinking suffered, as Marx's did not, from the problem of infinite regress, for his duality between the logical necessity of general truth and the invincible autonomy of individual truth was repeated within the realm of general truth itself. The realm of general truth is the realm of "the economic movement" which "amid all the endless host of accidents (i.e., of things and events . . .) finally asserts itself as necessary" by producing the historical "driving forces" common to the whole society, but this economic movement itself requires a massive kind of empirical historical study before it can play its heuristic role: [10]

All history must be studied afresh, the conditions of existence of the different formations of society must be individually ex-

---

[9] *Ibid.*, I, 458–59.
[10] Engels to Joseph Bloch, September 21, 1890, in *ibid.*, I, 381.

amined before the attempt is made to deduce from them the political, civil-legal, aesthetic, philosophic, religious, etc., notions corresponding to them. Only a little has been done here up to now because only a few people have got down to it seriously. In this field we can utilize masses of help.[11]

Indeed, Engels even felt that he had to excuse Marx for preferring the logical over the historical method in the realm of economic analysis, and he explicitly applied to economics, ostensibly "the key to the understanding of the whole history of society," the same ambiguous relationship between contingent and necessary truths that inhabited his notion of history as such:

> The logical method of treatment . . . is nothing else than the historical method; only divested of its historical form and disturbing fortuities. The chain of thought must begin with the same thing with which this history begins and its further course will be nothing else than the mirror-image of the historical course in abstract and theoretically consistent form. . . .[12]

The two methods were presumably linked by the dialectic, which was designed precisely to derive unity from heterogeneous individualities, but this simply meant that economics, far from being the key to any solution, became simply part of the wider problem that Engels had with the relating of the dialectic to history.

Second, Engels' version of historical materialism suffered from an ultimate vacillation between the logical and the empirical principles. His general statements on the role of these principles in history as a whole show that he thought of them in juxtaposition rather than in synthesis. "History has its own course, and as dialectically as it may finally turn out, still dialectic must often enough wait long upon history."[13] For a historical event to be a consequence of dialectical law, it must

[11] Engels to Conrad Schmidt, August 5, 1890, in *ibid.*, I, 380.
[12] Engels, "On Karl Marx's *Contribution to the Critique of Political Economy*" (1895), in *ibid.*, I, 368–69.
[13] Friedrich Engels, *Dialektik der Natur* (5th ed.; Berlin, 1961), p. 111.

be proved that it "in part has happened and in part must happen." [14]

It was this inability of Engels' to find a source of historical unity in either the integral force of economics or the extensive logic of the dialectic that drove him to look for it, finally, in the relations between the economic and the other historical activities of man. His focus on these relations marked a new stage in his search for synthesis, for the famous concessions that he made in them to the role of the superstructure in history show both his need to find in a reciprocating process the unity he could not find in a monistic principle, and his stubborn recognition of a concrete individuality in history that ultimately subverted unity in the process as in the principle.

Engels' overt purpose, in these later glosses on the Marxist philosophy of history, was to enlarge its scope by showing that political and ideological history had meaning for it and could be explained in terms of it. Engels now argued that "the various elements of the superstructure"—politics, ideology, and so forth—"also exercise their influence upon the course of the historical struggles" and that they "react back as an influence upon the whole development of society, even on its economic development," which is the "ultimately determining" but not the *"only* determining basis" of history. Engels insisted, moreover, that this reciprocal relationship was grounded in the very fundamentals of Marxism—that is, in the dialectic, which "proceeds in the form of interaction" and rejects all "metaphysical" notions of one-way "here cause and there effect." [15]

But actually, Engels' purpose in this reassessment of historical materialism went beyond such substantive reinterpretation. This reinterpretation entailed a fundamental revision of historical method, and Engels addressed himself both to this other dimension and to its metaphysical implications. This level of his concern reflected his interest in history as a discipline and it

[14] Quoted in Mayer, Engels, II, 434.
[15] For this discussion, see Engels' correspondence from 1890 to 1894 in Marx, *Selected Works,* I, 380–94, and Mayer, *Engels,* II, 432–56.

betrayed the persistence of duality behind the formula of "interaction." For the substantive relationship of economic to political and ideological history coincided, in Engels, with the methodological relationship of rational to empirical history. Whatever the inadequacies he discerned in economic history when he focused his attention upon it alone, it acquired the exclusive properties of logical rationality and necessity when he considered it in the context of history as a whole. "Economic relations, however much they may be influenced by the other political and ideological ones, are still ultimately the decisive ones, forming the red thread which runs through them and alone leads to understanding. . . . The necessity which here asserts itself amidst all accident is again ultimately economic necessity." [16] The political and ideological elements in history, then, fill the role of "accidents," which cannot be plotted rationally, but can only be known empirically. "The further the particular sphere which we are investigating is removed from the economic sphere and approaches that of pure abstract ideology, the more shall we find it exhibiting accidents in its development, the more will its curve run in a zig-zag." [17] Thus, underlying Engels' attempt to show the comprehensive unity of the interactive process between economics and superstructure in history lay the attempt to show both the metaphysical unity between necessity and freedom and its methodological corollary of the unity between rational analysis and empirical research. That "men make their history themselves, but . . . are governed by *necessity,* which is supplemented by and appears under the forms of *accident,*" was Engels' sharpened version of an early Marxian formula, and his employment of it in the later context of an enhanced superstructure indicated the larger role that he would now grant to the historical perception of man's purposive and "accidental" acts vis-à-vis the logical analysis of their unintended and "necessary" effects.[18]

---

[16] Engels to Heinz Starkenburg, January 25, 1894, in Marx, *Selected Works,* I, 392.

[17] *Ibid.,* I, 393.

[18] *Ibid.,* I, 392. Cf. Marx's: "Men make their own history, but they do

But to establish the dialectical unity of history, Engels had to proceed through two distinct steps. First, he had to buttress the new dignity which he was conferring on the political and ideological superstructure as a real pole in the dialectic by conferring a parallel dignity upon its analogous principles of metaphysical contingency and methodological empiricism. With this, as we have just seen, he had no difficulty. Second, however, he had to show the logic in the interaction between each of these three principles—superstructure, contingency, empiricism—with its opposite number—economics, necessity, rationalism—and here the parallelism among the three levels broke down. Whereas the substantive relationship of politics and ideology to economics was a difference of degree, the relationships of free will to determinism and of the unique event to rational totality were oppositions of kind. On the substantive level, Engels admitted the fault of the early joint philosophy of history to be merely a matter of emphasis—"Marx and I are ourselves partly to blame for the fact that younger writers sometimes lay more stress on the economic side than is due to it" [19]—and he proposed a revised formula for the relationship of economic to political and ideological history that was essentially quantitative in its dependence upon physical analogy. Thus, on the relationship of economics to politics in history:

> It is the interaction of two unequal forces: on the one hand the economic movement, on the other the new political power, which strives for as much independence as possible, and which, having once been established, is also endowed with a movement of its own. On the whole, the economic movement gets its way, but it has also to suffer reactions from the political movement which it established and endowed with relative independence itself. . . . [20]

---

not make it just as they please; they do not make it under circumstances chosen by themselves, but under circumstances directly found, given and transmitted from the past." *The Eighteenth Brumaire of Louis Bonaparte* (1852), in *ibid.*, II, 315.

[19] Engels to Joseph Bloch, September 21, 1890, in *ibid.*, I, 383.

[20] Engels to Conrad Schmidt, October 27, 1890, in *ibid.*, I, 384.

But the implicit methodology and metaphysics were some-thing else again. On the level of method, his self-criticism of the early joint theory went far beyond the gradational mode of his substantive structure and took the categorical mode of opposing content to form:

> We all laid and were bound to lay the main emphasis at first on the derivation of political, juridical, and other ideological notions, from basic economic facts. But in doing so we neglected the formal side—the way in which these notions come about—for the sake of the content.[21]

Engels thought, undoubtedly, that his two judgments—the em-phasis on economics and the neglect of form—were congruent, but actually they were not. If he had meant by "form" here simply a methodological synonym for the neglected superstruc-ture, then the judgments would indeed have been apposite. But from his use of the term both here and in other contexts, it is clear that by "form" he referred not to the realm of political and ideological events alone but to the point of their integration with the underlying economic force. He indicted for neglect of form both those who hypostatized economics and those who isolated ideology, and he defined form in synthetic terms: "As all the driving forces of the actions of any individual person must pass through his brain, and transform themselves into motives of his will in order to set him into action, so also all the needs of civil society . . . must pass through the will of the state in order to secure general validity in the form of laws. That is the formal aspect of the matter. . . ."[22]

Thus Engels' re-evaluation of "superstructure" and of "form" was not the same point attacked from two angles but two separate, sequential points. What he was saying, in essence, was this: because Marx and he had undervalued the facts of super-structure in history, they had had no occasion to proceed to the consequent basic problem of integrating these facts into the lawful economic movement. But—and this is why the distinc-

---

[21] Engels to Mehring, July 14, 1893, in Karl Marx and Friedrich Engels, *Correspondence, 1846–1895* (New York, 1933), pp. 510–11.

[22] *Ibid.*, pp. 510–12; Engels, *Feuerbach*, in Marx, *Selected Works*, I, 462.

tion between the levels is so crucial—Engels now found that the solution of the first problem rendered impossible the solution of the second. After prescribing the quantitative enhancement of the superstructure in the abstract recipe of "interaction," he could not, and indeed would not, devise a formula for either the method or the rationale of its integration with its economic base. In the face of this issue, he explicitly renounced the philosophy of history for history proper, since history inhabited the substantive realm in which political and ideological facts could be juxtaposed with economic conditions without confronting the implicit philosophical antinomies of method and of metaphysics. Not only did he claim for the early Marx and Engels that "when it was a case of presenting a section of history, that is, of a practical application, there the thing was different and no error was possible," but he could now write that "the Marxist conception of history . . . puts an end to philosophy in the realm of history." Its "proof is to be found in history itself. . . . It is no longer a question anywhere of inventing interconnections from out of our brains, but of discovering them in the facts." [23] Nor did he shrink, at the end, from taking the step even beyond this position, which exalted actual history as the exclusive source of historical materialism, to the ultimate declaration of historical independence which scaled down historical materialism to a mere hermeneutic tool for the interpretation of actual history. He rejoiced, Engels wrote in 1892, that historical materialism "finally begins to be used for what it really was—a guide to the study of history." [24]

Thus history came, for Engels, to be the only possible resolution for problems raised by his philosophy of history, and from this function stemmed its comprehensive quality. For it was precisely the inclusion of human events ranging the full spectrum from economic activities through military tactics to religious ideas that distinguished his historical works. But if Engels' history benefited from the frustrations of his philosophy of

---

[23] Engels to Joseph Bloch, September 21, 1890, in Marx, *Selected Works*, I, 383; Engels, *Feuerbach*, in *ibid.*, I, 468.

[24] Quoted in Mayer, *Engels*, II, 453.

history, it had to suffer from them as well, for it reflected the philosophical irresolutions it could not resolve. His history could construct a pattern that was unified according to the distinctive criteria of its own limited realm, a pattern based upon the simple temporal simultaneity and succession of conditions and events, but, by virtue of the very assumptions that went into the history, it could only exemplify Engels' methodological inability to build the individuality of empirical observations into the generality of a logical process and his metaphysical inability to reconcile the freedom of individual actions with the determinism of collective effects. For despite Engels' nominal substitution of history for philosophy of history as the medium of synthesis, his ultimate synthesis, in both its methodological and its metaphysical versions, excluded history as categorically as the philosophy of history.

On the level of method, Engels prescribed that "historical science assimilate the dialectic," but he then defined the relationship of fact and logic in such a way as to make it impossible for "historical science" to do so.[25] When he "expelled" philosophy from history (and from nature), he was segregating rather than destroying philosophy, for he still assigned it the valid function of "the theory of the laws of the thought process itself, logic and dialectics."[26] That he did not here indicate how this philosophical logic would "discover" the "inter-connections" that were supposed to reside in the historical facts from which philosophy had been excluded was no mere neglect. It was rooted in his fundamental conviction, articulated in another context, that the only kinds of facts that could be integrated into a logical process were facts of present and future experience:

> The empiricism of observation can never suffice to prove necessity. *Post hoc*, but not *propter hoc*. . . . But the proof of necessity lies in human activity, in experiment, in labor: If I can produce the *post hoc*, it becomes identical with the *propter hoc*.[27]

---

[25] Engels, *Dialektik der Natur*, p. 223.
[26] Engels, *Feuerbach*, in Marx, *Selected Works*, I, 468.
[27] Engels, *Dialektik der Natur*, p. 244.

It is easy to see how this logic of revolutionary activism could be applied to the experimental method of natural science, but it is easy to see too how inappropriate such a pragmatic method is to historical facts whose essence is precisely that they cannot be reproduced.

This gap between the facts of history and the laws of thought was at once confirmed by and grounded in the traces of historical metaphysics which continued to frame Engels' writing of history.[28] According to this metaphysics, the entire historical realm was necessarily condemned to the persistent tension between free will and determinism for the very simple reason that this tension could only be resolved in a kind of situation that has never yet come into existence. "Men make their history . . . not as yet with a collective will or according to a collective plan or even in a definitely defined given society," and until they do they will be governed, as they always have been governed, by a combination of "necessity" and "accident" that is Engels' terminology within history for the diremption of determinism and free will in the making of history.[29] All history hitherto, however remote or contemporary, consists fundamentally in the distinction between accident and necessity because these express in terms of historical *events* the distinction between the free individual will and the determined collective effect in the original historical *actions*. These relations hold not only for the connection between different kinds of historical events—that is, between necessary economic and accidental political or ideological events—but for the very structure of every historical event per se. For "the historical event" was itself

---

[28] "Metaphysics" is, of course, my label for this aspect of Engels' thought and not Engels' own, since, with Marx, he abjured metaphysics in any guise. I use it to designate that portion of their inverted Hegelianism which produced a rational schema of the historical process and an analysis of freedom and determinism and of contingency and necessity as its ultimate and formative realities. For an exhaustive philosophical analysis of the idealistic components in Engels' philosophy of history, see Rodolfo Mondolfo, *Le matérialisme historique d'après Fréderic Engels* (translated from Italian, Paris, 1917).

[29] Engels to Heinz Starkenburg, January 25, 1894, in Marx, *Selected Works*, I, 392.

a "resultant," "a collective mean" that was produced "unconsciously and without volition" by the "innumerable intersecting forces" of conscious and purposeful individual wills.[30] From the point of view of the individual, the event was an accident, since "what emerges is something that no one willed," but from the point of view of the society, the event was a necessity, since it was a collective result determined by the collective conditions of the event, and from this collective point of view it was the intentional action of the individual will that was accidental.

But Engels never clarified the relationship between the contingency and the necessity which he thus identified in history. He did not do so for the very good reason that he believed in the cancellation of the distinction between accident and necessity, but in terms that were inapplicable to history as it has been lived and as he interpreted it.[31] This cancellation, stemming admittedly from Hegel and stipulating "that necessity determines itself as accident and that . . . this accident is absolute necessity," Engels did apply to nature, but it could apply to human society only when a future revolution would synthesize individual and collective wills—an eventuality which lay obviously beyond history.[32] Engels' repeated resort, in human history, to the concepts of "accident" and "necessity," which he rejected in both nature and the human future as false metaphysical antitheses, betrayed the fundamental character of the disjunction between the individual origins and the collective results of all historical actions in his view of man's past. All previous societies, he wrote, have been governed both by "necessity" which has appeared "under the forms of accident" and by accident as such which has "supplemented" necessity.[33]

Engels postulated both a progressive tendency toward the synthetic transcendence of accident and necessity in an expanding circle of freedom and a stubborn persistence of accident

---

[30] Engels to Joseph Bloch, September 21, 1890, in *ibid.*, I, 382–83.

[31] "What can I reject more strongly than both these designations of thought?" Engels, *Dialektik der Natur*, p. 231.

[32] *Ibid.*, p. 234.

[33] Engels to Heinz Starkenburg, January 25, 1894, in Marx, *Selected Works*, I, 392.

and necessity as separate identities in the continuing social limitations upon that freedom. He subscribed both to a positive relationship between accident and necessity that was teleological in character and a negative relationship that was constituent in character. But he had no theoretical solution or even formulation for the subsequent problem of how these two sets of relations were in turn related. His theoretical restraint is perhaps explicable by the ambiguous working solution he actually gave the problem in his histories when he faced it in the concrete form of individual and group actions which had no demonstrable link with the collective "driving forces" of history and in fact deviated from the individual and group actions demonstrably entailed by these forces. His solution was to treat the apparently maverick actions alternately as indifferent or as related by dialectical negation to the main movement of history. The ambiguity was a fruitful one, for it enabled Engels to indulge freely in his passion for the specific materials of history and still to cover its descriptive details and narrative form with the logic of historical materialism.

And so we are led both by Engels' personal tastes and by his version of the Marxist philosophy of history to the history that he wrote. The foregoing considerations serve, moreover, not only as a backdrop for his historical writing but as an explanation of the surprises it contains. The mixed quality of this writing, indeed, is such as to require at least as much explanation as it provides. For if we turn to Engels' historical works with the aim of characterizing his historiography as a whole, we find that they are not simply Marxist tracts, nor are they simply empirical or scientific history—that, indeed, they are not anything simple. His history is characterized rather by the plurality of its salient traits and the divergent tendencies they denote. So divergent, in fact, are they that they even suffer arrangement into a series of contraries.

Engels wrote history primarily to illuminate the social conflicts of his own age, but he also went back through the early modern period into ancient and prehistory and immersed himself in the very different forms and issues of these eras. He wrote normative history in which he openly judged what his historical subjects did by what their social roles indicated they should have done, but he also wrote long stretches of autonomous history in which he permitted military, political, and cultural facts to speak for themselves. This differentiation held true, moreover, not only for the criteria but for the very arrangement and structure of his histories: the economic and social sections appeared at the beginning and were cast in an analytical mode, while the military, political, and cultural materials were segregated into their own later sections and were cast in a narrative mold. Again, the economic and social analysis covered long-term evolution; the rest was focused upon short-term revolution. Finally, his historical reference extended to all mankind, but his historical preference concentrated upon the German nation.

The upshot is a kind of historical writing that shares with Marx's own the schematism, the economic and social causation, the didactic purpose, the contemporary and revolutionary emphases so familiar now in Marxist historiography—and yet it has a distinctive texture of its own. The difference lies not simply in Engels' addiction to Germany in contrast to Marx's propensity for France, but in their characteristically divergent ways of executing their history. Marx's history has the texture of a plait, in which theory and fact, social structure and political events, are braided together in continuing contact. Engels' has the sound of factual nuggets jostling against one another inside a theory-ribbed receptacle.

Much of the duality that runs through Engels' historical composition is obviously explicable in terms of his own varied roles as revolutionary, social theorist, German burgher, and scholar *manqué*. Much of it is explicable, too, by the stresses which developed within his gloss on the Marxist philosophy of history. His personal tastes and his theoretical limits combined to give him a real appreciation of history as such, an appreciation that could embroil him in the methods and substance of historical inquiry without explicit reference to its ultimate

Marxist meaning. He complained when he had to write history without adequate sources, and he was proud when he could claim his historical "material" to be of his own research.[34] He was clearly apologetic because his *Peasant War in Germany* "does not pretend to present independently collected material," and for years thereafter he did collect such material for the radical revision which he planned but did not live long enough to make.[35] His attraction to history was such, moreover, that it was an important dimension of all his main works. Not only was much of the *Anti-Dühring* and the *Ludwig Feuerbach and the Outcome of Classical German Philosophy* cast in the form of intellectual history, but even the early *Condition of the Working Class in England* was "originally designed to form part of a more comprehensive work on English social history." [36]

But if the factors making for a certain intrinsicality in Engels' concern with German history are obvious enough, what is not so obvious is the relationship that he postulated between this kind of history and the Marxist framework that was supposed to explain it. Unquestionably, however separate the two lines of his history—the social analysis and the political narrative—look to us, they certainly did not seem so to him. He rejected as emphatically as Marx the leading lights of the new empirical and critical history in Germany—Ranke, Mommsen, Sybel— precisely because their principle of independence for the unique political event made of history "a wild confusion of unbridled aggressions." The autonomy of empirical history was thus intellectually intolerable to him, and Marx's version of the Hegelian dialectic satisfied a profound need by "bringing order into chaos" and revealing the "quiet . . . and real movement of history behind the noisy deeds." [37] But how to reconcile this need for a unifying principle with the respect for the integrity

---

[34] Engels to Marx, August 21, 1851, in V. Adoratsky (ed.), "Karl Marx/Friedrich Engels," *Historish-Kritische Gesamtausgabe* (Berlin, 1929), Part III, Vol. 1, p. 242; Frederick Engels, *The Origin of the Family, Private Property, and the State* (Chicago, 1902), p. 11.

[35] See below, p. 3.

[36] Engels, *The Condition of the Working Class in England*, p. 3.

[37] Mayer, *Engels*, II, 428–29.

of the historical fact that found expression in the forms of his own history writing and in his agreement with the historicist principle of "the right of every age and situation to its own stage of knowledge and of society"? [38] This was the problem that repeated concretely on the historical level what Engels had failed to resolve theoretically on the level of the philosophy of history. He did solve it on the concrete historical level through the kind of history that he chose to write about. In the context of his general problem, Engels' option for the history of German revolutions becomes itself not a question but an answer.

We have already noted Engels' inability to provide a theoretical formulation of this reconciliation, but however inadequate for itself, his philosophy of history does provide the key to how he could live with the duality in his practice of history. Indeed, the fruitfulness of Engels' German revolutionary histories, both for his dilemma and for our historical knowledge, springs from the appropriateness of their subject matter to the problematic theoretical assumptions with which he organized and interpreted it. The Germans have actually been dominated in their history by the tension between an ideal unity and an actual diversity. Germany shared only partially in the unifying social effects of western economic growth; it exhibited a gap between an autocratically oriented politics and a plurally divided society; it made its tradition of national community into an illusion, detached from its real political particularism; it alienated its ambitious cultural elite from an impermeable social and political reality. In all these ways German history did epitomize in fact the fundamental disjunction between reason and reality that Engels epitomized in theory, and it is no wonder that he was attuned to this history. That Engels did understand the German past in these terms and that this understanding did fill a need in his philosophy of history are confirmed by the brief (and neglected) essay on recent German history that he wrote for the Chartist *Northern Star* immediately after his conversion to historical materialism in 1845. The historical disjunctions that must be inferred from the more sophisticated tendency of

---

[38] *Ibid.,* II, 446.

his subsequent German histories took a more primitive and obvious form here: he reserved his unitary economic and social analysis for the European context of German developments and separated out the specifically German history into a straight narration of political conflict and cultural frustration.[39]

But to this divisiveness of his German preference Engels added the integrating influence of his option for revolutionary subjects. During most of the German past the connections both within and between each set of its tensions have been obscure, and the Germans have tended to pursue each of their compartmentalized economic, social, political, and cultural activities in apparent indifference to the others. But in times of revolution the insulation has been fretted away, and the kinds of activity which had seemed so independent became obviously implicated in a single process whose character and fate consisted precisely in the specific unfolding of the negative relationships which had for so long subsisted among them. Engels was perfectly aware of the power of revolution to expose the dialectical linkage within the apparent heterogeneity of men's usual concerns: "In history movement in the form of antitheses emerges only in all critical epochs of the leading nations. In such moments a people has only the choice between two horns of a dilemma—either-or." [40] Hence Engels' equation of revolutions with nature—"a revolution is a pure phenomenon of nature, which is led more according to physical laws than according to the rules which in ordinary times determine the development of society" [41]—takes on a historiographical meaning when we recall that for Engels it is in nature that history and dialectic have their most perfect union.[42]

In the history of the German revolutions Engels thus found a practical form of his historical theory that managed both to incarnate the divisions of the theory and yet to escape its anomalies. For the chronological relations of historical events

[39] "Deutsche Zustände," in Karl Marx/Friedrich Engels, *Werke* (Berlin, 1958), II, 564–84.

[40] Engels, *Dialektik der Natur*, p. 225.

[41] Engels to Marx, February 13, 1851, in Marx/Engels, *Gesamtausgabe*, Part III, Vol. 1, p. 149.

[42] See above, pp. xix–xx, xxviii–xxx.

supplied him with a connection among the diverse facts which he could not find in the logical relations of his dialectical theory. The outstanding common feature of the historical works that he devoted to revolution in Germany was the care which he bestowed upon the delineation of political and military actions and of political and religious programs with the purpose of showing how their overt political and ideological autonomy was explicable by the conscious alienation of their individual and group agents from their real social base. What stands out in his history of the Revolution of 1848 is not simply his identification of the various political groups and leaders with their cognate social classes, but his analysis of the economic, political, and intellectual factors that obscured their view of their class position at that particular time, and his narrative description of the political events whose fortuitous and irrational character stemmed precisely from their social opacity. The very occasion for Engels' history of the German Peasants' War revealed its role as a synthesizer in practice of what was disjoined in theory. Engels used it to demonstrate the coherence behind the apparent incoherence of 1848 by a historical analogy that provided a limiting case of the contingency and the multiplicity necessarily infecting the acts and ideas of men who did not understand the economic and social basis of what they did and thought.

It is easy to see, in his choice of subjects, how Engels could think that history itself resolved the dilemma of the philosophy of history by manifesting social determinism in such a way as to spare the duality between necessity and freedom. But even in these choice histories Engels vacillated repeatedly between the explanation of his historical agents' false consciousness as a necessary consequence of an immature economic development and his explanation of it as a contingent product of temporary circumstances and human failings. In the last analysis, this fruitful ambiguity is precisely what is most remarkable about Engels' history: it re-echoed while it resolved the problems in the theory that spawned it.

Germany had had two revolutions by Engels' time—the Peasants' War of 1525 and the Revolution of 1848—and he wrote the histories of both. The circumstances in which he wrote them furnish an object lesson for the way in which the classic works of men outgrow the incidentals of their origin and take on a life of their own. It follows that these works have not only a content but a history of their own, and it is to the outer history of Engels' revolutionary histories that we now turn.

The editorial origins of the two volumes were similar. Engels wrote each work as a series of magazine articles. *The Peasant War in Germany* was published in the telescoped May to October (1850) issue of the *Neue Rheinische Zeitung* which Marx and Engels edited in London and had printed in Hamburg. *Germany: Revolution and Counter-Revolution* appeared sporadically between October, 1851, and September, 1852, in the socially minded Charles A. Dana's *New York Tribune*. Both works were written for reasons that were extraneous to their contents: Engels wrote *The Peasant War* just after the disappointments of 1848–49 and in expectation of a new revolutionary surge. His twin purposes were, correspondingly, to trace the genealogy of the bourgeois and petty bourgeois traitors of the recent revolution and to stimulate the hoped-for proletarian vanguard of the coming revolution. He wrote *Germany: Revolution and Counter-Revolution* because Marx, who had agreed to comment on the German situation for the *Tribune,* was too busy or too unsure of his English or too convinced that Germany was Engels' bailiwick—Marx never specified which—to do it himself. The articles were sent to Dana through Marx and were published under the latter's name, but the Marx-Engels correspondence reveals Engels' authorship and even indicates that Marx sent them along unaltered.[43] The final external similarity of the two works lies in their parallel editorial histories: both were published in volume form by Marxist

---

[43] Substantive discussion of the articles is entirely absent from the lengthy published correspondence for this period. Remarks about them abound, but always in the sense of complaints about Dana's cavalier treatment of them or about the imminent deadlines requiring Engels' immediate dispatch. Together with the absence of discussion between friends who discussed everything else, this constant pressure confirms the conclusion from internal evidence that *Germany: Revolution and Counter-*

disciples—*The Peasant War* in 1870 and *Germany: Revolution and Counter-Revolution* in 1896—and both have since been kept in circulation as part of the Marxist canon through divers translations and reprintings.

But if the works have followed parallel courses in their capacity as models for the historical application of Marxism, they have had divergent destinies in their capacity as contributions to European history. The divergence in their historical reputations has occurred in our own generation, for after a long period of their joint neglect by all but Marxist intellectuals like Karl Kautsky and Franz Mehring and Soviet historians like D. Riazanov [44] the postwar era has witnessed the new but limited academic use of *The Peasant War* in a non-Soviet, Marxist, professional historiography, and the new broad appreciation of *Germany: Revolution and Counter-Revolution* in professional Marxist and non-Marxist historiography alike.

The one-sided revival of *The Peasant War* stems exclusively from the development of a Marxist academic historiography in the German Democratic Republic—that is, Communist East Germany. The official penetration of Marxism into the East German universities has introduced a new phase in the posthumous career of Engels' book because their professional historians have extended its role from a specific example of general Marxist history to the Marxist interpretation of specific history. Thereby, for the first time, the particular historical result of the work rather than its general theoretical approach has become

---

Revolution was all Engels'. The one apparent exception to this was Engels' request, on April 29, 1852, for a memorandum from Marx, but characteristically what Engels wanted was not help on the historical sections of the work but on "the revolutionary prospects of Germany" and "the position of our Party," which would conclude the series of articles. Marx agreed to write such a memorandum, but he never did, pleading the pressure of family affairs as his excuse. See Marx/Engels, *Gesamtausgabe,* Part III, Vol. 1, pp. 229–392, especially pp. 343, 345, 403.

[44] Thus Karl Kautsky, *Communism in Central Europe in the Time of the Reformation* (translated from German; London, 1897); Franz Mehring's edition of Engels, *Der deutsche Bauernkrieg* (Berlin, 1920); D. Riazanov's edition of Engels, *The Peasant War in Germany* (English translation; New York, 1926).

the subject of academic discussion. A. Meusel's *Thomas Müntzer und seine Zeit* (1952), the East German translation of the Russian study by M. M. Smirin, *Die Volksreformation des Thomas Münzer und der grosse Bauernkrieg* (1952), and Heinz Kamnitzer's *Zur Vorgeschichte des Deutschen Bauernkrieges* (1953) have explicitly brought Engels into the historical scholarship on the Peasants' War as the progenitor of its social interpretation. Again, the recent (1952) East German re-edition of Wilhelm Zimmermann's old (1840–44) *Der Grosse Deutsche Bauernkrieg* is certainly associated with Engels' express and laudatory citation of the book as his own chief source.

That Engels' history of the Peasant War has received no such recognition among non-Marxist historians comes as no surprise, but what does need explaining is their continued failure to accord it any recognition at all beyond the dubious honor of an occasional refutation. There would appear to be three reasons for this combination of neglect and hostility in the attitude of contemporary non-Marxist historians to this work of Engels— the first technical and the other two substantive.

First, then, Engels' "material," as he himself admitted, all came out of Zimmermann, and historians do better to consult Zimmermann, where it has vitality, than Engels, where it is pap. Actually, however, they tend to consult neither of these, but rather the recent and standard Günther Franz, *Der deutsche Bauernkrieg* (4th ed., 1956), which epitomizes the results of subsequent research with its stress upon the social diversity of the peasants' revolt and its restrictions upon any uniform interpretation of the movement.

A second reason for the disregard of Engels in this field is the partial historiographical success of what he himself did obviously contribute to the understanding of the peasant revolution by "showing the religious and political controversies of that epoch as a reflection of the class struggles that were taking place simultaneously." [45] As the very label affixed to the revolt attests and the perennial socialist interest in it confirms, the social

---

[45] See below, p. 3.

motif of the movement is so indisputable that the kind of emphasis initiated by Engels has long since been built into all interpretations of the age. As *a* dimension, consequently, it rates no credit line.

But finally, and most fundamentally, Engels' work on the Peasant War of the sixteenth century has been particularly slighted because it ambitiously applies the economic interpretation to a pre-industrial age, an application that non-Marxist historians find singularly inappropriate. Engels posed his social thesis not simply as a dimension but as a prime cause of the peasants' revolt, and in this form non-Marxist historians have rejected it or ignored it because they have found it wrong or irrelevant. In the proportioning of causes they have tended to emphasize the primacy of state-building in triggering mass action and of religion in driving Engels' hero, Thomas Müntzer. They have also disputed the notion of a general tendency toward peasant economic and social misery, cited a mixture of progress and decline, and correspondingly made the economic and social dimensions contributory rather than primary. Although the difference seems to be one of mere proportions, the upshot is a position categorically opposed to Engels', for the contemporary non-Marxist historians see unity precisely in the politics and the religion wherein he saw diversity, and they see factual multiplicity in the economics and society wherein he saw rational coherence.

Despite its dubious status in non-Marxist historiography, Engels' *Peasant War in Germany* does remain a historical classic still worth reading. Three factors justify its longevity. First, it initiated a prominent tradition of socialist history on the era of the Peasant War, running through Karl Kautsky, E. Belfort Bax, and Roy Pascal to the current official Marxist studies.[46] It is a tradition serious enough, in the recent judgment of a respected

[46] For other socialist accounts of the Peasants' War (in addition to Engels' and Kautsky's, cited above), see E. Belfort Bax, *The Peasants War in Germany* (London, 1899), and Roy Pascal, *The Social Basis of the Reformation* (London, 1933).

German scholar, to rival the non-Marxist tradition and to leave the interpretation of the Peasant War still moot between them.[47] It should be added, as a subordinate consideration, that the Marxist line is not only becoming more respectable academically but has always been more convenient scholastically. Of the historical works devoted wholly or mainly to the Peasants' War, the only ones in English are those from the socialist tradition. The best of the non-Marxist tradition, old and new alike, remain in their original German. This tradition is available in English only through more inclusive works in which the Peasants' War is one topic among others.[48]

The second factor which warrants the attribution of classic status to Engels' *Peasant War in Germany* is more convincing, for it bears upon an essential and distinctive quality of the book itself. In the actual working out of his economic thesis through his religious material, Engels formulated relationships of practical interests to religious ideals that are more important for the connections they make than for the putative economic primacy from which he began. Undoubtedly, Engels' early religious experience and his lifelong conviction of a kinship between religion and communism helped him to approach, in the context of the religiosity of the Peasants' War, as close as he would ever

---

[47] Wilhelm Treue, "Wirtschafts- und Sozialgeschichte vom 16. bis zum 18. Jahrhundert," in Bruno Gebhardt, *Handbuch der deutschen Geschichte* (8th ed.; Stuttgart, 1955), II, 376–77.

[48] For standard German accounts, in addition to Zimmermann and Franz (cited above), see Adolf Waas, *Die grosse Wendung im deutschen Bauernkrieg* (Munich and Berlin, 1939), and Willy Andreas, *Deutschland vor der Reformation* (6th ed.; Stuttgart, 1959). For recent works in English with sections on the Peasants' War, see Hajo Holborn, *A History of Modern Germany: the Reformation* (New York, 1959); Harold John Grimm, *The Reformation Era, 1500–1650* (New York, 1954); George H. Williams, *The Radical Reformation* (London, 1962); *The New Cambridge Modern History*: Vol. II, *The Reformation* (Cambridge, 1958). Of the older accounts, see especially Leopold von Ranke, *History of the Reformation in Germany* (English translation; New York, 1905); Preserved Smith, *The Age of the Reformation* (New York, 1920); J. Selwyn Schapiro, *The Reformation and Social Reform* (New York, 1909); J. Janssen, *A History of the German People from the Close of the Middle Ages* (English translation; London, 1905–10).

get to an integral relationship among the variegated historical activities of man.[49] The connection between the radical sects and the "peasant-plebeian" classes—the connection that embodied Engels' most penetrating historical perception—remains the one definite relationship that has been accepted by historians on both sides of the Marxist divide. In general, moreover, even if Engels' priority of social interests and his one-to-one correlation of the other religious confessions with social classes have found no such acceptance, the relevance of the social dimension to the religious conflicts of the Reformation era is beyond cavil and the discovery of how this relationship actually worked remains one of the live issues for European historiography.

Third, and finally, *The Peasant War in Germany* embodies Engels' Marxist dilemma in a form that can help every student of history to know himself. Engels himself unwittingly pointed out the lesson to be learned from the work in a later summary of the historical principles that had gone into it. When placed in juxtaposition these principles make explicit the fundamental paradox of history that Engels' work, unpretentious as it is, does exemplify. The paradox consists in the necessarily variant views of historical events taken by the men who made the events and the historian who re-creates them, and it is Engels' glory to have cast his Marxism into a sixteenth-century shape that makes clear the ultimate ambiguity of the historian's situation.

Engels, on the one hand, understood the point of view of the men who made the long stretch of pre-industrial history, and he recognized their right to put their own stamp upon that history. Because these historical subjects viewed "thoughts as . . . developing independently and subject only to their own laws," and because the determination of this thought process by "material life conditions remains of necessity unknown to these persons," the men of the pre-industrial era constrain "every social and political movement to take on a theological form."

On the other hand, however, Engels also fully recognized the right of the modern historian to read back into this same pre-

---

[49] See the translation of Engels' "On the Early History of Christianity" and editorial comments in Lewis S. Feuer (ed.), *Marx and Engels: Basic Writings on Politics and Philosophy* (New York, 1959), pp. 168–94, 412.

industrial era the knowledge of the primacy of "material life conditions," although this is a knowledge that only the industrialism of the historian's own age made possible. The historian need only perform this reinterpretation, as Engels felt he himself had, and what had been "the riddle" of the driving forces of history is thereby solved for all preceding periods as well as for his own.[50] Needless to say, Engels remained too much of a Hegelian believer in the retroactive power of knowledge to have himself been aware of the problem posed by this combination of principles. But to others not so comfortably endowed his *Peasant War in Germany* will remain a case study in the problem of how far the historian can go in opposing to his subjects' interpretations of themselves contrary interpretations stemming from subsequently acquired knowledge which the subjects did not and could not have had about themselves.

Germany: Revolution and Counter-Revolution poses no such historiographical problem. As a history of the German Revolution of 1848 in which, by the common consent of all recent historians, social interests and conflicts did in fact play a conscious and crucial role, the work has been recognized as a classic by historians of all persuasions. In part, undoubtedly, its repute and utility rest on considerations extraneous to its value as a historical study, for it functions as a primary source both for the revolution of which Engels was an intelligent contemporary witness and for the revolutionary party in which he was a leading participant. But even when these functions are discounted and the question is only of its status as a historical study, both its repute and its utility remain eminent. Its eminence does not rest especially upon its technique, for if the materials from newspapers and other contemporary accounts of the revolution make it superior in this respect to *The Peasant War in Germany*, they are hardly distinctive enough to account for the precedence which it has recently enjoyed over all the contemporary and even many of the subsequent histories of the 1848 revolution in Germany. The eminence of the work rests rather upon the ascending role that the social interpretation

---

[50] Engels, *Feuerbach*, in Marx, *Selected Works*, I, 459, 465–66.

pioneered by Engels has played in the historiography of the revolution.

Down to the end of World War II the standard interpretations of the German Revolution of 1848 centered on the political issues of liberalism and democracy, monarchy and republic, particularism and nationalism, federalism and centralism, a smaller and a larger Germany.[51] But the postwar generation of historians, seeking to explain the futility of German idealism in terms of its relations to practical interests, eagerly took up Engels' social interpretation of the revolution as a scheme which could get relevant answers out of the old material without waiting for the necessary new researches. The flexibility which we have seen to be characteristic of Engels' revolutionary history—the separate treatment and acknowledgment given such political factors as particularism and nationalism and to such ideological factors as the philosophies of idealism and liberalism, combined with the confident assurance that they were related, if only by negation, to the dimly perceived class conflict[52]—was perfectly suited to both the material and the needs of the postwar historians. That the East German writing on 1848 should have cited Engels in the style of scripture is to be expected, but a whole galaxy of non-Marxist historians, including even so notable a representative of the nationalist school as Friedrich Meinecke, both passed favorable judgment upon him and relied upon his judgments, not simply as a witness or participant but as a historian.[53]

---

[51] Especially Erich Brandenburg, *Die deutsche Revolution 1848* (2d ed.; Leipzig, 1919), and Veit Valentin *Geschichte der deutschen Revolution 1848–49* (2 vols.; Berlin, 1930–31), abridged English translation, *1848: Chapters of German History* (London, 1940).

[52] See above, pp. xxviii–xxx.

[53] For postwar East German histories of 1848, see Jürgen Kuczynski, *Die wirtschaftlichen und sozialen Voraussetzungen der Revolution von 1848–1849* (Berlin, 1848); Karl Obermann, *Die deutschen Arbeiter in der ersten bürgerlichen Revolution* (Berlin, 1950). For favorable non-Marxist comments on, or citations of, Engels, see A. J. P. Taylor, *The Course of German History* (New York, 1946), p. 77; G. Barraclough, *The Origins of Modern Germany* (Oxford, 1947), p. 416; Friedrich Meinecke, *1848: eine Sekuläbetrachtung* (Berlin, 1948), *passim*; Wilhelm Mommsen, *Grösse und Versagen des deutschen Bürgertums* (2d ed., Munich, 1964), p. 127;

Where *Germany: Revolution and Counter-Revolution* has now been superseded by new insights and researches, it has been extended rather than refuted. Even the more independent of the recent interpretations—those of Stadelmann and Hamerow that stress the role of the lower middle class in the revolution—are social interpretations that are tangential rather than opposed to Engels.[54] But the most impressive evidence of the continuing validity of Engels' work is the high value which is placed upon it in Jacques Droz's monumental *Les révolutions allemandes de 1848* (1957), now undoubtedly the standard work in the field. Droz has publicized his debt to Engels through frequent citations at crucial points—citations that are all the more impressive for the fine balance of Droz's interpretation among the social, political, and intellectual elements of the revolution.[55] But Droz has gone further and has paid Engels the supreme compliment that a historian of one generation can pay to a predecessor: one of Droz's major reinterpretations has restored to prominence the workers' revolutionary role first adumbrated by Engels and minimized by his successors. There are, to be sure, particular emphases in *Germany: Revolution and Counter-Revolution* that are unacceptable today—the wholesome condemnation of the traitorous bourgeoisie; the rigid concentration on Prussia and Austria as the only significant arenas of action; the dismissal of the Frankfurt National Assembly as the "parliament of an imaginary country" that created "an imaginary government," passed "imaginary resolutions," and was of interest only to "the collector of literary and antiquarian curiosities"; and the deprecation of Slav nationalities and cultures. These were occasions when Engels could not hold the equilibrium between the Marxism that was his key and the historical reality that was his

---

Koppel S. Pinson, *Modern Germany: Its History and Civilization* (2d ed.; New York, 1966), pp. 79, 106, 626.

[54] Rudolf Stadelmann, *Soziale und politische Geschichte der Revolution von 1848* (Munich, 1948); Theodore S. Hamerow, *Restoration, Revolution, Reaction: Economics and Politics in Germany 1815–71* (Princeton, 1958).

[55] Jacques Droz, *Les révolutions allemandes de 1848* (Paris, 1957), pp. 64, 99–100, 616, 628.

passion. But the failure of a revolution is a sign of an actual imbalance in the historical situation, and to this extent Engels' own imbalances were appropriate to the ill-fated revolutions he so shrewdly chose to describe.

In the final analysis, the value of Engels' historical writing must be assessed by two distinct criteria. As a substantive application of historical materialism, its validity rises and falls with the factual force of economic and social interests in the historical events under consideration. From this point of view, his interpretation is relevant to both the German revolutions, but in different ways: it illuminates certain individual events of the sixteenth-century revolution and the general course of the nineteenth-century revolution.

But beyond the literal truth or falsity of the economic interpretation, Engels' historical writing has a more universal function that must be assessed by a more fundamental standard of judgment. Engels was one of those rare historians who converted a philosophy of history which conditioned history from outside of history into a historical principle which was operative within the historical process itself. By thus engaging the strands of rationality and continuity in the kaleidoscopic manifold of history, Engels put the basic issue of the philosophy of history—whether there are any constant factors in the making or knowing of history—into a form that historians cannot avoid. From this point of view, his two histories of the German revolutions are complementary: *Germany: Revolution and Counter-Revolution* is a case study in the coherence of the history that men made; *The Peasant War in Germany* is a case study in the coherence of the knowledge that the historian has of it. These variants of the issue recapitulated two whole epochs in the philosophy of history: the long previous epoch when the philosophers of history had looked for laws in history, and the epoch to come when they were to look for universals in the way historians know about history. Because Engels stood at the turning point of these two epochs, his historical works epitomize the strengths and weaknesses of any synthetic approach to the diversity of historical experience.

LEONARD KRIEGER

xlvi

Contents

Contents

THE PEASANT WAR
IN GERMANY

Author's Preface to the Second Edition

THIS work was written in London in the summer of 1850, under the vivid impression of the counter-revolution that had just been completed. It appeared in 1850 in the fifth and sixth issues of the *Neue Rheinische Zeitung*, a political economic review edited by Karl Marx in Hamburg. My political friends in Germany desire to see it in book form, and I hereby fulfil that desire, since, unfortunately, it still has the interest of timeliness.

The work does not pretend to present independently collected material. Quite the contrary, all the material relating to the peasant revolts and to Thomas Muenzer has been taken from Zimmermann whose book, although showing gaps here and there, is still the best presentation of the facts. Moreover, old Zimmermann enjoyed his subject. The same revolutionary instinct which makes him here the advocate of the oppressed classes, made him later one of the best in the extreme left wing of Frankfurt.

If, nevertheless, the Zimmermann representation lacks internal coherence; if it does not succeed in showing the religious and political controversies of that epoch as a reflection of the class struggles that were taking place simultaneously; if it sees in the class struggles only oppressors and oppressed, good and evil, and the final victory of evil; if its insight into social conditions which determined both the outbreak and the outcome of the struggle is extremely poor, it was the fault of the time in which that book came into existence. Nevertheless, for its time, and among the German idealistic works on history, it stands out as written in a very realistic vein.

3

This book, while giving the historic course of the struggle only in its outlines, undertakes to explain the origin of the peasant wars, the attitude of the various parties which appear in the war, the political and religious theories through which those parties strove to make clear to themselves their position; and finally, the result of the struggle as determined by the historical-social conditions of life, to show the political constitution of Germany of that time, the revolt against it; and to prove that the political and religious theories were not the causes, but the result of that stage in the development of agriculture, industry, land and waterways, commerce and finance, which then existed in Germany. This, the only materialistic conception of history, originates, not from myself but from Marx, and can be found in his works on the French Revolution of 1848–49, published in the same review, and in his *Eighteenth Brumaire of Louis Bonaparte.*

The parallel between the German Revolutions of 1525 and of 1848–49 was too obvious to be left entirely without attention. However, together with an identity of events in both cases, as for instance, the suppression of one local revolt after the other by the army of the princes, together with a sometimes comic similitude in the behaviour of the city middle-class, the difference is quite clear.

"Who profited by the Revolution of 1525? The princes. Who profited by the Revolution of 1848? The big princes, Austria and Prussia. Behind the princes of 1525 there stood the lower middle-class of the cities, held chained by means of taxation. Behind the big princes of 1850, there stood the modern big bourgeoisie, quickly subjugating them by means of the State debt. Behind the big bourgeoisie stand the proletarians."

I am sorry to state that in this paragraph too much honour was given to the German bourgeoisie. True, it had the opportunity of "quickly subjugating" the monarchy by means of the State debt. Never did it avail itself of this opportunity.

Austria fell as a boon into the lap of the bourgeoisie after the war of 1866, but the bourgeoisie does not understand how to

4

govern. It is powerless and inefficient in everything. Only one thing is it capable of doing: to storm against the workers as soon as they begin to stir. It remains at the helm only because the Hungarians need it.

And in Prussia? True, the State debt has increased by leaps and bounds. The deficit has become a permanent feature. The State expenditures keep growing, year in and year out. The bourgeoisie have a majority in the Chamber. No taxes can be increased and no debts incurred without their consent. But where is their power in the State? It was only a couple of months ago, when a deficit was looming, that again they found themselves in the most favourable position. They could have gained considerable concessions by persevering. What was their reaction? They considered it a sufficient concession when the Government *allowed* them to lay at its feet nine millions, not for one year alone, but to be collected indefinitely every year.

I do not want to blame the "national liberals" of the Chamber more than is their due. I know they have been forsaken by those who stand behind them, by the mass of the bourgeoisie. This mass does not wish to govern. 1848 is still in its bones.

Why the German bourgeoisie has developed this remarkable trait, will be discussed later.

In general, however, the above quotation has proved perfectly true. Beginning from 1850, the small States were in constant retreat, serving only as levers for Prussian and Austrian intrigues. Austria and Prussia were engaged in ever-stronger struggles for supremacy. Finally, the fearful clash of 1866 took place. Austria, retaining all its provinces, subjugated, directly and indirectly, the entire north of Prussia, while leaving the fate of the three southern States in the air.

In all these grand activities of the States, only the following are of particular importance for the German working class:

First, that universal suffrage has given the workers the power to be directly represented in the legislative assemblies.

Second, that Prussia has set a good example by swallowing three crowns by the grace of God. That after this operation her own crown is maintained by the grace of God as pure as she claims it to be, not even the national liberals believe any more.

Third, that there is only one serious enemy of the Revolution in Germany at the present time—the Prussian government.

Fourth, that the Austro-Germans will now be compelled to ask themselves what they wish to be, Germans or Austrians; whom they wish to adhere to, to Germany or her extraordinary transleithanian appendages. It has been obvious for a long time that they will have to give up one or the other. Still, this has been continually glossed over by the petty-bourgeois democracy.

As to other important controversies concerning 1866 which were threshed out between the "national-liberals" and the people's party *ad nauseam,* coming years will show that the two standpoints fought so bitterly simply because they were the opposite poles of the same stupidity.

In the social conditions of Germany, the year 1866 has changed almost nothing. A few bourgeois reforms: uniform measures and weights, freedom of movement, freedom of trade, etc.,—all within limits befitting bureaucracy, do not even come up to that of which other western European countries have been in possession for a long while, and leaves the main evil, the system of bureaucratic concessions, unshaken. As to the proletariat, the freedom of movement, and of citizenship, the abolition of passports and other such legislation is made illusory by the current police practice.

What is much more important than the grand manoeuvres of the State in 1866 is the growth of German industry and commerce, of the railways, the telegraph, and ocean steamship navigation since 1848. This progress may be lagging behind that of England or even France, but it is unheard of for Germany, and has done more in twenty years than would have been previously possible in a century. Germany has been drawn, earnestly and irrevocably, into world commerce. Capital invested in industry has multiplied rapidly. The position of the bourgeoisie has improved accordingly. The surest sign of industrial prosperity—speculation—has blossomed richly, princes and dukes being chained to its triumphal chariot. German capital is now constructing Russian and Rumanian railways, whereas, only fifteen years ago, the German railways went a-begging to English entrepreneurs. How, then, is it possible that the bourgeoisie has not conquered political power, that it behaves in so cowardly a manner toward the government?

It is the misfortune of the German bourgeoisie to have come too late,—quite in accordance with the beloved German tradition. The period of its ascendancy coincides with the time when the bourgeoisie of the other western European countries is politically on the downward path. In England, the bourgeoisie could place its real representative, Bright, into the government only by extending the franchise which in the long run is bound to put an end to its very domination. In France, the bourgeoisie, which for two years only, 1849–50, had held power as a class under the republican régime, was able to continue its social existence only by transferring its power to Louis Bonaparte and the army. Under present conditions of enormously increased interdependence of the three most progressive European countries, it is no more possible for the German bourgeoisie extensively to utilize its political power while the same class has outlived itself in England and France. It is a peculiarity of the bourgeoisie, distinguishing it from all other classes, that a point is being reached in its development after which every increase in its power, that is, every enlargement of its capital, only tends to make it more and more incapable of retaining political dominance. *"Behind the big bourgeoisie stand the proletarians."* In the degree as the bourgeoisie develops its industry, its commerce, and its means of communication, it also produces the proletariat. At a certain point, which must not necessarily appear simultaneously and on the same stage of development everywhere, it begins to note that this, its second self, has outgrown it. From then on, it loses the power for exclusive political dominance. It looks for allies with whom to share its authority, or to whom to cede all power, as circumstances may demand.

In Germany, this turning point came for the bourgeoisie as early as 1848. The bourgeoisie became frightened, not so much by the German, as by the French proletariat. The battle of June, 1848, in Paris, showed the bourgeoisie what could be expected. The German proletariat was restless enough to prove to the bourgeoisie that the seed of revolution had been sown also in German soil. From that day, the edge of bourgeois political action was broken. The bourgeoisie looked around for allies. It sold itself to them regardless of price, and there it remains.

These allies are all of a reactionary turn. It is the king's power, with his army and his bureaucracy; it is the big feudal nobility; it is the smaller Junker; it is even the clergy. The bourgeoisie has made so many compacts and unions with all of them to save its dear skin, that now it has nothing more to barter. And the more the proletariat developed, the more it began to feel as a class and to act as one, the feebler became the bourgeoisie. When the astonishingly bad strategy of the Prussians triumphed over the astonishingly worse strategy of the Austrians at Sadowa, it was difficult to say who gave a deeper sign of relief, the Prussian bourgeois, who was a partner to the defeat at Sadowa, or his Austrian colleague.

Our upper middle-class of 1870 acted in the same fashion as did the moderate middle-class of 1525. As to the small bourgeoisie, the master artisans and merchants, they remain unchanged. They hope to climb up to the big bourgeoisie, and they are fearful lest they be pushed down into the ranks of the proletariat. Between fear and hope, they will in times of struggle seek to save their precious skin and to join the victors when the struggle is over. Such is their nature.

The social and political activities of the proletariat have kept pace with the rapid growth of industry since 1848. The rôle of the German workers, as expressed in their trade unions, their associations, political organisations and public meetings, at elections, and in the so-called Reichstag, is alone a sufficient indication of the transformation which came over Germany in the last twenty years. It is to the credit of the German workers that *they alone* have managed to send workers and workers' representatives into the Parliament—a feat which neither the French nor the English had hitherto accomplished.

Still, even the proletariat shows some resemblance to 1525. The class of the population which entirely and permanently depends on wages is now, as then, a minority of the German people. This class is also compelled to seek allies. The latter can be found only among the petty bourgeoisie, the low grade proletariat of the cities, the small peasants, and the wage-workers of the land.

The petty bourgeoisie has been mentioned above. This class is entirely unreliable except when a victory has been won. Then its noise in the beer saloons is without limit. Nevertheless, there are good elements among it, who, of their own accord, follow the workers.

The *lumpenproletariat*, this scum of the decaying elements of all classes, which establishes headquarters in all the big cities, is the worst of all possible allies. It is an absolutely venal, an absolutely brazen crew. If the French workers, in the course of the Revolution, inscribed on the houses: *Mort aux voleurs!* (Death to the thieves!) and even shot down many, they did it, not out of enthusiasm for property, but because they rightly considered it necessary to hold that band at arm's length. Every leader of the workers who utilises these gutter-proletarians as guards or supports, proves himself by this action alone a traitor to the movement.

The small peasants (bigger peasants belong to the bourgeoisie) are not homogeneous. They are either in serfdom bound to their lords and masters, and inasmuch as the bourgeoisie has failed to do its duty in freeing those people from serfdom, it will not be difficult to convince them that salvation, for them, can be expected only from the working class; or they are tenants, whose situation is almost equal to that of the Irish. Rents are so high that even in times of normal crops the peasant and his family can hardly eke out a bare existence; when the crops are bad, he virtually starves. When he is unable to pay his rent, he is entirely at the mercy of the landlord. The bourgeoisie thinks of relief only under compulsion. Where, then, should the tenants look for relief outside of the workers?

There is another group of peasants, those who own a small piece of land. In most cases they are so burdened with mortgages that their dependence upon the usurer is equal to the dependence of the tenant upon the landlord. What they earn is practically a meagre wage, which, since good and bad crops alternate, is highly uncertain. These people cannot have the least hope of getting anything out of the bourgeoisie, because it is the bourgeoisie, the capitalist usurers, that squeeze the life-blood out of them. Still, the peasants cling to their property, though in reality it does not belong to them, but to the usurers. It will be necessary to make it clear to these people that only when a government of the people will have transformed all mortgages into a debt to the State, and thereby lowered the rent, will they be able to free themselves from the usurer. This, however, can be accomplished only by the working class.

Wherever middle and large land ownership prevails, the wage-workers of the land form the most numerous class. This is the case throughout the entire north and east of Germany, and it is here that the industrial workers of the city find their most numerous and natural allies. In the same way as the capitalist is opposed to the industrial worker, the large land-owner or large tenant is opposed to the wage-workers of the land. The measures that help the one must also help the other. The industrial workers can free themselves only by turning the capital of the bourgeoisie, that is, the raw materials, machines and tools, the foodstuffs necessary for production, into social property, their own property, to be used by them in common. Similarly, the wage-workers of the land can be freed from their hideous misery only when the main object of their work, the land itself, will be withdrawn from the private property of the large peasants and still larger feudal masters, and transformed into social property to be cultivated by an association of land workers on a common basis. And here we come to the famous decision of the International Socialist Congress in Basle: That it is in the interest of society to transform property on land into common national property. This decision was made primarily for those countries where there is large land ownership, with large agricultural enterprises, with one master and many wage-workers in every estate. It is these conditions that still prevail in Germany, and next to England, the decision was *most timely* for Germany. The agricultural proletariat, the wage-workers of the land, is the class from which the bulk of the armies of the princes is being recruited. It is the class which, thanks to universal suffrage, sends into Parliament the great mass of feudal masters and Junkers. However, it is also the class nearest to the industrial workers of the city. It shares their conditions of living, and it is still deeper steeped in misery than the city workers. This class, powerless because split and scattered, but possessing a hidden power which is so well known to the government and nobility that they purposely allow the schools to deteriorate in order that the rural population should remain unenlightened, must be called to life and drawn into the movement. This is the most urgent task of the German labour movement. From the day when the mass of the workers of the land have learned to understand their own interests, a reactionary, feudal, bureaucratic or bourgeois government in Germany becomes an impossibility.

Addendum to Preface to the Second Edition

THE preceding lines were written over four years ago, but they are valid also at present. What was true after Sadowa and the partition of Germany, is being confirmed also after Sedan and the erection of the Holy German Empire of Prussian nationality. Little indeed are the "world shaking" activities of the States in the realm of so-called big politics in a position to change the trend of historic development.

What these grand activities of the States *are* in a position to accomplish is to hasten the tempo of historic movement. In this respect, the originators of the above-mentioned "world-shaking" events have made involuntary successes which to themselves appear highly undesirable, but which, however, they must take into the bargain, for better or worse.

Already the war of 1866 had shaken the old Prussia to its foundations. After 1848 it was difficult to bring the rebellious industrial element of the western provinces, bourgeois as well as proletarian, under the old discipline. Still, somehow, this was accomplished, and the interests of the Junkers of the eastern provinces, together with those of the army, again became dominant in the State. In 1866 almost all the northwest of Germany became Prussian. Besides the incurable moral injury to the Prussian crown, by the fact that it had swallowed up three other crowns by the grace of God, the centre of gravity of the monarchy had moved considerably westward. The four million Rhinelanders and Westphalians were reinforced, first, by four million Germans annexed through the North German Alliance directly, and then by six million annexed indirectly. In 1870, however, eight million southwest Germans were added, so that, in the "new monarchy," the fourteen and a half million old Prussians (all the six East Elbian provinces, among them, two million Poles) were opposed by twenty-five million who had long outgrown the old Prussian junker feudalism. So it happened that the very victories of the Prussian army displaced the entire foundation of the Prussian State edifice; the junker dominance became ever more intolerable, even for the government itself. At the same time, however, the struggle between the bourgeoisie and the workers made inevitable by the impetuous growth of industry, relegated to the background the struggle between junkers and bourgeoisie, so that the inner social foundations of the old State suffered a complete transformation. Ever since 1840, the condition making possible the existence of the slowly rotting monarchy was the struggle between nobility and bourgeoisie, wherein the monarchy retained equilibrium. From the moment, however, when it was no more a question of protecting the nobility against the onslaught of the bourgeoisie, but of protecting all propertied classes against the onslaught of the working-class, the absolute monarchy had to turn to that form of state which was expressly devised for this specific purpose,—the Bonapartist monarchy. This change of Prussia towards Bonapartism I have discussed in another place (*Wohnungsfrage*). What I did not stress there, and what is very important in this connection, is that this change was the greatest progress made by Prussia after 1848, which only shows how backward Prussia was in point of modern development. It is a fact that the Prussian State still was a semi-feudal State, whereas Bonapartism is, at all events, a modern form of state which presupposes the abolition of feudalism. Thus Prussia must decide to do away with its numerous remnants of feudalism, to sacrifice its junkerdom as such. This, naturally, is being done in the mildest possible form, and under the tune of the favourite melody, "Always slowly forward." An example of such "reform" work is the notorious organisation of districts, which, removing the feudal privileges of the individual Junker in relation to his estate, restores them as special privileges of the big landowners in relation to the entire district. The substance remains, it being only translated from the feudal into the bourgeois dialect. The old Prussian Junker is forcibly being transformed into something akin to the English squire. He need not have offered so much resistance, because the one is just as foolish as the other.

Thus it was the peculiar feat of Prussia not only to culminate, by the end of this century, her bourgeois revolution begun in 1808–13 and continued in 1848, but to culminate it in the present form of Bonapartism. If everything goes well, and the world remains nice and quiet, and we all become old enough, we can still perhaps live to see—about 1900—the government of Prussia actually relinquishing all feudal institutions, and Prussia finally reaching a point where France stood in 1792.

Speaking positively, the abolition of feudalism means the introduction of bourgeois conditions. In the measure as the privileges of the nobility fall, legislation becomes more and more bourgeois. Here, again, we meet with the chief point at issue, the attitude of the German bourgeoisie towards the government. We have seen that the government is compelled to introduce these slow and petty reforms, but in its relation to the bourgeoisie, the government portrays these small concessions as sacrifices in favour of the bourgeoisie, as concessions yielded by the crown with difficulty and pain, and for which the bourgeoisie must, in return, yield something to the government. The bourgeoisie, on the other hand, though quite aware of this state of affairs, allows itself to be fooled. This is the source of the tacit agreement which is the basis of all Reichstag and Chamber debates. On the one hand, the government reforms the laws at a snail pace tempo in the interests of the bourgeoisie; it removes the impediments to industry emanating from the multiplicity of small states; it creates unity of coinage, of measures and weights; it gives freedom of trade, etc.; it grants the freedom of movement; it puts the working power of Germany at the unlimited disposal of capital; it creates favourable conditions for trade and speculation. On the other hand, the bourgeoisie

14

leaves in the hands of the government all actual political power; it votes taxes, loans and recruits; it helps to frame all new reform laws in a way that the old police power over undesirable individuals shall remain in full force. The bourgeoisie buys its gradual social emancipation for the price of immediate renunciation of its own political power. Naturally, the motive which makes such agreement acceptable to the bourgeoisie is not the fear of the government but the fear of the proletariat.

Miserable as the bourgeoisie appears in the political realm, it cannot be denied that as far as industry and commerce are concerned, the bourgeoisie fulfils its historic duty. The growth of industry and commerce mentioned already in the introduction to the second edition has been going on with even greater vigour. What has taken place in the Rhenish-Westphalian industrial region since 1869 is unprecedented for Germany, and it reminds one of the rapid growth in the English manufacturing districts at the beginning of this century. The same thing will happen in Saxony and Upper Silesia, in Berlin, Hanover, and the southern States. At last we have world trade, a really big industry, and a really modern bourgeoisie. But we have also had a real crisis, and we have a truly mighty proletariat. For the future historian of Germany, the battle roar of 1859–64 on the field of Spicheren, Mars la Tour, Sedan, and the rest, will be of much less importance than the unpretentious, quiet, and constantly forward-moving development of the German proletariat. Immediately after 1870, the German workers stood before a grave trial—the Bonapartist war provocation and its natural sequence, the general national enthusiasm in Germany. The German workers did not allow themselves to be illusioned for a moment. Not a trace of national chauvinism made itself manifest among them. In the midst of a mania for victory, they remained cool, demanding "equitable peace with the French Republic and no annexations," and not even the state of siege was in a position to silence them. No glory of battle, no phraseology of German "imperial magnificence" attracted them. Their sole aim remained the liberation of the entire European prole-

15

tariat. We may say with full assurance that in no country have the workers stood such a difficult test with such splendid results.

The state of siege of wartime was followed by trials for treason, *lèse majesté,* and contempt of officers and by ever increasing police atrocities practised in peace time. The *Volksstaat* had three or four editors in prison simultaneously; the other papers, in the same ratio. Every known party speaker had to face court at least once a year, and was usually convicted. Deportations, confiscations, suppressions of meetings rapidly followed one another, but all to no avail. The place of every prisoner or deportee was immediately filled by another. For one suppressed gathering, two others were substituted, wearing out arbitrary police power in one locality after the other by endurance and strict conformity to the law. Persecution defeated its own purpose. Far from breaking the workers' party or even bending it, it attracted ever new recruits, and strengthened the organisation. In their struggle against the authorities and the individual bourgeois, the workers manifested an intellectual and moral superiority. Particularly in their conflicts with the employers of labour did they show that they, the workers, were now the educated class, while the capitalists were dupes. In their fights, a sense of humour prevailed, showing how sure they were of their cause, and how superior they felt. A struggle thus conducted on historically prepared soil must yield great results. The success of the January (1874) elections stood out, unique in the history of the modern labour movement, and the astonishment aroused by them throughout Europe was perfectly deserved.

The German workers have two important advantages compared with the rest of Europe. First, they belong to the most theoretical people of Europe; second, they have retained that sense of theory which the so-called "educated" people of Germany have totally lost. Without German philosophy, particularly that of Hegel, German scientific Socialism (the only scientific Socialism extant) would never have come into existence. Without a sense for theory, scientific Socialism would have never

16

become blood and tissue of the workers. What an enormous advantage this is, may be seen on the one hand from the indifference of the English labour movement towards all theory, which is one of the reasons why it moves so slowly in spite of the splendid organisation of the individual unions; on the other hand, from the mischief and confusion created by Proudhonism in its original form among the Frenchmen and Belgians, and in its caricature form, as presented by Bakunin, among the Spaniards and Italians.

The second advantage is that, chronologically speaking, the Germans were the last to appear in the labour movement. In the same manner as German theoretical Socialism will never forget that it rests on the shoulders of Saint Simon, Fourier and Owen, the three who, in spite of their fantastic notions and Utopianism, belonged to the most significant heads of all time and whose genius anticipated numerous things the correctness of which can now be proved in a scientific way, so the practical German labour movement must never forget that it has developed on the shoulders of the English and French movements, that it had utilised their experience, acquired at a heavy price, and that for this reason it was in a position to avoid their mistakes which in their time were unavoidable. Without the English trade unions and the French political workers' struggles preceding the German labour movement, without the mighty impulse given by the Paris Commune, where would we now be?

It must be said to the credit of the German workers that they have utilised the advantages of their situation with rare understanding. For the first time in the history of the labour movement the struggle is being so conducted that its three sides, the theoretical, the political and the practical economical (opposition to the capitalists), form one harmonious and well-planned entity. In this concentric attack, as it were, lies the strength and invincibility of the German movement.

It is due to this advantageous situation on the one hand, to the insular peculiarities of the British, and to the cruel suppression of the French movements on the other, that for the present moment the German workers form the vanguard of the proletarian struggle. How long events will allow them to occupy this post of honour cannot be foreseen. But as long as they are placed in it, let us hope that they will discharge their duties in the proper manner. It is the specific duty of the leaders to gain an ever clearer understanding of the theoretical problems, to free themselves more and more from the influence of traditional phrases inherited from the old conception of the world, and constantly to keep in mind that Socialism, having become a science, demands the same treatment as every other science—it must be studied. The task of the leaders will be to bring understanding, thus acquired and clarified, to the working masses, to spread it with increased enthusiasm, to close the rank of the party organisations and of the labour unions with ever greater energy. The votes cast in favour of the Socialists last January may represent considerable strength, but they still are far from being the majority of the German working class; and encouraging as may be the successes of the propaganda among the rural population, more remains to be done in this field. The slogan is not to flinch in the struggle. The task is to wrest from after the other. In the first place, however, it is necessary to the enemy's hands one seat after the other, one electoral district retain a real international spirit which permits of no chauvinism, which joyfully greets each new step of the proletarian movement, no matter in which nation it is made. If the German workers proceed in this way, they may not march exactly at the head of the movement—it is not in the interest of the movement that the workers of one country should march at the head of all—but they will occupy an honourable place on the battle line, and they will stand armed for battle when other unexpected grave trials or momentous events will demand heightened courage, heightened determination, and the will to act.

Friedrich Engels

London, July 1, 1874

I

THE German people are by no means lacking in revolutionary tradition. There were times when Germany produced characters that could match the best men in the revolutions of other countries; when the German people manifested an endurance and energy which, in a centralised nation, would have brought the most magnificent results; when the German peasants and plebeians were pregnant with ideas and plans which often made their descendants shudder.

In contrast to present-day enfeeblement which appears everywhere after two years of struggle (since 1848) it is timely to present once more to the German people those awkward but powerful and tenacious figures of the great peasant war. Three centuries have flown by since then, and many a thing has changed; still the peasant war is not as far removed from our present-day struggles as it would seem, and the opponents we have to encounter remain essentially the same. Those classes and fractions of classes which everywhere betrayed 1848 and 1849, can be found in the rôle of traitors as early as 1525, though on a lower level of development. And if the robust vandalism of the peasant wars appeared in the movement of the last years only sporadically, in the Odenwald, in the Black Forest, in Silesia, it by no means shows a superiority of the modern insurrection.

Let us first review briefly the situation in Germany at the beginning of the Sixteenth Century.

German industry had gone through a considerable process of

19

growth in the Fourteenth and Fifteenth Centuries. The local industry of the feudal countryside was superseded by the guild organisation of production in the cities, which produced for wider circles and even for remote markets. Weaving of crude woollen stuffs and linens had become a well-established, ramified branch of industry, and even finer woollen and linen fabrics, as well as silks, were already being produced in Augsburg. Outside of the art of weaving, there had arisen those branches of industry, which, approaching the finer arts, were nurtured by the demands for luxuries on the part of the ecclesiastic and lay lords of the late mediaeval epoch: gold- and silver-smithing, sculpture and wood-carving, etching and wood-engraving, armour-making, medal-engraving, wood-turning, etc., etc. A series of more or less important discoveries culminating in the invention of gunpowder and printing had considerably aided the development of the crafts. Commerce kept pace with industry. The Hanseatic League, through its century-long monopoly of sea navigation, had brought about the emergence of the entire north of Germany out of mediaeval barbarism; and even when, after the end of the Sixteenth Century, the Hanseatic League had begun to succumb to the competition of the English and the Dutch, the great highway of commerce from India to the north still lay through Germany, Vasco da Gama's discoveries notwithstanding. Augsburg still remained the great point of concentration for Italian silks, Indian spices, and all Levantine products. The cities of upper Germany, namely, Augsburg and Nuernberg, were the centres of opulence and luxury remarkable for that time. The production of raw materials had equally progressed. The German miners of the Fifteenth Century had been the most skilful in the world, and agriculture was also shaken out of its mediaeval crudity through the blossoming forth of the cities. Not only had large stretches of land been put under cultivation, but dye plants and other imported cultures had been introduced, which in turn had a favourable influence on agriculture as a whole.

Still, the progress of national production in Germany had not kept pace with the progress of other countries. Agriculture lagged far behind that of England and Holland. Industry lagged far behind the Italian, Flemish and English, and as to sea navigation, the English, and especially the Dutch, were already driving the Germans out of the field. The population was still very sparse. Civilisation in Germany existed only in spots, around the centres of industry and commerce; but even the interests of these individual centres diverged widely, with hardly any point of contact. The trade relations and markets of the South differed from those of the North; the East and the West had almost no intercourse. No city had grown to become the industrial and commercial point of gravity for the whole country, such as London was for England. Internal communication was almost exclusively confined to coastwise and river navigation and to a few large commercial highways, like those from Augsburg and Nuernberg through Cologne to the Netherlands, and through Erfurt to the North. Away from the rivers and highways of commerce there was a number of smaller cities which, excluded from the great trade centres, continued a sluggish existence under conditions of late mediaeval times, consuming few non-local articles, and yielding few products for export. Of the rural population, only the nobility came into contact with wide circles and new wants; the mass of the peasants never overstepped the boundaries of local relations and local outlook.

While in England, as well as in France, the rise of commerce and industry had brought about a linking of interests over the entire country, the political centralisation of Germany had succeeded only in the grouping of interests according to provinces and around purely local centres. This meant political decentralisation which later gained momentum through the exclusion of Germany from world commerce. In the degree as the purely feudal empire was falling apart, bonds of unity were becoming weakened, great feudal vassals were turning into almost independent princes, and cities of the empire on the one hand, the knights of the empire on the other, were forming alliances either against each other, or against the princes or the emperor. The imperial power, now uncertain as to its own position, vacillated between the various elements opposing the empire, and was constantly losing authority; the attempt at centralisation, in the manner of Louis XI, brought about nothing but the holding together of the Austrian hereditary lands, this in spite of all intrigues and violent actions. The final winners, who could not help winning in this confusion, in this helter-skelter of numerous conflicts, were the representatives of centralisation amidst disunion, the representatives of local and provincial centralisation, the princes, beside whom the emperor gradually became no more than a prince among princes.

Under these conditions the situation of the classes emerging from mediaeval times had considerably changed. New classes had been formed besides the old ones.

Out of the old nobility came the princes. Already they were almost independent of the emperor, and possessed the major part of sovereign rights. They declared war and made peace of their own accord, they maintained standing armies, called local councils, and levied taxes. They had already drawn a large part of the lower nobility and cities under their lordly power; they did everything in their power to incorporate in their lands all the rest of the cities and baronies which still remained under the empire. Towards such cities and baronies they appeared in the rôle of centralisers, while as far as the imperial power was concerned, they were the decentralising factor. Internally, their reign was already autocratic, they called the estates only when they could not do without them. They imposed taxes, and collected money whenever they saw fit. The right of the estates to ratify taxes was seldom recognised, and still more seldom practised. And even when they were called, the princes ordinarily had a majority, thanks to the knights and the prelates which were the two estates freed from taxes, participating, nevertheless, in their consumption. The need of the princes for money grew with the taste for luxuries, with the increase of the courts and the standing armies, with the mounting costs of administration. The taxes were becoming more and more oppressive. The cities being in most cases protected against them by privileges, the entire weight of the tax burden fell upon the peasants, those under the princes themselves, as well as the serfs and bondsmen of the knights bound by vassalage to the princes; wherever direct taxation was insufficient, indirect taxes were introduced; the most skilful machinations of the art of finance were utilised to fill the gaping holes of the fiscal system. When nothing else availed, when there was nothing to pawn and no free imperial city was willing to grant credit any longer, one resorted to coin manipulations of the basest kind, one coined depreciated money, one set a higher or lower rate of legal tender most convenient for the prince. Trading in city and other privileges, subsequently to be taken away by force, in order that they might again be sold, seizing every attempt at opposition as an excuse for incendiarism and robbery of every kind, etc., etc., were lucrative and quite ordinary sources of income for the princes of those times. The administration of justice was also a constant and not unimportant article of trade for the princes. In brief, the subjects who, besides the princes, had to satisfy the private appetites of their magistrates and bailiffs as well, were enjoying the full taste of the "fatherly" system. Of the mediaeval feudal hierarchy, the knighthood of moderate possessions had almost entirely disappeared; it had either climbed up to the position of independence of small princes, or it had sunk into the ranks of the lower nobility. The lower nobility, the knighthood, was fast moving towards extinction. A large portion of it had already become pauperised, and lived on its services to the princes, either in military or in civil capacity; another portion was bound by vassalage to the sovereignty of the prince; a very small portion was directly under the empire. The development of military science, the rising importance of infantry, the spread of firearms, had dwarfed their military importance as heavy cavalry, at the same time destroying the invincibility of their castles. The knights had become superfluous through the progress of industry, just as the artisans had become obviated by the same progress. The dire need of the knighthood for money added considerably to their ruin. The luxurious life in the castles, the competition in magnificence at tournaments and feasts, the price of armaments and of horses all increased with the progress of civilisation, whereas the sources of income of the knights and barons, increased but little, if at all. Feuds with accompanying plunders and incendiarism, lying in ambush, and similar noble occupations, became in the course of time too dangerous. The cash payments of the knights' subjects brought in hardly more than before. In order to satisfy mounting requirements, the noble masters resorted to the same means as were practised by the princes; the peasantry was being robbed by the masters with greater dexterity every year. The serfs were being wrung dry. The bondsmen were burdened with ever new payments of various descriptions upon every possible occasion. Serf labour, dues, ground rents, land sale taxes, death taxes, protection moneys and so on, were increased at will in spite of old agreements. Justice was denied or sold for money, and wherever the knight could not obtain the peasant's money otherwise, he threw him into the tower without much ado, and compelled him to pay ransom.

With the other classes, the lower nobility courted no friendly relations either. Vassal knights strove to become vassals of the empire; vassals of the empire strove to become independent. This led to incessant conflicts with the princes. The knighthood looked upon the clergy with their resplendent grandeur as upon a powerful but superfluous class. It envied them their large estates and their riches held secure by celibacy and the church constitution. With the cities, the knighthood was continually on the war path; it owed them money, it fed on plundering their territory, on robbing their merchants, on the ransom paid for prisoners captured in conflicts. The struggle of the knighthood against all these estates became more vehement as the estates themselves began to realise that the money question was a life problem for them.

The clergy, representatives of the ideology of mediaeval feudalism, felt the influence of the historic transformation no less acutely. The invention of the art of printing, and the requirements of extended commerce, robbed the clergy not only of its monopoly of reading and writing, but also of that of higher education. Division of labour was being introduced also into the realm of intellectual work. The newly arising class of jurists drove the clergy out of a series of very influential positions. The clergy was also beginning to become largely superfluous, and it acknowledged this fact by growing lazier and more ignorant. The more superfluous it became, the more it grew in numbers, thanks to the enormous riches which it still kept on augmenting by fair means or foul.

The clergy was divided into two distinct groups. The feudal hierarchy of the clergy formed the aristocratic group—bishops and archbishops, abbots, priors and other prelates. These high church dignitaries were either imperial princes themselves, or they reigned as vassals of other princes over large areas with numerous serfs and bondsmen. They not only exploited their subjects as recklessly as the knighthood and the princes, but they practised this in an even more shameful manner. They used not only brutal force, but all the intrigues of religion as well; not only the horrors of the rack, but also the horror of excommunication, or refusal of absolution; they used all the intricacies of the confessional in order to extract from their subjects the last penny, or to increase the estates of the church. Forging of documents was a widespread and beloved means of extortion in the hands of those worthy men, who, receiving from their subjects feudal payments, taxes and tithes, were still in constant need of money. The manufacture of miracle-producing saints' effigies and relics, the organisation of praying-centres endowed with the power of salvation, the trade in indulgences was resorted to in order to squeeze more payments out of the people. All this was practised long and with not little success.

The prelates and their numerous gendarmerie of monks which grew with the spread of political and religious baiting, were the objects of hatred not only of the people but also of the nobility. Being directly under the empire, the prelates were in the way of the princes. The fast living of the corpulent bishops and abbots with their army of monks, roused the envy of the nobility and the indignation of the people who bore the burden. Hatred was intensified by the fact that the behaviour of the clergy was a slap in the face of their own preaching.

The plebeian faction of the clergy consisted of preachers, rural and urban. The preachers were outside the feudal hierarchy of the church and participated in none of its riches. Their activities were less rigorously controlled and, important as they were for the church, they were for the moment far less indispensable than the police services of the barracked monks. Consequently, they were paid much less than the monks, and their prebends were far from lucrative. Being of a middle-class or plebeian origin, they were nearer to the life of the masses, thus being able to retain middle-class and plebeian sympathies, in spite of their status as clergy. While the participation of the monks in the movements of their time was the exception, that of the plebeian clergy was the rule. They gave the movement its theorists and ideologists, and many of them, representatives of the plebeians and peasants, died on the scaffold. The hatred of the masses for the clergy seldom touched this group.

What the emperor was to the princes and nobility, the pope was to the higher and lower clergy. As the emperor received the "common penny," the imperial taxes, so the pope was paid the general church taxes, out of which he defrayed the expenses of the luxurious Roman court. In no country were his taxes collected with such conscientiousness and rigour as in Germany, due to the power and the number of the clergy. The annates were collected with particular severity when a bishopric was to become vacant. With the growth of the court's demands, new means for raising revenues were invented, such as the traffic in relics and indulgences, jubilee collections, etc. Large sums of money were thus yearly transported from Germany to Rome, and the increased pressure fanned not only the hatred towards the clergy, but it also aroused national feelings, particularly among the nobility, the then most national class.

In the cities, the growth of commerce and handicraft produced three distinct groups out of the original citizenry of mediaeval times.

The city population was headed by the *patrician families*, the so-called "honourables." Those were the richest families. They alone sat in the council, and held all the city offices. They not

26

only administered all the revenues of the city, but they also consumed them. Strong in their riches and their ancient aristocratic status, recognised by emperor and empire, they exploited in every possible way the city community as well as the peasants belonging to the city. They practised usury in grain and money; they secured for themselves monopolies of various kinds; they gradually deprived the community of every right to use the city forests and meadows, and used them directly for their own private benefit. They imposed road, bridge and gate payments and other duties; they sold trade and guild privileges, master and citizen rights; and they traded with justice. The peasants of the city area were treated by them with no more consideration than by the nobility and the clergy. On the contrary, the city magistrates and bailiffs, mostly patricians, brought into the villages, together with aristocratic rigidity and avarice, a certain bureaucratic punctuality in collecting duties. The city revenues thus collected were administered in a most optional fashion; city bookkeeping was as neglectful and confused as possible; defraudation and treasury deficits were the order of the day. How easy it was for a comparatively small caste, surrounded by privileges, and held together by family ties and community of interests, to enrich itself enormously out of the city revenues, will be understood when one considers the numerous frauds and swindles which 1848 witnessed in many city administrations.

The patricians took care to make dormant the rights of the city community everywhere, particularly as regards finance. Later, when the extortions of these gentlemen became too severe, the communities started a movement to bring at least the city administration under their control. In most cities they actually regained their rights, but due, on the one hand, to the eternal squabbles between the guilds and, on the other, to the tenacity of the patricians and their protection by the empire and the governments of the allied cities, the patrician council members soon restored by shrewdness or force their dominance in the councils. At the beginning of the Sixteenth Century, the communities of all the cities were again in the opposition.

The city opposition against the patricians was divided into two factions which stood out very clearly in the course of the peasant war.

The *middle-class opposition,* the predecessor of our modern liberals, embraced the richer middle-class, the middle-class of moderate means, and a more or less appreciable section of the poorer elements, according to local conditions. This opposition demanded control over the city administration and participation in the legislative power either through a general assemblage of the community or through representatives (big council, city committee). Further, it demanded modification of the patrician policy of favouring a few families which were gaining an exceptional position inside the patrician group. Aside from this, the middle-class opposition demanded the filling of some council offices by citizens of their own group. This party, joined here and there by dissatisfied elements of impoverished patricians, had a large majority in all the ordinary general assemblies of the community and in the guilds. The adherents of the council and the more radical opposition formed together only a minority among the real citizens.

We shall see how, in the course of the Sixteenth Century, this moderate, "law-abiding," well-off and intelligent opposition played exactly the same rôle and exactly with the same success as its heir, the constitutional party in the movements of 1848 and 1849. The middle-class opposition had still another object of heated protest: the clergy, whose loose way of living and luxurious habits aroused its bitter scorn. The middle-class opposition demanded measures against the scandalous behaviour of those illustrious people. It demanded that the inner jurisdiction of the clergy and its right to levy taxes should be abolished, and that the number of the monks should be limited.

The *plebeian opposition* consisted of ruined members of the middle-class and that mass of the city population which possessed no citizenship rights: the journeymen, the day labourers, and the numerous beginnings of the *lumpenproletariat* which can be found even in the lowest stages of development of city life. This low-grade proletariat is, generally speaking, a phenomenon which, in a more or less developed form, can be found in all the phases of society hitherto observed. The number of people without a definite occupation and a stable domicile was at that time gradually being augmented by the decay of feudalism in a society in which every occupation, every realm of life, was intrenched behind a number of privileges. In no modern country was the number of vagabonds so great as in Germany, in the first half of the Sixteenth Century. One portion of these tramps joined the army in war-time, another begged its way through the country, a third sought to eke out a meagre living as day-labourers in those branches of work which were not under guild jurisdiction. All three groups played a rôle in the peasant war; the first in the army of the princes to whom the peasant succumbed, the second in the conspiracies and in the troops of the peasants where its demoralising influence was manifested every moment; the third, in the struggles of the parties in the cities. It must be borne in mind, however, that a large portion of this class, namely, the one living in the cities, still retained a considerable foundation of peasant nature, and had not developed that degree of venality and degradation which characterise the modern civilised low-grade proletariat.

It is evident that the plebeian opposition of the cities was of a mixed nature. It combined the ruined elements of the old feudal and guild societies with the budding proletarian elements of a coming modern bourgeois society; on the one hand, impoverished guild citizens, who, due to their privileges, still clung to the existing middle-class order, on the other hand, driven out peasants and ex-officers who were yet unable to become proletarians. Between these two groups were the journeymen, for the time being outside official society and so close to the standard of living of the proletariat as was possible under the industry of the times and the guild privileges, but, due to the same privileges, almost all prospective middle-class master artisans. The party affiliations of this mixture were, naturally, highly uncertain, and varying from locality to locality. Before the peasant war, the plebeian opposition appeared in the political struggles, not as a party, but as a shouting, rapacious tail-end to the middle-class opposition, a mob that could be bought and sold for a few barrels of wine. It was the revolt of the peasants that transformed them into a party, and even then they were almost everywhere dependent upon the peasants, both in demands and in action—a striking proof of the fact that the cities of that time were greatly dependent upon the country. In so far as the plebeian opposition acted independently, it demanded extension of city trade privileges over the rural districts, and it did not like to see the city revenues curtailed by abolition of feudal burdens in the rural area belonging to the city, etc. In brief, in so far as it appeared independently, it was reactionary. It submitted to its own middle-class elements, and thus formed a characteristic prologue to the tragic comedy staged by the modern petty-bourgeoisie in the last three years under the head of democracy.

Only in Thuringia and in a few other localities was the plebeian faction of the city carried away by the general storm to such an extent that its embryo proletarian elements for a brief time gained the upper hand over all the other factors of the movement. This took place under the direct influence of Muenzer in Thuringia, and of his disciples in other places. This episode, forming the climax of the entire peasant war, and grouped around the magnificent figure of Thomas Muenzer, was of very brief duration. It is easily understood why these elements collapse more quickly than any other, why their movement bears an outspoken, fantastic stamp, and why the expression of their demands must necessarily be extremely indefinite. It was this group that found least firm ground in the then existing conditions.

At the bottom of all the classes, save the last one, was the huge exploited mass of the nation, *the peasants*. It was the peasant who carried the burden of all the other strata of society: princes, officialdom, nobility, clergy, patricians and middle-class. Whether the peasant was the subject of a prince, an imperial baron, a bishop, a monastery or a city, he was everywhere treated as a beast of burden, and worse. If he was a serf, he was entirely at the mercy of his master. If he was a bondsman, the legal deliveries stipulated by agreement were sufficient to crush him; even they were being daily increased. Most of his time, he had to work on his master's estate. Out of that which he earned in his few free hours, he had to pay tithes, dues, ground rents, war taxes, land taxes, imperial taxes, and other payments. He could neither marry nor die without paying the master. Aside from his regular work for the master, he had to gather litter, pick strawberries, pick bilberries, collect snail-shells, drive the game for the hunting, chop wood, and so on. Fishing and hunting belonged to the master. The peasant saw his crop destroyed by wild game. The community meadows and woods of the peasants had almost everywhere been forcibly taken away by the masters. And in the same manner as the master reigned over the peasant's property, he extended his wilfulness over his person, his wife and daughters. He possessed the right of the first night. Whenever he pleased, he threw the peasant into the tower, where the rack waited for him just as surely as the investigating attorney waits for the criminal in our times. Whenever he pleased, he killed him or ordered him beheaded. None of the instructive chapters of the Carolina which speaks of "cutting of ears," "cutting of noses," "blinding," "chopping of fingers," "beheading," "breaking on the wheel," "burning," "pinching with burning tongs," "quartering," etc., was left unpractised by the gracious lord and master at his pleasure. Who could defend the peasant? The courts were manned by barons, clergymen, patricians, or jurists, who knew very well for what they were being paid. Not in vain did all the official estates of the empire live on the exploitation of the peasants.

Incensed as were the peasants under terrific pressure, it was still difficult to arouse them to revolt. Being spread over large areas, it was highly difficult for them to come to a common understanding; the old habit of submission inherited from generation to generation, the lack of practise in the use of arms in many regions, the unequal degree of exploitation depending on the personality of the master, all combined to keep the peasant quiet. It is for these reasons that, although local insurrections of peasants can be found in mediaeval times in large numbers, not one general national peasant revolt, least of all in Germany, can be observed before the peasant war. Moreover, the peasant alone could never make a revolution as long as they were confronted by the organised power of the princes, nobility and the cities. Only by allying themselves with other classes could they have a chance of victory, but how could they have allied themselves with other classes when they were equally exploited by all?

At the beginning of the Sixteenth Century the various groups of the empire, princes, nobility, clergy, patricians, middle-class, plebeians and peasants formed a highly complicated mass with the most varied requirements crossing each other in different directions. Every group was in the way of the other, and stood continually in an overt or covert struggle with every other group. A splitting of the entire nation into two major camps, as witnessed in France at the outbreak of the first revolution, and as at present manifest on a higher stage of development in the most progressive countries, was under such conditions a rank impossibility. Something approaching such division took place only when the lowest stratum of the population, the one exploited by all the rest, arose, namely, the plebeians and the peasants. The tangle of interests, views and endeavours of that time will be easily understood when one remembers what a confusion was manifested in the last two years in a society far less complicated and consisting only of feudal nobility, bourgeoisie, petty-bourgeoisie, peasants and proletariat.

II

THE grouping of the numerous and variegated groups into bigger units was at that time made impossible by decentralisation, by local and provincial independence, by industrial and commercial isolation of the provinces from each other, and by poor means of communication. This grouping develops only with the general spread of revolutionary, religious and political ideas, in the course of the Reformation. The various groups of the population which either accept or oppose those ideas, concentrate the nation, very slowly and only approximately indeed, into three large camps, the reactionary or Catholic, the reformist middle-class or Lutheran, and the revolutionary elements. If we discover little logic even in this great division of the nation, if the first two camps include partly the same elements, it is due to the fact that most of the official groupings brought over from the Middle Ages had begun to dissolve and to become decentralised, which circumstance gave to the same groups in different localities a momentary opposing orientation. In the last years we have so often met with similar facts in Germany that we will not be surprised at this apparent mixture of groups and classes under the much more complicated conditions of the Sixteenth Century.

The German ideology of to-day sees in the struggles to which the Middle Ages had succumbed nothing but violent theological bickerings, this notwithstanding our modern experiences. Had the people of that time only been able to reach an understanding concerning the celestial things, say our patriotic historians and wise statesmen, there would have been no ground whatever for struggle over earthly affairs. These ideologists were gullible enough to accept on their face value all the illusions which an epoch maintains about itself, or which the ideologists of a certain period maintained about that period. This class of people, which saw in the revolution of 1789 nothing but a heated debate over the advantages of a constitutional monarchy as compared with absolutism, would see in the July Revolution a practical controversy over the untenability of the empire by the grace of God, and in the February Revolution, an attempt at solving the problem of a republic or monarchy, etc. Of the *class struggles* which were being fought out in these convulsions, and whose mere expression is being every time written as a political slogan on the banner of these class struggles, our ideologists have no conception even at the present time, although manifestations of them are audible enough not only abroad, but also from the grumbling and the resentment of many thousands of home proletarians.

In the so-called religious wars of the Sixteenth Century, very positive material class-interests were at play, and those wars were class wars just as were the later collisions in England and France. If the class struggles of that time appear to bear religious earmarks, if the interests, requirements and demands of the various classes hid themselves behind a religious screen, it little changes the actual situation, and is to be explained by conditions of the time.

The Middle Ages had developed out of raw primitiveness. It had done away with old civilisation, old philosophy, politics and jurisprudence, in order to begin anew in every respect. The only thing which it had retained from the old shattered world was Christianity and a number of half-ruined cities deprived of their civilisation. As a consequence, the clergy retained a monopoly of intellectual education, a phenomenon to be found in every primitive stage of development, and education itself had acquired a predominantly theological nature.

In the hands of the clergy, politics and jurisprudence, as well as other sciences, remained branches of theology, and were treated according to the principles prevailing in the latter. The dogmas of the church were at the same time political axioms, and Bible quotations had the validity of law in every court. Even after the formation of a special class of jurists, jurisprudence long remained under the tutelage of theology. This supremacy of theology in the realm of intellectual activities was at the same time a logical consequence of the situation of the church as the most general force co-ordinating and sanctioning existing feudal domination.

It is obvious that under such conditions, all general and overt attacks on feudalism, in the first place attacks on the church, all revolutionary, social and political doctrines, necessarily became theological heresies. In order to be attacked, existing social conditions had to be stripped of their aureole of sanctity.

The revolutionary opposition to feudalism was alive throughout all the Middle Ages. According to conditions of the time, it appeared either in the form of mysticism, as open heresy, or of armed insurrection. As mysticism, it is well known how indispensable it was for the reformers of the Sixteenth Century. Muenzer himself was largely indebted to it. The heresies were partly an expression of the reaction of the patriarchal Alpine shepherds against the encroachments of feudalism in their realm (Waldenses), partly an opposition to feudalism of the cities that had outgrown it (The Albigenses, Arnold of Brescia, etc.), and partly direct insurrections of peasants (John Ball, the master from Hungary in Picardy, etc.). We can omit, in this connection, the patriarchal heresy of the Waldenses, as well as the insurrection of the Swiss, which by form and contents, was a reactionary attempt at stemming the tide of historic development, and of a purely local importance. In the other two forms of mediaeval heresy, we find as early as the Twelfth Century the precursors of the great division between the middle-class and the peasant-plebeian opposition which caused the collapse of the peasant war. This division is manifest throughout the later Middle Ages.

The heresy of the cities, which is the actual official heresy of the Middle Ages, directed itself primarily against the clergy, whose riches and political importance it attacked. In the very same manner as the bourgeoisie at present demands a *"gouvernement à bon marché"* (cheap government), so the middle-class of mediaeval times demanded first of all an *"église à bon marché* (cheap church). Reactionary in form, as is every heresy which sees in the further development of church and dogma only a degeneration, the middle-class heresy demanded the restoration of the ancient simple church constitution and the abolition of an exclusive class of priests. This cheap arrangement would eliminate the monks, the prelates, the Roman court, in brief, everything which was expensive for the church. In their attack against papacy, the cities, themselves republics although under the protection of monarchs, expressed for the first time in a general form the idea that the normal form of government for the bourgeoisie was the republic. Their hostility towards many a dogma and church law is partly explained by the foregoing and partly by their conditions. Why they were so bitter against celibacy, no one has given a better explanation than Boccaccio. Arnold of Brescia in Italy and Germany, the Albigenses in south France, John Wycliffe in England, Huss and the Calixtines in Bohemia, were the chief representatives of this opposition. That the opposition against feudalism should appear here only as an opposition against religious feudalism, is easily understood when one remembers that, at that time, the cities were already a recognised estate sufficiently capable of fighting lay feudalism with its privileges either by force of arms or in the city assemblies.

Here, as in south France, in England and Bohemia, we find the lower nobility joining hands with the cities in their struggle against the clergy and in their heresies, a phenomenon due to the dependence of the lower nobility upon the cities and to the community of interests of both groups as against the princes and the prelates. The same phenomenon is found in the peasant war.

A totally different character was assumed by that heresy which was a direct expression of the peasant and plebeian demands, and which was almost always connected with an insurrection. This heresy, sharing all the demands of middle-class heresy relative to the clergy, the papacy, and the restoration of the ancient Christian church organisation, went far beyond them. It demanded the restoration of ancient Christian equality among the members of the community, this to be recognised as a rule for the middle-class world as well. From the equality of the children of God it made the implication as to civil equality, and partly also as to equality of property. To make the nobility equal to the peasant, the patricians and the privileged middle-class equal to the plebeians, to abolish serfdom, ground rents, texes, privileges, and at least the most flagrant differences of property—these were demands put forth with more or less definiteness and regarded as naturally emanating from the ancient Christian doctrine. This peasant-plebeian heresy, in the fullness of feudalism, e. g., among the Albigenses, hardly distinguishable from the middle-class opposition, grew in the course of the Fourteenth and Fifteenth Centuries to be a strongly defined party opinion appearing independently alongside the heresy of the middle-class. This is the case with John Ball, preacher of the Wat Tyler insurrection in England alongside the Wycliffe movement. This is also the case with the Taborites alongside the Calixtines in Bohemia. The Taborites showed even a republican tendency under theocratic colouring, a view later developed by the representatives of the plebeians in Germany in the Fifteenth and at the beginning of the Sixteenth Century.

This form of heresy was joined in by the dream visions of the mystic sects, such as the Scourging Friars, the Lollards, etc., which in times of suppression continued revolutionary tradition.

The plebeians of that time were the only class outside of the existing official society. It was outside the feudal, as well as outside the middle-class organisation. It had neither privileges nor property; it was deprived even of the possessions owned by peasant or petty bourgeois, burdened with crushing duties as much as they might be; it was deprived of property and rights in every respect; it lived in such a manner that it did not even come into direct contact with the existing institutions, which ignored it completely. It was a living symptom of the dissolution of the feudal and guild middle-class societies, and it was at the same time the first precursor of modern bourgeois society.

This position of the plebeians is sufficient explanation as to why the plebeian opposition of that time could not be satisfied with fighting feudalism and the privileged middle-class alone; why, in fantasy, at least, it reached beyond modern bourgeois society then only in its inception; why, being an absolutely propertyless faction, it questioned institutions, views and conceptions common to every society based on division of classes. The chiliastic dream-visions of ancient Christianity offered in this respect a very serviceable starting-point. On the other hand, this reaching out beyond not only the present but also the future, could not help being violently fantastic. At the first practical application, it naturally fell back into narrow limits set by prevailing conditions. The attack on private property, the demand for community of possession had to solve itself into a crude organisation of charity; vague Christian equality could result in nothing but civic equality before the law; abolition of all officialdom transformed itself finally in the organisation of republican governments elected by the people. Anticipation of communism by human fantasy was in reality anticipation of modern bourgeois conditions.

This anticipation of coming stages of historic development, forced in itself, but a natural outcome of the life conditions of the plebeian group, is first to be noted in Germany, in the teachings of Thomas Muenzer and his party. Already the Taborites showed a kind of chiliastic community of property, but this was a purely military measure. Only in the teachings of Muenzer did these communist notions find expression as the desires of a vital section of society. Through him they were formulated with a certain definiteness, and were afterwards found in every great convulsion of the people, until gradually they merged with the modern proletarian movement. Something similar we observe in the Middle Ages, where the struggles of the free peasants against increasing feudal domination merged with the struggles of the serfs and bondsmen for the complete abolition of the feudal system.

While the first of the three large camps, the conservative Catholics, embraced all the elements interested in maintaining the existing imperial power, the ecclesiastical and a section of the lay princes, the richer nobility, the prelates and the city patricians—the middle-class moderate Lutheran reform gathered under its banner all the propertied elements of the opposition, the mass of the lower nobility, the middle-class and even a portion of the lay princes who hoped to enrich themselves through the confiscation of the church estates and to seize the opportunity for establishing greater independence from the empire. As to the peasants and plebeians, they grouped themselves around the revolutionary party whose demands and doctrines found their boldest expression in Muenzer.

Luther and Muenzer, in their doctrines, in their characters, in their actions, accurately embodied the tenets of their separate parties.

Between 1517 and 1525, Luther had gone through the same transformations as the German constitutionalists between 1846 and 1849. This has been the case with every middle-class party which, having marched for a while at the head of the movement, has been overwhelmed by the plebeian-proletarian party pressing from the rear.

When in 1517 opposition against the dogmas and the organisation of the Catholic church was first raised by Luther, it still had no definite character. Not exceeding the demands of the earlier middle-class heresy, it did not exclude any trend of opinion which went further. It could not do so because the first moment of the struggle demanded that all opposing elements be united, the most aggressive revolutionary energy be utilised, and the totality of the existing heresies fighting the Catholic orthodoxy be represented. In a similar fashion, our liberal bourgeoisie of 1847 were still revolutionary. They called themselves socialists and communists and they discussed emancipation of the working class. Luther's sturdy peasant nature asserted itself in the stormiest fashion in the first period of his activities. "If the raging madness [of the Roman churchmen] were to continue, it seems to me no better counsel and remedy could be found

against it than that kings and princes apply force, arm themselves, attack those evil people who have poisoned the entire
world, and once and for all make an end to this game, *with
arms, not with words.* If thieves are being punished with
swords, murderers with ropes, and heretics with fire, why do we
not seize, with arms in hand, all those evil teachers of perdition,
those popes, bishops, cardinals, and the entire crew of Roman
Sodom? Why do we not wash our hands in their blood?"

This revolutionary ardour did not last long. The lightning
thrust by Luther caused a conflagration. A movement started
among the entire German people. In his appeals against the
clergy, in his preaching of Christian freedom, peasants and
plebeians perceived the signal for insurrection. Likewise, the
moderate middle-class and a large section of the lower nobility
joined him, and even princes were drawn into the torrent.
While the former believed the day had come in which to wreak
vengeance upon all their oppressors, the latter only wished to
break the power of the clergy, the dependence upon Rome, the
Catholic hierarchy, and to enrich themselves through the confiscation of church property. The parties became separated from
each other, and each found a different spokesman. Luther had
to choose between the two. Luther, the protégé of the Elector of
Saxony, the respected professor of Wittenberg who had become
powerful and famous overnight, the great man who was surrounded by a coterie of servile creatures and flatterers, did not
hesitate a moment. He dropped the popular elements of the
movement, and joined the train of the middle-class, the nobility
and the princes. Appeals to a war of extermination against
Rome were heard no more. Luther was now preaching *peaceful
progress* and passive resistance. (Cf. *To the nobility of the
German nation,* 1520, etc.) Invited by Hutten to visit him and
Sickingen in the castle of Ebern, the centre of the noble conspiracy against clergy and princes, Luther replied: "*I should not
like to see the Gospel defended by force and bloodshed.* The
world was conquered by the Word, the Church has maintained
itself by the Word, the Church will come into its own again

through the Word, and as Antichrist gained ascendency without violence, so without violence he will fall."

Out of this turn of mind, or, to be more exact, out of this definite delineation of Luther's policy, sprang that policy of bartering and haggling over institutions and dogmas to be retained or reformed, that ugly diplomatising, conceding, intriguing and compromising, the result of which was the Augsburg Confession, the final draft of the constitution of the reformed middle-class church. It was the same petty trading which, in the political field, repeated itself *ad nauseam* in the recent German national assemblies, unity gatherings, chambers of revision, and in the parliaments of Erfurt. The Philistine middle-class character of the official reformation appeared in these negotiations most clearly.

There were valid reasons why Luther, now the recognised representative of middle-class reform, chose to preach lawful progress. The mass of the cities had joined the cause of moderate reform; the lower nobility became more and more devoted to it; one section of the princes joined it, another vacillated. Success was almost certain at least in a large portion of Germany. Under continued peaceful development the other regions could not in the long run withstand the pressure of moderate opposition. Violent convulsions, on the other hand, were bound to result in a conflict between the moderates and the extreme plebeian and peasant party, thus to alienate the princes, the nobility, and a number of cities from the movement and to leave open the alternative of either the middle-class party being overshadowed by the peasants and plebeians, or the entire movement being crushed by Catholic restoration. How middle-class parties, having achieved the slightest victory, attempt to steer their way between the Scylla of revolution and the Charybdis of restoration by means of lawful progress, we have had occasions enough to observe in the events of recent times.

It was in the nature of the then prevailing social and political conditions that the results of every change were advantageous to the princes, increasing their power. Thus it came about that the middle-class reform, having parted ways with the plebeian and peasant elements, fell more and more under the control of the reform princes. Luther's subservience to them increased, and the people knew very well what they were doing when they accused him of having become a slave of the princes as were all the others, and when they pursued him with stones in Orlamuende.

When the peasant war broke out, becoming more predominant in regions with Catholic nobility and princes, Luther strove to maintain a conciliatory position. He resolutely attacked the governments. He said it was due to their oppression that the revolts had started, that not the peasants alone were against them, but God as well. On the other hand, he also said that the revolt was ungodly and against the Gospel. He advised both parties to yield, to reach a peaceful understanding.

Notwithstanding these sincere attempts at conciliation, however, the revolt spread rapidly over large areas, including such sections as were dominated by Protestant Lutheran princes, nobles and cities, and rapidly outgrew the middle-class "circumspect" reform. The most determined faction of the insurgents under Muenzer opened their headquarters in Luther's very proximity, in Thuringia. A few more successes, and Germany would have been one big conflagration, Luther would have been surrounded, perhaps piked as a traitor, and middle-class reform would have been swept away by the tides of a peasant-plebeian revolution. There was no more time for circumspection. In the face of the revolution, all old animosities were forgotten. Compared with the hordes of peasants, the servants of the Roman Sodom were innocent lambs, sweet-tempered children of God. Burgher and prince, noble and clergyman, Luther and the pope united "against the murderous and plundering hordes of the peasants." "They should be knocked to pieces, strangled and stabbed, secretly and openly, by everybody who can do it, just as one must kill a mad dog!" Luther cried. "Therefore, dear gentlemen, hearken here, save there, stab, knock, strangle them at will, and if thou diest, thou art blessed; no better death canst thou ever attain." No false mercy was to be practised in relation to the peasants. "Whoever hath pity on those whom God pities not, whom He wishes punished and destroyed, shall be classed among the rebellious himself." Later, he said, the peasants would learn to thank God when they had to give away one cow in order that they might enjoy the other in peace. Through the revolution, he said, the princes would learn the spirit of the mob which could reign by force only. "The wise man says: '*Cibus, onus et virgam asino.*' The heads of the peasants are full of chaff. They do not hearken to the Word, and they are senseless, so they must hearken to the virga and the gun, and this is only just. We must pray for them that they obey. Where they do not, there should not be much mercy. Let the guns roar among them, or else they will make it a thousand times worse."

It is the same language that was used by our late socialist and philanthropic bourgeoisie, when, after the March days the proletariat also demanded its share in the fruits of victory.

Luther had given the plebeian movement a powerful weapon—a translation of the Bible. Through the Bible, he contrasted feudal Christianity of his time with moderate Christianity of the first century. In opposition to decaying feudal society, he held up the picture of another society which knew nothing of the ramified and artificial feudal hierarchy. The peasants had made extensive use of this weapon against the forces of the princes, the nobility, and the clergy. Now Luther turned the same weapon against the peasants, extracting from the Bible a veritable hymn to the authorities ordained by God—a feat hardly exceeded by any lackey of absolute monarchy. Princedom by the grace of God, passive resistance, even serfdom, were being sanctioned by the Bible. Thus Luther repudiated not only the peasant insurrection but even his own revolt against religious and lay authority. He not only betrayed the popular movement to the princes, but the middle-class movement as well.

Need we mention other bourgeois who recently gave us examples of repudiating their own past?

Let us now compare the plebeian revolutionary, Muenzer, with the middle-class reformist, Luther.

Thomas Muenzer was born in Stolberg, in the Harz, in 1498. It is said that his father died on the scaffold, a victim of the wilfulness of the Count of Stolberg. In his fifteenth year, Muenzer organised at the Halle school a secret union against the Archbishop of Magdeburg and the Roman Church in general. His scholarly attainments in the theology of his time brought him early the doctor's degree and the position of chaplain in a Halle nunnery. Here he began to treat the dogmas and rites of the church with the greatest contempt. At mass he omitted the words of the transubstantiation, and ate, as Luther said, the almighty gods unconsecrated. Mediaeval mystics, especially the chiliastic works of Joachim of Calabria, were the main subject of his studies. It seemed to Muenzer that the millennium and the day of judgment over the degenerated church and the corrupted world, as announced and pictured by that mystic, had come in the form of the Reformation and the general restlessness of his time. He preached in his neighbourhood with great success. In 1520 he went to Zwickau as the first evangelist preacher. There he found one of those dreamy chiliastic sects which continued their existence in many localities, hiding behind an appearance of humility and detachment, the rankly growing opposition of the lower strata of society against existing conditions, and with the growth of agitation, beginning to press to the foreground more boldly and with more endurance. It was the sect of the Anabaptists headed by Nicolas Storch. The Anabaptists preached the approach of the Day of Judgment and of the millennium; they had "visions, convulsions, and the spirit of prophecy." They soon came into conflict with the council of Zwickau. Muenzer defended them, though he had never joined them unconditionally, and had rather brought them under his own influence. The council took decisive steps against them, they were compelled to leave the city, and Muenzer departed with them. This was at the end of 1521.

He then went to Prague and, in order to gain ground, attempted to join the remnants of the Hussite movement. His proclamations, however, made it necessary for him to flee Bohemia also. In 1522, he became preacher at Altstedt in Thuringia. Here he started with reforming the cult. Before even Luther dared to go so far, he entirely abolished the Latin language, and ordered the entire Bible, not only the prescribed Sunday Gospels and epistles, to be read to the people. At the same time, he organised propaganda in his locality. People flocked to him from all directions, and soon Altstedt became the centre of the popular anti-priest movement of entire Thuringia.

Muenzer at that time was still theologian before everything else. He directed his attacks almost exclusively against the priests. He did not, however, preach quiet debate and peaceful progress, as Luther had begun to do at that time, but he continued the early violent preachments of Luther, appealing to the princes of Saxony and the people to rise in arms against the Roman priests. "Is it not Christ who said: 'I have come to bring, not peace, but the sword'? What can you [the princes of Saxony] do with that sword? You can do only one thing: If you wish to be the servants of God, you must drive out and destroy the evil ones who stand in the way of the Gospel. Christ ordered very earnestly (Luke, 19, 27): 'But these mine enemies, that would not that I should reign over them, bring hither, and slay them before me.' Do not resort to empty assertions that the power of God could do it without aid of our sword, since then it would have to rust in its sheath. We must destroy those who stand in the way of God's revelation, we must do it mercilessly, as Hezekiah, Cyrus, Josiah, Daniel and Elias destroyed the priests of Baal, else the Christian Church will never come back to its origins. We must uproot the weeds in God's vineyard at the time when the crops are ripe. God said in the Fifth Book of Moses, 7, 'Thou shalt not show mercy unto the idolators, but ye shall break down their altars, dash in pieces their graven images and burn them with fire that I shall not be wroth at you.'"

But these appeals to the princes were of no avail, whereas the revolutionary agitation among the people grew day by day. Muenzer, whose ideas became more definitely shaped and more courageous, now definitely relinquished the middle-class reformation, and at the same time appeared as a direct political agitator.

His theologic-philosophic doctrine attacked all the main points not only of Catholicism but of Christianity as such. Under the cloak of Christian forms, he preached a kind of pantheism, which curiously resembles the modern speculative mode of contemplation, and at times even taught open atheism. He repudiated the assertion that the Bible was the only infallible revelation. The only living revelation, he said, was reason, a revelation which existed among all peoples at all times. To contrast the Bible with reason, he maintained, was to kill the spirit by the latter, for the Holy Spirit of which the Bible spoke was not a thing outside of us; the Holy Spirit was our reason. Faith, he said, was nothing else but reason become alive in man, therefore, he said, pagans could also have faith. Through this faith, through reason come to live, man became godlike and blessed, he said. Heaven was to be sought in this life, not beyond, and it was, according to Muenzer, the task of the believers to establish Heaven, the kingdom of God, here on earth. As there is no Heaven in the beyond, he asserted, so there is no Hell in the beyond, and no damnation, and there are no devils but the evil desires and cravings of man. Christ, he said, was a man, as we are, a prophet and a teacher, and his "Lord's Supper" is nothing but a plain meal of commemoration wherein bread and wine are being consumed with mystic additions.

Muenzer preached these doctrines mostly in a covert fashion, under the cloak of Christian phraseology which the new philosophy was compelled to utilise for some time. The fundamental heretic idea, however, is easily discernible in all his writings, and it is obvious that the biblical cloak was for him of much less importance than it was for many a disciple of Hegel in modern times. Still, there is a distance of three hundred years between Muenzer and modern philosophy.

Muenzer's political doctrine followed his revolutionary religious conceptions very closely, and as his theology reached far beyond the current conceptions of his time, so his political doctrine went beyond existing social and political conditions.

46

As Muenzer's philosophy of religion touched upon atheism, so his political programme touched upon communism, and there is more than one communist sect of modern times which, on the eve of the February Revolution, did not possess a theoretical equipment as rich as that of Muenzer of the Sixteenth Century. His programme, less a compilation of the demands of the then existing plebeians than a genius's anticipation of the conditions for the emancipation of the proletarian element that had just begun to develop among the plebeians, demanded the immediate establishment of the kingdom of God, of the prophesied millennium on earth. This was to be accomplished by the return of the church to its origins and the abolition of all institutions that were in conflict with what Muenzer conceived as original Christianity, which, in fact, was the idea of a very modern church. By the kingdom of God, Muenzer understood nothing else than a state of society without class differences, without private property, and without superimposed state powers opposed to the members of society. Al existing authorities, as far as they did not submit and join the revolution, he taught, must be overthrown, all work and all property must be shared in common, and complete equality must be introduced. In his conception, a union of the people was to be organised to realise this programme, not only throughout Germany, but throughout entire Christendom. Princes and nobles were to be invited to join, and should they refuse, the union was to overthrow or kill them, with arms in hand, at the first opportunity.

Muenzer immediately set to work to organise the union. His preachings assumed a still more militant character. He attacked, not only the clergy, but with equal passion the princes, the nobility and the patricians. He pictured in burning colours the existing oppression, and contrasted it with the vision of the millennium of social republican equality which he created out of his imagination. He published one revolutionary pamphlet after another, sending emissaries in all directions, while he personally organised the union in Altstedt and its vicinity.

The first fruit of this propaganda was the destruction of St. Mary's Chapel in Mellerbach near Altstedt, according to the command of the Bible (Deut. 7, 5): "Ye shall break down their altars, and dash in pieces their pillars, and hew down their Asherim, and burn their graven images with fire." The princes of Saxony came in person to Altstedt to quell the upheaval, and they called Muenzer to the castle. There he delivered a sermon, which they had never heard from Luther, "that easy living flesh of Wittenberg," as Muenzer called him. He insisted that the ungodly rulers, especially the priests and monks who treated the Gospel as heresy, must be killed; for confirmation he referred to the New Testament. The ungodly have no right to live, he said, save by the mercy of the chosen ones. If the princes would not exterminate the ungodly, he asserted, God would take their sword from them because the right to wield the sword belongs to the community. The source of the evil of usury, thievery and robbery, he said, were the princes and the masters who had taken all creatures into their private possession—the fishes in the water, the birds in the air, the plants in the soil. And the usurpers, he said, still preached to the poor the commandment, "Thou shalt not steal," while they grabbed everything, and robbed and crushed the peasant and the artisan. "When, however, one of the latter commits the slightest transgression," he said, "he has to hang, and Dr. Liar says to all this: Amen." The masters themselves created a situation, he argued, in which the poor man was forced to become their enemy. If they did not remove the causes of the upheaval, how could things improve in times to come? he asked. "Oh, my dear gentlemen, how the Lord will smite with an iron rod all these old pots! When I say so, I am considered rebellious. So be it!" (Cf. Zimmermann's *Peasant War*, II, 75.)

Muenzer had the sermon printed. His Altstedt printer was punished by Duke Johann of Saxony with banishment. His own writings were to be henceforth subjected to the censorship of the ducal government in Weimar. But he paid no heed to this order. He immediately published a very inciting paper in the imperial city of Muehlhausen, wherein he admonished the people "to widen the hole so that all the world may see and

48

comprehend who our fools are who have blasphemously turned our Lord into a painted mannikin." He concluded with the following words: "All the world must suffer a big jolt. The game will be such that the ungodly will be thrown off their seats and the downtrodden will rise." As a motto, Thomas Muenzer, "the man with the hammer," wrote the following on the title page: "Beware, I have put my words into thy mouth; I have lifted thee above the people and above the empires that thou mayest uproot, destroy, scatter and overthrow, and that thou mayest build and plant. A wall of iron against the kings, princes, priests, and for the people hath been erected. Let them fight, for victory is wondrous, and the strong and godless tyrants will perish."

The breach between Muenzer and Luther with his party had taken place long before that. Luther himself was compelled to accept some church reforms which were introduced by Muenzer without consulting him. Luther watched Muenzer's activities with the nettled distrust of a moderate reformer towards an energetic far-aiming radical. Already in the spring of 1524, in a letter to Melanchthon, that model of a hectic stay-at-home Philistine, Muenzer wrote that he and Luther did not understand the movement at all. They were seeking, he said, to choke it by adherence to the letter of the Bible, and their doctrine was worm-eaten. "Dear brethren," he wrote, "stop your delaying and hesitating. The time has come, the summer is knocking at our doors. Do not keep friendship with the ungodly who prevent the Word from exercising its full force. Do not flatter your princes in order that you may not perish with them. Ye tender, bookish scholars, do not be wroth, for I cannot do otherwise."

Luther had more than once invited Muenzer to an open debate. The latter, however, being always ready to accept battle in the presence of the people, did not have the slightest desire to plunge into a theological squabble before the partisan public of the Wittenberg University. He had no desire "to bring the testimony of the spirit before the high school of learning exclusively." If Luther was sincere, he wrote, let him use his influence to stop the chicaneries against his, Muenzer's, printers, and to lift the censorship in order that their controversy might be freely fought out in the press.

When the above-mentioned revolutionary brochure appeared, Luther openly denounced Muenzer. In his "Letter to the Princes of Saxony Against the Rebellious Spirit," he declared Muenzer to be an instrument of Satan, and demanded of the princes to intervene, and drive the instigators of the upheaval out of the country, since, he said, they did not confine themselves to preaching their evil doctrine, but incited to insurrection, to violent lawless action against the authorities.

On August 1st, Muenzer was compelled to appear before the princes in the castle of Weimar, to defend himself against the accusation of incendiary machinations. There were highly compromising facts quoted against him; his secret union had been traced; his hand was discovered in the organisation of the pitmen and the peasants. He was being threatened with banishment. Upon returning to Altstedt, he learned Duke Georg of Saxony demanded his extradition. Union letters in his handwriting had been intercepted, wherein he called Georg's subjects to armed resistance against the enemies of the Gospel. The council would have extradited him had he not left the city.

In the meantime, the rising agitation among the peasants and the plebeians had enormously lightened Muenzer's task of propaganda. In the person of the Anabaptists he found invaluable agents. This sect, having no definite dogmas, held together by common opposition against all ruling classes and by the common symbol of second baptism, ascetic in their mode of living, untiring, fanatic and intrepid in propaganda, had grouped itself more closely around Muenzer. Made homeless by constant persecutions, its members wandered over the length and breadth of Germany, announcing everywhere the new gospel wherein Muenzer had made clear to them their own demands and wishes. Numberless Anabaptists were put on the rack, burned or otherwise executed. But the courage and endurance of these emissaries were unshaken, and the success of their activities amidst the rapidly rising agitation of the people was enormous.

That was one of the reasons why, on his flight from Thuringia, Muenzer found the ground prepared wherever he turned.

In Nuernberg, a peasant revolt had been nipped in the bud a month previous. Here Muenzer conducted his propaganda under cover. Soon there appeared persons who defended his most audacious theological doctrines of the non-obligatory power of the Bible and the meaninglessness of sacraments, declaring Christ to have been a mere man, and the power of lay authorities to be ungodly. "We see there Satan stalking, the spirit of Altstedt!" Luther exclaimed. In Nuernberg, Muenzer printed his reply to Luther. He accused him of flattering the princes and supporting the reactionary party by his moderate position. "The people will free themselves in spite of everything," he wrote, "and then the fate of Dr. Luther will be that of a captive fox." The city council ordered the paper confiscated, and Muenzer was compelled to leave the city. From there he went through Suabia to Alsace, then to Switzerland, and then back to the Upper Black Forest where the insurrection had started several months before, precipitated largely by the Anabaptist emissaries. There is no doubt that this propaganda trip of Muenzer's added much to the organisation of the people's party, to a clear formulation of its demands and to the final general outbreak of the insurrection in April, 1525. It was through this trip that the dual nature of Muenzer's activities became more and more pronounced—on the one hand, his propaganda among the people whom he approached in the only language then comprehensible to the masses, that of religious prophecy; on the other hand, his contact with the initiated, to whom he could disclose his ultimate aims. Even previous to this journey he had grouped around himself in Thuringia a circle of the most determined persons, not only from among the people, but also from among the lower clergy, a circle whom he had put at the head of the secret organisation. Now he became the centre of the entire revolutionary movement of southwest Germany, organising connections between Saxony and Thuringia through Franconia and Suabia up to Alsace and the Swiss frontier and counting among his disciples and the heads of the organisation such men as Hubmaier of Waldshut, Conrad Grebel of Zurich, Franz Rabmann of Griessen, Schappelar of Memmingen, Jakob Wehe of Leipheim, and Dr. Mantel in Stuttgart, the most revolutionary of priests. He kept himself mostly in Friessen on the Schaffhausen frontier, undertaking journeys through the Hegau, Klettgau, etc. The bloody persecutions undertaken by the alarmed princes and masters everywhere against this new plebeian heresy, aided not a little in fanning the rebellious spirit and closing the ranks of the organisation. In this way, Muenzer passed five months in upper Germany. When the outbreak of the general movement was at hand, he returned to Thuringia, where he wished to lead the movement personally. There we will find him later.

We shall see how truly the character and the behaviour of the two party heads reflected the position of their respective parties. Luther's indecision, his fear of the movement, assumed serious proportions; his cowardly servility towards the princes corresponded closely to the hesitating, vacillating policy of the middle-classes. The revolutionary energy and decisiveness of Muenzer, on the other hand, was seen in the most advanced faction of the plebeians and peasants. The difference was that while Luther confined himself to an expression of the ideas and wishes of a majority of his class and thereby acquired among it a very cheap popularity, Muenzer, on the contrary, went far beyond the immediate ideas and demands of the plebeians and peasants, organising out of the then existing revolutionary elements a party, which, as far as it stood on the level of his ideas and shared his energy, still represented only a small minority of the insurgent masses.

III

About fifty years after the suppression of the Hussite movement, the first symptoms of a budding revolutionary spirit became manifest among the German peasants.

The first peasant conspiracy came into being in 1476, in the bishopric of Wuerzburg, a country already impoverished "by bad government, manifold taxes, payments, feuds, enmity, war, fires, murders, prison, and the like," and continually plundered by bishops, clergy and nobility in a shameless manner. A young shepherd and musician, Hans Boeheim of Niklashausen, also called the "Drum-Beater" and "Hans the Piper," suddenly appeared in Taubergrund in the rôle of a prophet. He related that the Virgin had appeared to him in a vision, that she told him to burn his drum, to cease serving the dance and the sinful gratification of the senses, and to exhort the people to do penance. Therefore, he said, everybody should purge himself of sin and the vain lusts of the world, forsake all adornments and embellishments, and make a pilgrimage to the Madonna of Niklashausen to attain forgiveness.

Already among these precursors of the movement we notice an asceticism which is to be found in all mediaeval uprisings that were tinged with religion, and also in modern times at the beginning of every proletarian movement. This austerity of behaviour, this insistence on relinquishing all enjoyment of life, contrasts the ruling classes with the principle of Spartan equality. Nevertheless, it is a necessary transitional stage, without which the lowest strata of society could never start a movement. In order to develop revolutionary energy, in order to become conscious of their own hostile position towards all other elements of society, in order to concentrate as a class, the lower strata of society must begin with stripping themselves of everything that could reconcile them to the existing system of society. They must renounce all pleasures which would make their subdued position in the least tolerable and of which even the severest pressure could not deprive them.

This plebeian and proletarian asceticism differs widely, both by its wild fanatic form and by its contents, from the middle-class asceticism as preached by the middle-class Lutheran morality and by the English Puritans (to be distinguished from the independent and farther-reaching sects) whose whole secret is middle-class thrift. It is quite obvious that this plebeian-proletarian asceticism loses its revolutionary character when the development of modern productive forces increases the number of commodities, thus rendering Spartan equality superfluous, and on the other hand, the very position of the proletariat in society, and thereby the proletariat itself becomes more and more revolutionary. Gradually, this asceticism disappears from among the masses. Among the sects with which it survives, it degenerates either into bourgeois parsimony or into high-sounding virtuousness which, in the end, is nothing more than Philistine or guild-artisan niggardliness. Besides, renunciation of pleasures need not be preached to the proletariat for the simple reason that it has almost nothing to renounce.

Hans the Piper's call to penitence found a great response. All the prophets of rebellion started with appeals against sin, because, in fact, only a violent exertion, a sudden renunciation of all habitual forms of existence could bring into unified motion a disunited, widely scattered generation of peasants grown up in blind submission. A pilgrimage to Niklashausen began and rapidly increased, and the greater the masses of people that joined the procession, the more openly did the young rebel divulge his plans. The Madonna of Niklashausen, he said, had announced to him that henceforth there should be neither king nor princes, neither pope nor other ecclesiastic or lay authority. Every one should be a brother to each other, and win his bread by the toil of his hands, possessing no more than his neighbour. All taxes, ground rents, serf duties, tolls and other payments and deliveries should be abolished forever. Forests, waters and meadows should be free everywhere.

The people received this new gospel with joy. The fame of the prophet, "the message of our Mother," spread everywhere, even in distant quarters. Hordes of pilgrims came from the Odenwald, from Main, from Kocher and Jaxt, even from Bavaria and Suabia, and from the Rhine. Miracles supposed to have been performed by the Piper were being related; people fell on their knees before the prophet, praying to him as to a saint; people fought for small strips from his cap as for relics or amulets. In vain did the priests fight him, denouncing his visions as the devil's delusions and his miracles as hellish swindles. But the mass of believers increased enormously. The revolutionary sect began to organise. The Sunday sermons of the rebellious shepherd attracted gatherings of 40,000 and more to Niklashausen.

For several months Hans the Piper preached before the masses. He did not intend, however, to confine himself to preaching. He was in secret communication with the priest of Niklashausen and with two knights, Kunz of Thunfeld and his son, who accepted the new gospel and were singled out as the military leaders of the planned insurrection. Finally, on the Sunday preceding the day of St. Kilian, when the shepherd believed his power to be strong enough, he gave the signal. He closed his sermon with the following words: "And now go home, and weigh in your mind what our Holiest Madonna has announced to you, and on the coming Saturday leave your wives and children and old men at home, but you, you men, come back here to Niklashausen on the day of St. Margaret, which is next Saturday, and bring with you your brothers and friends, as many as they may be. Do not come with pilgrims' staves, but covered with weapons and ammunition, in one hand a candle, in the other a sword and a pike or halberd, and the Holy Virgin will then announce to you what she wishes you to do." But before the peasants came in masses, the horsemen of the bishop seized the prophet of rebellion at night, and brought him to the Castle of Wuerzburg. On the appointed day, 34,000 armed peasants appeared, but the news had a discouraging effect on the mass; the majority went home, the more initiated retained about 16,000 with whom they moved to the castle under the leadership of Kunz of Thunfeld and his son Michael. The bishop, by means of promises, persuaded them to go home, but as soon as they began to disperse, they were attacked by the bishop's horsemen, and many were imprisoned. Two were decapitated, and Hans the Piper was burned. Kunz of Thunfeld fled, and was allowed to return only at the price of ceding all his estates to the monastery. Pilgrimages to Niklashausen continued for some time, but were finally suppressed.

After this first attempt, Germany remained quiet for some time; but at the end of the century rebellions and conspiracies of the peasants started anew.

We shall pass over the Dutch peasant revolt of 1491 and 1492 which was suppressed by Duke Albrecht of Saxony in the battle near Heemskerk; also the revolt of the peasants of the Abbey of Kempten in Upper Suabia which occurred simultaneously, and the Frisian revolt under Shaard Ahlva, about 1497, which was also suppressed by Albrecht of Saxony. These revolts were mostly too far from the scene of the actual Peasant War. In part they were struggles of hitherto free peasants against the attempt to force feudalism upon them. We now pass to the two great conspiracies which prepared the Peasant War: the *Union Shoe* and the *Poor Konrad.*

The rise in the price of commodities which had called forth the revolt of the peasants in the Netherlands, brought about, in 1493, in Alsace, a secret union of peasants and plebeians with a sprinkling of the purely middle-class opposition party, and a certain amount of sympathy even among the lower nobility. The seat of the union was the region of Schlettstadt, Sulz, Dambach, Rossheim, Scherweiler, etc. The conspirators demanded the plundering and extermination of the Jews, whose usury then, as now, sucked the blood of the peasants of Alsace, the introduction of a jubilee year to cancel all debts, the abolition of taxes, tolls and other burdens, the abolition of the ecclesiastical and Rottweil (imperial) court, the right to ratify taxation, the reduction of the priests' incomes to a prebend of between fifty and sixty guilders, the abolition of the auricular confession, and the establishment in the communities of courts elected by the communities themselves. The conspirators planned, as soon as they became strong enough, to overpower the stronghold of Schlettstadt, to confiscate the treasuries of the monasteries and the city, and from there to arouse the whole of Alsace. The banner of the union to be unfurled at the moment of insurrection, contained a peasant's shoe with long leather strings, the so-called Union Shoe, which gave a symbol and a name to the peasant conspiracies of the following twenty years.

The conspirators held their meetings at night on the lonesome Hungerberg. Membership in the Union was connected with the most mysterious ceremonies and threats of severest punishment against traitors. Nevertheless, the movement became known about Easter Week of 1493, the time appointed for the attack on Schlettstadt. The authorities immediately intervened. Many of the conspirators were arrested and put on the rack, to be quartered or decapitated. Many were crippled by chopping their hands and fingers, and driven out of the country. A large number fled to Switzerland. The Union Shoe, however, was far from being annihilated and continued its existence in secret. Numerous exiles, spread over Switzerland and south Germany, became its emissaries. Finding everywhere the same oppression and the same inclination towards revolt, they spread the Union Shoe over the territory of present-day Baden. The greatest admiration is due the tenacity and endurance with which the peasants of upper Germany conspired for thirty years after 1493, with which they overcame the obstacles to a more centralised organisation in spite of the fact that they were scattered over the countryside, and with which, after numberless dispersions, defeats, executions of leaders, they renewed their conspiracies over and over again, until an opportunity came for a mass upheaval.

In 1502, the bishopric of Speyer, which at that time embraced also the locality of Bruchsal, showed signs of a secret movement among the peasants. The Union Shoe had here reorganised itself with considerable success. About 7,000 men belonged to the organisation whose centre was Untergrombach, between Bruchsal and Weingarten, and whose ramifications reached down the Rhine to the Main, and up to the Margraviate of Baden. Its articles provided: No ground rent, tithe, tax or toll to be paid to the princes, the nobility or the clergy; serfdom to be abolished; monasteries and other church estates to be confiscated and divided among the people, and no other authority to be recognised aside from the emperor.

We find here for the first time expressed among the peasants the two demands of secularising the church estates in favour of the people and of a unified and undivided German monarchy—demands which henceforth will be found regularly in the more advanced faction of the peasants and plebeians.

In Thomas Muenzer's programme, the division of the church estates was transformed into confiscation in favour of common property, and the unified German *empire,* into the unified and undivided *republic.*

The renewed Union Shoe had, as well as the old, its own secret meeting places, its oath of silence, its initiation ceremonies, and its union banner with the legend, "Nothing but God's Justice." The plan of action was similar to that of the Alsatian Union. Bruchsal, where the majority of the population belonged to the Union, was to be overpowered. A union army was to be organised and dispatched into the surrounding principalities as moving points of concentration.

The plan was betrayed by a clergyman to whom one of the conspirators revealed it in the confessional. The governments immediately resorted to counter action. How widespread the Union had become, is apparent from the terror which seized the various imperial estates in Alsace and in the Union of Suabia. Troops were concentrated, and mass arrests were made. Emperor Maximilian, "the last of the knights," issued the most blood-thirsty, punitive decree against the undertaking of the peasants. Hordes of peasants assembled here and there, and armed resistance was offered, but the isolated peasant troops could not hold ground for a long time. Some of the conspirators were executed and many fled, but the secrecy was so well preserved that the majority, and also the leaders, could remain unmolested in their own localities or in the countries of the neighbouring masters.

After this new defeat, there followed a prolonged period of apparent quiet in the class struggles. The work, however, was continued in an underground way. Already, in the first years of the Sixteenth Century, *Poor Konrad* was formed in Suabia, apparently in connection with the scattered members of the Union Shoe. In the Black Forest, the Union Shoe continued in isolated circles until, ten years later, an energetic peasant leader succeeded in uniting the various threads and combining them into a great conspiracy. Both conspiracies became public, one shortly after the other, in the restless years from 1513 to 1515, in which the Swiss, Hungarian and Slovenian peasants made a series of significant insurrections.

The man who restored the Upper Rhenish Union Shoe was Joss Fritz of Untergrombach, a fugitive from the conspiracy of 1502, a former soldier, in all respects an outstanding figure. After his flight, he had kept himself in various localities between the Lake Constance and the Black Forest, and finally settled as a vassal near Freiburg in Breisgau, where he even became a forester. Interesting details as to the manner in which he reorganised the Union from this point of vantage and as to the skill with which he managed to attract people of different character, are contained in the investigations. It was due to the diplomatic talent and the untiring endurance of this model conspirator that a considerable number of people of the most divergent classes became involved in the Union: knights, priests, burghers, plebeians and peasants, and it is almost certain that he organised several grades of the conspiracy, one more or less sharply divided from the other. All serviceable elements were utilised with the greatest circumspection and skill. Outside of the initiated emissaries who wandered over the country in various disguises, the vagrants and beggars were used for subordinate missions. Joss stood in direct communication with the beggar kings, and through them he held in his hand the numerous vagabond population. In fact, the beggar kings played a considerable rôle in his conspiracy. Very original figures they were, these beggar kings. One roamed the country with a girl using her seemingly wounded feet as a pretext for begging; he wore more than eight insignia on his hat—the fourteen deliverers, St. Ottilie, Our Mother in Heaven, etc.; besides, he wore a long red beard, and carried a big knotty stick with a dagger and pike. Another, begging in the name of St. Velten, offered spices and worm-seeds; he wore a long iron-coloured coat, a red barret, with the Baby of Trient attached thereto, a sword at his side, and many knives and a dagger on his girdle. Others had artificial open wounds, besides similar picturesque attire. There were at least ten of them, and for the price of two thousand guilders they were supposed to set fire simultaneously in Alsace, in the Margraviate of Baden, and in Breisgau, and to put themselves, with at least 2,000 men of their own, under the command of Georg Schneider, the former Captain of the Lansquenets, on the day of the Zabern Parish Fair in Rozen, in order to conquer the city. A courier service from station to station was established between real members of the union. Joss Fritz and his chief emissary, Stoffel of Freiburg, continually riding from place to place, reviewed the armies of the neophytes at night. There is ample material in the documents of the court investigations relative to the spread of the Union in the Upper Rhine and Black Forest regions. The documents contain many names of members from the various localities in that region, together with descriptions of persons. Most of those mentioned were journeymen, peasants and innkeepers, a few nobles, priests (like that of Lehen himself), and unemployed Lansquenets. This composition shows the more developed character that the Union Shoe had assumed under Joss Fritz. The plebeian element of the cities began to assert itself more and more. The ramifications of the conspiracy went over into Alsace, present-day Baden, up to Wuerttemberg and the Main. Larger meetings were held from time to time on remote mountains such as the Kniebis, etc., and the affairs of the Union were discussed. The meetings of the chiefs, often participated in by local members as well as by delegates of the more remote localities, took place on the Hartmatte near Lehen, and it was here that the fourteen articles of the Union were adopted: No master besides the emperor, and (according to some) the pope; abolition of the Rottweil imperial court; limitation of the church court to religious affairs; abolition of all interest which had been paid so long that it equalled the capital; an interest of 5 per cent as the highest permissible rate; freedom of hunting, fishing, grazing, and wood cutting; limitation of the priests to one prebend for each; confiscation of all church estates and monastery gems in favour of the union; abolition of all inequitable taxes and tolls; eternal peace within entire Christendom, energetic action against all opponents of the Union; Union taxes; seizure of a strong city, such as Freiburg, to serve as the centre of the Union; opening of negotiations with the emperor as soon as the Union hordes were gathered, and with Switzerland in case the emperor declined—these were the points agreed upon. We see that the demands of the peasants and plebeians assumed a more and more definite and decisive form, although concessions had to be made in the same measure to the more moderate and timid elements as well.

The blow was to be struck about Autumn, 1513. Nothing was lacking but a Union banner, and Joss Fritz went to Heilbrun to have it painted. It contained, besides all sorts of emblems and pictures, the Union Shoe and the legend "God help thy divine justice." While he was away, a premature attempt was made to overwhelm Freiburg, but the attempt was discovered. Some indiscretions in the conduct of the propaganda put the council of Freiburg and the Margrave of Baden on the right track. The betrayal of two conspirators completed the series of disclosures. Presently the Margrave, the council of Freiburg, and the imperial government of Ensisheim sent out their spies and soldiers. A number of Union members were arrested, tortured and executed. But the majority escaped once more, Joss Fritz among them. The Swiss government now persecuted the fugitives with great assiduity and even executed many of them. However, it could not prevent the majority of the fugitives from keeping themselves continually in the vicinity of their homes and gradually returning there. The Alsace government in Ensisheim was more cruel than the others. It ordered very many to be decapitated, broken on the wheel, and quartered. Joss Fritz kept himself mainly on the Swiss bank of the Rhine, but he also went often to the Black Forest without ever being apprehended.

Why the Swiss made common cause with the neighbouring governments this time is apparent from the peasant revolt that broke out the following year, 1514, in Berne, Sollothurne and Lucerne, and resulted in a purging of the aristocratic governments and the institution of patricians. The peasants also forced through some privileges for themselves. If these Swiss local revolts succeeded, it was simply due to the fact that there was still less centralisation in Switzerland than in Germany. The local German masters were all subdued by the peasants of 1525, and if they succumbed, it was due to the organised mass armies of the princes. These latter, however, did not exist in Switzerland.

Simultaneously with the Union Shoe in Baden, and apparently in direct connection with it, a second conspiracy was formed in Wuerttemberg. According to documents, it had existed since 1503, but since the name Union Shoe became too dangerous after the dispersal of the Untergrombach conspirators, it adopted the name of Poor Konrad. Its seat was the valley of Rems underneath the mountain of Hohenstaufen. Its existence had been no mystery for a long time, at least among the people. The shameless pressure of Duke Ulrich's government, and the series of famine years which so greatly aided the outbreaks of 1513 and 1514, had increased the number of conspirators. The newly imposed taxes on wine, meat and bread, as well as a capital tax of one penny yearly for every guilder, caused the new outbreak. The city of Schorndorf, where the heads of the complot used to meet in the house of a cutler named Kaspar Pregizer, was to be seized first. In the spring of 1514, the rebellion broke out. Three thousand, and, according to others, five thousand peasants appeared before the city, and were persuaded by the friendly promises of the Duke's officers to move on. Duke Ulrich, having promised the abolition of the new tax, came riding fast with eighty horsemen, to find that everything was quiet in consequence of the promise. He promised to convene a diet where all complaints would be examined. The chiefs of the organisation, however, knew very well that Ulrich sought only to keep the people quiet until he had recruited and concentrated enough troops to be able to break his word and collect the taxes by force. They issued from Kaspar Pregizer's house, "the office of Poor Konrad," a call to a Union congress, this call having the support of emissaries everywhere. The success of the first uprising in the valley of Rems had everywhere strengthened the movement among the people. The papers and the emissaries found a favourable response, and so the congress held in Untertuerkhein on May 28, was attended by numerous representatives from all parts of Wuerttemberg. It was decided immediately to proceed with the propaganda and to strike a decisive blow in the valley of Rems at the first opportunity in order to spread the uprising from that point in every direction. While Bantelshans of Dettingen, a former soldier, and Singerhans of Wuertingen, a prominent peasant, were bringing the Suabian Alp into the Union, the uprising broke out on every side. Though Singerhans was suddenly attacked and seized, the cities of Backnang, Winnenden, and Markgroenningen fell into the hands of the peasants combined with the plebeians, and the entire territory from Weinsberg to Blaubeuren and from there up to the frontiers of Baden, was in open revolt. Ulrich was compelled to yield. However, while he was calling the Diet for June 25, he sent out a circular letter to the surrounding princes and free cities, asking for aid against the uprising, which, he said, threatened all princes, authorities and nobles in the empire, and which "strangely resembled the Union Shoe."

In the meantime, the Diet, representing the cities, and many delegates of the peasants who also demanded seats in the Diet, convened on June 18 in Stuttgart.

The prelates were not there as yet. The knights had not been invited. The opposition of the city of Stuttgart, as well as two threatening hordes of peasants at Leonberg nearby in the valley of Rems, strengthened the demands of the peasants. Their delegates were admitted, and it was decided to depose and punish three of the hated councillors of the Duke—Lamparter, Thumb and Lorcher, to add to the Duke a council of four knights, four burghers and four peasants, to grant him a civil list, and to confiscate the monasteries and the endowments in favour of the State treasury.

Duke Ulrich met these revolutionary decisions with a coup d'état. On June 21, he rode with his knights and councillors to Tuebingen, where he was followed by the prelates. He ordered the middle-class to come there as well. This was obeyed, and there he continued the session of the Diet without the peasants. The burghers, confronted with military terrorism, betrayed their allies, the peasants. On July 8, the Tuebingen agreement came into being, which imposed on the country almost a million of the Duke's debt, imposed on the Duke some limitations of power which he never fulfilled, and disposed of the peasants with a few meagre general phrases and a very definite penal law against insurrection. Of course, nothing was mentioned about peasant representation in the Diet. The plain people cried "Treason!" but the Duke, having acquired new credits after his debts were taken over by the estates, soon gathered troops while his neighbours, particularly the Elector Palatine, were sending military aid. Thus, by the end of July, the Tuebingen agreement had been accepted all over the country, and a new oath taken. Only in the valley of Rems did Poor Konrad offer resistance. The Duke, who rode there in person, was almost killed. A peasant camp was formed on the mountain of Koppel. But the affair dragged on, most of the insurgents running away for lack of food; later the remaining ones also went home after concluding an ambiguous agreement with some representatives of the Diet. Ulrich, whose army had in the meantime been strengthened by voluntarily offered troops of the cities which, having attained their demands, now fanatically turned against the peasants, attacked the valley of Rems contrary to the terms of the agreement, and plundered its cities and villages. Sixteen hundred peasants were captured, sixteen of them decapitated, and the rest receiving heavy fines in favour of Ulrich's treasury. Many remained in prison for a long time. A number of penal laws were issued against a renewal of the organisation, against all gatherings of peasants, and the nobility of Suabia formed a special union for the suppression of all attempts at insurrection. Meantime, the chief leaders of Poor Konrad had succeeded in escaping into Switzerland, whence most of them returned home singly, after the lapse of a few years.

Simultaneously with the Wuerttemberg movement, symptoms of new Union Shoe activities became manifest in Breisgau and in the Margraviate of Baden. In June, an insurrection was attempted at Buehl, but it was immediately dispersed by Margrave Philipp—the leader, Gugel-Bastian of Freiburg, having been seized and executed on the block.

In the spring of the same year, 1514, a general peasant war broke out in Hungary. A crusade against the Turks was being preached, and, as usual, freedom was promised to the serfs and bondsmen who would join it. About 60,000 congregated, and were to be under the command of György Dózsa, a Szekler, who had distinguished himself in the preceding Turkish wars and even attained nobility. The Hungarian knights and magnates, however, looked with disfavour upon the crusade which threatened to deprive them of their property and slaves. They hastily followed the individual hordes of peasants, and took back their serfs by force and mistreated them. When the army of crusaders learned about it, all the fury of the oppressed peasants was unleashed. Two of the men, enthusiastic advocates of the crusade, Lawrence Mészáros and Barnabas, fanned the fire, inciting the hatred of the army against the nobility by their revolutionary speeches. Dózsa himself shared the anger of his troops against the treacherous nobility. The army of crusaders became an army of the revolution, and Dózsa assumed leadership of the movement.

He camped with his peasants in the Rakos field near Pest. Hostilities were opened with encounters between the peasants

65

and the people of the nobility in the surrounding villages and in the suburbs of Pest. Soon there were skirmishes, and then followed Sicilian Vespers for all the nobility who fell into the hands of the peasants, and burning of all the castles in the vicinity. The court threatened in vain. When the first acts of the people's justice towards the nobility had been accomplished under the walls of the city, Dózsa proceeded to further operations. He divided his army into five columns. Two were sent to the mountains of Upper Hungary in order to effect an insurrection and to exterminate the nobility. The third, under Ambros Szaleves, a citizen of Pest, remained on the Rakos to guard the capital. The fourth and fifth were led by Dózsa and his brother Gregor against Szegedin.

In the meantime, the nobility gathered in Pest, and called to its aid Johann Zapolya, the *voivode* of Transylvania. The nobility, joined by the middle-class of Budapest, attacked and annihilated the army on the Rakos, after Szaleves with the middle-class elements of the peasant army had gone over to the enemy. A host of prisoners were executed in the most cruel fashion. The rest were sent home minus their noses and ears.

Dózsa suffered defeat before Szegedin and moved to Czanad which he captured, having defeated an army of the nobility under Batory Istvan and Bishop Esakye, and having perpetrated bloody repressions on the prisoners, among them the Bishop and the royal Chancellor Teleky, for the atrocities committed on the Rakos. In Czanad he proclaimed a republic, abolition of the nobility, general equality and sovereignty of the people, and then moved toward Temesvar, to which place Batory had rushed with his army. But during the siege of this fortress which lasted for two months and while he was being reinforced by a new army under Anton Hosza, his two army columns in Upper Hungary suffered defeat in several battles at the hand of the nobility, and Johann Zapolya, with his Transylvanian army, moved against him. The peasants were attacked by Zapolya and dispersed. Dózsa was captured, roasted on a red hot throne, and his flesh eaten by his own people, whose lives were granted to them only under this condition. The dispersed peasants, reassembled by Lawrence and Hosza, were defeated again, and whoever fell into the hands of the enemies were either impaled or hanged. The peasants' corpses hung in thousands along the roads or at the entrances of burned-down villages. According to reports, about 60,000 either fell in battle, or were massacred. The nobility took care that at the next session of the Diet, the enslavement of the peasants should again be recognised as the law of the land.

The peasant revolt in Carinthia, Carniola and Styria, the "windy marshes," which broke out at the same time, originated in a conspiracy akin to the Union Shoe, organised as early as 1503 in that region, wrung dry by imperial officers, devastated by Turkish invasions, and tortured by famines. It was this conspiracy that made the insurrection possible. Already in 1513, the Slovenian as well as the German peasants of this region had once more raised the war banner of the Stara Prawa (The Old Rights). They allowed themselves to be placated that time, and when in 1514 they gathered anew in large masses, they were again persuaded to go home by a direct promise of the Emperor Maximilian to restore the old rights. Still, the war of vengeance by the deceived people broke out in the Spring of 1515 with much more vigour. Here, as in Hungary, castles and monasteries were destroyed, captured nobles being tried and executed by peasant juries. In Styria and Carinthia, the emperor's captain Dietrichstein soon succeeded in crushing the revolt. In Carniola, it could be suppressed only through an attack from the Rain (Autumn, 1516) and through subsequent Austrian atrocities which formed a worthy counterpart to the infamies of the Hungarian nobility.

It is clear why, after a series of such decisive defeats, and after these mass atrocities of the nobility, the German peasants remained quiescent for a long time. Still, neither conspiracies nor local uprisings were totally absent. Already in 1516 most of the fugitives of the Union Shoe and Poor Konrad had returned to Suabia and to the upper Rhine. In 1517 the Union Shoe was again in full swing in the Black Forest. Joss Fritz himself, who still carried in his bosom the old Union Shoe banner of 1513, traversed the Black Forest in various directions, and developed great activity. The conspiracy was being organised anew. Meetings were again held on the Kniebis as they had been four years before. Secrecy, however, was not maintained. The governments learned the facts and interfered. Many were captured and executed. The most active and intelligent members were compelled to flee, among them Joss Fritz, who, although still not captured, seems, however, to have died in Switzerland a short time afterwards. At any rate, his name is not mentioned again.

IV

WHILE the fourth Union Shoe organisation was being suppressed in the Black Forest, Luther, in Wittenberg, gave the signal to a movement which was destined to draw all the estates into its torrent, and to shake the whole empire. The theses of this Augustinian from Thuringia had the effect of lightning in a powder magazine. The manifold and contradictory strivings of the knights and the middle-class, the peasants and the plebeians, the princes craving for sovereignty, the lower clergy, secretly playing at mysticism and the learned writer's opposition of a satirical and burlesque nature, found in Luther's theses a common expression around which they grouped themselves with astounding rapidity. This alliance of all the opposing elements, though formed overnight and of brief duration, suddenly revealed the enormous power of the movement, and gave it further impetus.

But this very rapid growth of the movement was also destined to develop the seeds of discord which were hidden in it. It was destined to tear asunder at least those portions of the aroused mass which, by their very situation in life, were directly opposed to each other, and to put them in their normal state of mutual hostility. Already in the first years of the Reformation, the assembling of the heterogeneous mass of the opposition around two central points became a fact. Nobility and middle-class grouped themselves unconditionally around Luther. Peasants and plebeians, as yet failing to see in Luther a direct enemy, formed a separate revolutionary party of the opposition. This was nothing new, since now the movement had become much more general, much broader in scope and deeper than it was in the pre-Luther times, which necessarily brought about a sharp antagonism and an open struggle between the two parties. This direct opposition soon became apparent. Luther and Muenzer, fighting in the press and in the pulpit, were as much opposed to each other as were the armies of princes, knights and cities (consisting, as they did, mainly of Lutherans or of forces at least inclined towards Lutherism), and the hordes of peasants and plebeians routed by those armies.

The divergence of interests of the various elements accepting the Reformation became apparent even before the Peasant War in the attempt of the nobility to realise its demands as against the princes and the clergy.

The situation of the German nobility at the beginning of the Sixteenth Century has been depicted above. The nobility was losing its independence to the ever-increasing power of the lay and clerical princes. It realised that in the same degree as it was going down as a group in society, the power of the empire was going down as well, dissolving itself into a number of sovereign principalities. The collapse of the nobility coincided, in its own opinion, with the collapse of the German nation. Added to it was the fact that the nobility, especially that section of it which was under the empire, by virtue of its military occupation and its attitude towards the princes, directly represented the empire and the imperial power. The nobility was the most national of the estates, and it knew that the stronger were the imperial power and the unity of Germany, and the weaker and less numerous the princes, the more powerful would the nobility become. It was for that reason that the knighthood was generally dissatisfied with the pitiful political situation of Germany, with the powerlessness of the empire in foreign affairs, which increased in the same degree as, by inheritance, the court was adding to the empire one province after the other, with the intrigues of foreign powers inside of Germany and with the plottings of German princes with foreign countries against the power of the empire. It was for that reason, also, that the demands of the nobility instantly assumed the form of a demand for the reform of the empire, the victims of which were to be the princes and the higher clergy. Ulrich of Hutten, the theoretician of the German nobility, undertook to formulate this demand in combination with Franz von Sickingen, its military and diplomatic representative.

The reform of the empire as demanded by the nobility was conceived by Hutten in a very radical spirit and expressed very clearly. Hutten demanded nothing else than the elimination of all princes, the secularisation of all church principalities and estates, and the restoration of *a democracy of the nobility* headed by a monarchy,—a form of government reminiscent of the heyday of the late Polish republic. Hutten and Sickingen believed that the empire would again become united, free and powerful, should the rule of the nobility, a predominantly military class, be reestablished, the princes, the elements of disintegration, removed, the power of the priests annihilated, and Germany torn away from under the dominance of the Roman Church.

Founded on serfdom this democracy of the nobility, the prototype of which could be found in Poland and, in the empires conquered by the Germanic tribes, at least in their first centuries, is one of the most primitive forms of society, and its normal course of development is to become an extensive feudal hierarchy, which was a considerable advance. Such a powerful democracy of the nobility had already become an impossibility in Germany of the Sixteenth Century, first of all because there existed at that time important and powerful German cities and there was no prospect of an alliance between nobility and the cities such as brought about in England the transformation of the feudal order into a bourgeois constitutional monarchy. In Germany, the old nobility survived, while in England it was exterminated by the Wars of the Roses, only twenty-eight families remaining, and was superseded by a new nobility of middle-class derivation and middle-class tendencies. In Germany, serfdom was still the common practice, the nobility drawing its income from *feudal* sources, while in England serfdom had been virtually eliminated, and the nobility had become plain middle-class land owners, with a *middle-class* source of income—the ground rent. Finally, that centralisation of absolute monarchial power which in France had existed and kept growing since Louis XI due to the clash of interests between nobility and middle-class, was impossible in Germany where conditions for national centralisation existed in a very rudimentary form, if at all.

Under these conditions, the greater was Hutten's determination to carry out his ideals in practice, the more concessions was he compelled to make, and the more clouded did his plan of reforming the empire become. Nobility, alone, lacked power to put the reform through. This was manifest from its weakness in comparison with the princes. Allies were to be looked for, and these could only be found either in the cities, or among the peasantry and the influential advocates of reform. But the cities knew the nobility too well to trust them, and they rejected all forms of alliance. The peasants justly saw in the nobility, which exploited and mistreated them, their bitterest enemy, and as to the theoreticians of reform, they made common cause with the middle-class, the princes, or the peasants. What advantages, indeed, could the nobility promise the middle-class or the peasants from a reform of the empire whose main task it was to lift the nobility into a higher position? Under these circumstances Hutten could only be silent in his propaganda writings about the future interrelations between the nobility, the cities and the peasants, or to mention them only briefly, putting all evils at the feet of the princes, the priests, and the dependence upon Rome, and showing the middle-class that it was in their interests to remain at least neutral in the coming struggle between the nobility and the princes. No mention was ever made by Hutten of abolishing serfdom or other burdens imposed upon the peasants by the nobility.

The attitude of the German nobility towards the peasants of that time was exactly the same as that of the Polish nobility towards its peasants in the insurrections since 1830. As in the modern Polish upheavals, the movement could have been brought to a successful conclusion only by an alliance of all the opposition parties, mainly the nobility and the peasants. But of all alliances, this one was entirely impossible on either side. The nobility was not ready to give up its political privileges and its feudal rights over the peasants, while the revolutionary peasants could not be drawn by vague prospects into an alliance with the nobility, the class which was most active in their oppression. The nobility could not win over the German peasant in 1522, as it failed in Poland in 1830. Only total abolition of serfdom, bondage and all privileges of nobility could have united the rural population with it. The nobility, like every privileged class, had not, however, the slightest desire to give up its privileges, its favourable situation, and the major parts of its sources of income.

Thus it came about that when the struggle broke out, the nobles were alone in the field against the princes. It was obvious that the princes, who, for two centuries had been taking the ground from under the nobility's feet, would this time also gain a victory without much effort.

The course of the struggle itself is well known. Hutten and Sickingen, already recognised as the political and millitary chiefs of the middle German nobility, organised in Landau, in 1522, a union of the Rhenish, Suabian and Franconian nobility for the duration of six years, ostensibly for self-defense. Sickingen assembled an army, partly out of his own means and partly in combination with the neighbouring knights. He organised the recruiting of armies and reinforcements in Franconia, along the Lower Rhine, in the Netherlands and in Westphalia, and in September, 1522, he opened hostilities by declaring a feud against the Elector-Archbishop of Trier. While he was stationed near Trier, his reinforcements were cut off by a quick intervention of the princes. The Landgrave of Hesse and the Elector Palatine went to the aid of the Archbishop of Trier, and Sickingen was hastily compelled to retreat to his castle, Landstuhl. In spite of all the efforts of Hutten and the remainder of his friends, the united nobility, intimidated by the concentrated and quick action of the princes, left him in the lurch. Sickingen was mortally wounded, surrendered Landstuhl, and soon afterwards he died. Hutten was compelled to flee to Switzerland, where he died a few months later on the Isle of Ufnau, on the Lake of Zurich.

With this defeat, and with the death of both leaders the power of the nobility as a body, independent of the princes, was broken. From then on the nobility appeared only in the service and under the leadership of the princes. The Peasant War, which soon broke out, drove the nobles still more deeply under the direct or indirect protection of the princes. It proved that the German nobility preferred to continue the exploitation of the peasants under princely sovereignty, rather than overthrow the princes and priests through an open alliance with the *emancipated* peasants.

V

FROM the moment when Luther's declaration of war against the Catholic hierarchy set into motion all the opposition elements of Germany, not a year passed without the peasants coming forth with their demands. Between 1518 and 1523, one local revolt followed another in the Black Forest and in upper Suabia. Beginning in the Spring of 1524, these revolts assumed a systematic character. In April of that year, the peasants of the Abbey of Marchthal refused serf labour and duties; in May of the same year, the peasants of St. Blasien refused serf payments; in June, the peasants of Steinheim near Memmingen declared they would pay neither the tithe nor other duties; in July and August, the peasants of Thurgau rebelled and were quieted partly through the mediation of Zurich, partly through the brutality of the confederacy which executed many of them. Finally, a decisive uprising took place in the Margraviate of Stuehlingen, which may be looked upon as the *real beginning of the Peasant War.*

The peasants of Stuehlingen suddenly refused deliveries to the Landgrave and assembled in strong numbers. On October 24, 1524, they moved towards Waldshut under Hans Mueller of Bulgenbach. Here they organised an evangelical fraternity, jointly with the city middle-class. The latter joined the organisation the more willingly since they were in conflict with the government of Upper Austria over the religious persecutions of their preacher, Balthaser Hubmaier, a friend and disciple of Thomas Muenzer's. A union tax of three kreutzer weekly was imposed. It was an enormous sum for the value of money of that time. Emissaries were sent out to Alsace, to the Moselle, to the entire Upper Rhine and to Franconia, to bring peasants everywhere into the Union. The aims of the Union were proclaimed as follows: abolition of feudal power; destruction of all castles and monasteries; elimination of all masters outside of the emperor. The German tricolour was the banner of the Union.

The uprising spread rapidly over the entire territory of present-day Baden. A panic seized the nobility of Upper Suabia, whose military forces were all engaged in Italy, in a war against Francis I of France. Nothing remained for it but to gain time by protracted negotiations, meanwhile collecting money and recruiting troops, pending the moment when it would feel strong enough to punish the peasants for their audacity by "burning and scorching, plundering and murdering." From that moment there began that systematic betrayal, that consistent recourse to perfidiousness and secret malice, which distinguished the nobility and the princes throughout the entire Peasant War, and which was their strongest weapon against decentralised peasants. The Suabian Union, comprising the princes, the nobility, and the imperial cities of Southwest Germany, tried conciliatory measures without guaranteeing the peasants real concessions. The latter continued their movement. Hans Mueller of Bulgenbach marched, from September 30 to the middle of October, through the Black Forest up to Urach and Furtwangen, increased his troops to 3,500 and took a position near Eratingen, not far from Stuehlingen. The nobility had no more than 1,700 men at their disposal, and even those were divided. It had to agree to an armistice, which was concluded in the camp at Eratingen. The peasants were promised a peaceful agreement, either directly between the interested parties, or by means of an arbitrator, and an investigation of complaints by the court at Stockach. The troops of both the nobility and the peasants were dispersed.

The peasants formulated sixteen articles, the acceptance of which was to be demanded of the court at Stockach. The articles were very moderate. They included abolition of the hunting right, of serf labour, of excessive taxes and master

76

privileges in general, protection against wilful arrests and against partisan courts. The peasants' demands went no farther.

Nevertheless, immediately after the peasants went home, the nobility demanded continuation of all contested services pending the court decision. The peasants refused, advising the masters to go to the court. Thus the conflict was renewed, the peasants reassembled, and the princes and masters once again concentrated their troops. This time the movement spread far over the Breisgau and deep into Wuerttemberg. The troops under Georg Truchsess of Waldburg, the Alba of the Peasant War, observed the peasants' movements, attacked individual reinforcements, but did not dare to attack the main force. Georg Truchsess negotiated with the peasant chiefs, and here and there he effected agreements.

By the end of December, proceedings began before the court at Stockach. The peasants protested against the court, composed entirely of nobles. In reply, an imperial edict to this effect was read. The proceedings lagged, while the nobility, the princes and the Suabian Union authorities were arming themselves. Archduke Ferdinand who dominated, besides hereditary lands then still belonging to Austria, also Wuerttemberg, the Black Forest and Southern Alsace, ordered the greatest severity against the rebellious peasants. They were to be captured, mercilessly tortured and killed; they were to be exterminated in the most expeditious manner; their possessions to be burned and devastated, and their wives and children driven from the land. It was in that way that the princes and masters kept the armistice, and this is what passed for amicable arbitration and investigation of grievances. Archduke Ferdinand, to whom the house of Welser of Augsburg advanced money, armed himself very carefully. The Suabian Union ordered a special tax, and a contingent of troops to be called in three installments.

The foregoing rebellions coincided with the five months' presence of Thomas Muenzer in the Highland. Though there are no direct proofs of his influence over the outbreak and the course of the movement, it is, nevertheless, indirectly ascertained. The most outspoken revolutionaries among the peasants were mostly his disciples, defending his ideas. The Twelve Articles, as well as the Letter of Articles of the Highland peasants, were ascribed to him by all the contemporaries, although the first was certainly not composed by Muenzer. Already, on his way back to Thuringia, he issued a decisive revolutionary manifesto to the insurgent peasants.

Duke Ulrich, who, since 1519, had been an exile from Wuerttemberg, was now intriguing to regain his land with the aid of the peasants. Since the beginning of his exile he had been trying to utilise the revolutionary party, and had supported it continuously. In most of the local disturbances taking place between 1520 and 1524 in the Black Forest and in Wuerttemberg, his name appeared. Now he armed himself directly for an attack on Wuerttemberg to be launched out of his castle, Hohentweil. However, he was only utilised by the peasants without influencing them, and without enjoying their confidence.

The winter passed without anything decisive happening on either side. The princely masters were in hiding. The peasant revolt was gaining scope. In January, 1525, the entire country between the Danube, the Rhine and the Lech, was in a state of fermentation. In February, the storm broke. While the Black Forest Hegau troops, under Hans Mueller of Bulgenbach, were conspiring with Ulrich of Wuerttemberg, partly sharing his futile march on Stuttgart (February and March, 1525), the peasants arose on February 9 in Ried above Ulm, assembled in a camp near Baltringen which was protected by marshes, hoisted the red flag, and formed, under the leadership of Ulrich Schmid, the Baltringen troop. They were 10,000 to 12,000 strong.

On February 25, the Upper Allgaeu troops, 7,000 strong, assembled at Schusser, moved by the rumour that troops were marching against the dissatisfied elements who had appeared in this locality as everywhere else. The people of Kempten, who had conducted a fight against their archbishop throughout the winter, assembled on the 26th and joined the peasants. The cities of Memmingen and Kaufbeuren joined the movement on certain conditions. The ambiguity of the position of the cities in this movement was already apparent. On March 7, the twelve Memmingen articles were proclaimed in Memmingen for all the peasants of Upper Allgaeu.

A message from the Allgaeu peasants brought about the formation on Lake Constance of the Lake Troop under Eitel Hans. This troop also grew fast. Its headquarters were in Bermatingen.

The peasants also arose in Lower Allgaeu in the region of Ochsenhausen and Schellenberg, in the localities of Zeil and Waldburg, and in the estates of Truchsess. The movement started in the early days of March. This Lower Allgaeu troop, which consisted of 7,000 men, camped near Wurzach.

All these troops adopted the Memmingen articles, which, it must be noted, were still more moderate than the Hegau articles, manifesting, as they did, a remarkable lack of determination in points relating to the attitude of the armed troops towards the nobility and the governments. Such determination, wherever manifested, appeared only in the later stages of the war, when the peasants learned to know from experience the mode of action of their enemies.

A sixth troop was formed on the Danube, simultaneously with the others. From the entire region, Ulm to Donauwoerth, from the valleys of the Iller, Roth and Biber, the peasants came to Leipheim, and opened camp there. From fifteen localities, every able-bodied man had come, while reinforcements were drawn from 117 places. The leader of the Leipheim troop was Ulrich Schoen. Its preacher was Jakob Wehe, the priest of Leipheim.

Thus, at the beginning of March, there were between 30,000 and 40,000 insurgent peasants of Upper Suabia in six camps under arms. The peasant troops were a heterogeneous lot. Muenzer's revolutionary party was everywhere in the minority but it formed the backbone of the peasant camps. The mass of the peasants were always ready to venture compacts with the masters wherever they were promised those concessions which they hoped to force upon their enemies by their menacing attitude. Moreover, as the uprising dragged on and the princes' armies began to approach, the peasants became weary. Most of those who still had something to lose, went home. Added to all the difficulties was the fact that the vagabond masses of the low grade proletariat had joined the troops. This made discipline more difficult, and demoralised the peasants, as the vagabonds were an unreliable element, coming and going all the time. This, alone, is sufficient explanation why, at the beginning, the peasants remained everywhere on the defensive, why they were becoming demoralised in their camps, and why, aside from tactical shortcomings and the rarity of good leaders, they could not match the armies of the princes.

While the troops were assembling, Duke Ulrich invaded Wuerttemberg from Hohentweil with recruited troops and a number of Hegau peasants. Were the peasants now to proceed from the other side, from Waldburg against Truchsess' troops, the Suabian Union would have been lost. But because of the defensive attitude of the peasant troops, Truchsess soon succeeded in concluding an armistice with those of Baltringen, Allgaeu, and the Lake, starting negotiations and fixing a date for terminating the whole undertaking, namely, Judica Sunday (April 2). In the meantime, he was able to proceed against Duke Ulrich, to besiege Stuttgart, compelling him to leave Wuerttemberg as early as March 17. Then he turned against the peasants, but the Lansquenets revolted in his own army and refused to proceed against the peasants. Truchsess succeeded in placating the disgruntled soldiers and moved towards Ulm, where new reinforcements were being gathered. He left an observation post at Kirchheim under the supervision of Teck.

At last the Suabian Union, with free hands and in command of the first contingents, threw off its mask, declaring itself "to be ready, with arms in hand and with the aid of God, to change that which the peasants wilfully ventured."

The peasants adhered strictly to the armistice. On Judica Sunday they submitted their demands, the famous Twelve Articles, for consideration. They demanded the election and removal of clergymen by the communities; the abolition of the small tithe and the utilisation of the large tithe, after subtraction of the priests' salaries, for public purposes; the abolition of serfdom, of fishing and hunting rights, and of death tolls; the limitation of excessive bonded labour, taxes and ground rents; the restitution of the forests, meadows and privileges forcibly withdrawn from the communities and individuals, and the elimination of wilfulness in the courts and the administration. It is obvious that the moderate conciliatory section still had the upper hand among the peasant troops. The revolutionary party had formulated its programme earlier, in the *Letter of Articles.* It was an open letter to all the peasantry, admonishing them to join "the Christian Alliance and Brotherhood" for the purpose of removing all burdens either by goodness, "which will hardly happen," or by force, and threatening all those who refuse to join with the "lay anathema," that is, with expulsion from the society and from any intercourse with the Union members. All castles, monasteries and priests' endowments were also, according to the Letter, to be placed under lay anathema unless the nobility, the priests and the monks relinquished them of their own accord, moved into ordinary houses like other people, and joined the Christian Alliance. We see that this radical manifesto which obviously had been composed *before* the Spring insurrection of 1525, deals in the first place with the revolution, with complete victory over the ruling classes, and that the "lay anathema" only designates those oppressors and traitors that were to be killed, the castles that were to be burned, and the monasteries and endowments that were to be confiscated, their jewels to be turned into cash.

Before the peasants succeeded in presenting their Twelve Articles to the proper courts of arbitration, they learned that the agreement had been broken by the Suabian Union and that its troops were approaching. Steps were taken immediately by the peasants. A general meeting of all Allgaeu, Baltringen and Lake peasants was held at Geisbeuren. The four divisions were combined and reorganised into four columns. A decision was made to confiscate the church estates, to sell their jewels in favour of the warchest, and to burn the castles. Thus, aside from the official Twelve Articles, the Letter of the Articles became the rule of warfare, and Judica Sunday, designated for the conclusion of peace negotiations, became *the date of general uprising.*

The growing agitation everywhere, the continued local conflicts of the peasants with the nobility, the news of a growing revolt in the Black Forest for the preceding six months and of its spread up to the Danube and the Lech, are sufficient to explain the rapid succession of peasant revolts in two-thirds of Germany. The fact, however, that the partial revolts took place simultaneously, proves that there were men at the head of the movement who had organised it through Anabaptists and other emissaries. Already in the second half of March, disorders broke out in Wuerttemberg, in the lower regions of the Neckar and the Odenwald, and in Upper and Middle Franconia. April 2, Judica Sunday, however, had already been named everywhere as the day of the general uprising, and everywhere the decisive blow, the revolt of the masses, fell in the first week of April. Th Allgaeu, Hegau and Lake peasants sounded the alarm bells on April 1, calling into the camp a mass meeting of all able-bodied men, and together with the Baltringen peasants, they immediately opened hostilities against the castles and monasteries.

In Franconia, where the movement was grouped around six centres, the insurrection broke out everywhere in the first days of April. In Noerdlingen two peasant camps were formed about that time, and the revolutionary party of the city under Anton Forner, aided by the peasants, gained the upper hand, appointing Forner the Mayor, and completing a union between the city and the peasants. In the region of Anspach, the peasants revolted everywhere between April 1 and 7, and from here the revolts spread as far as Bavaria. In the region of Rottenburg, the peasants were already under arms on March 22. In the city of Rottenburg the rule of the honourables was overthrown by the lower middle-class and plebeians under Stephan of Menzingen, but since the peasant dues were the chief source of revenue for the city, the new government was able to maintain a vacillating and equivocal attitude towards the peasants. In the Grand Chapter of Wurzburg there was a general uprising, early in April, of the peasants and the small cities. In the bishopric of

Bamberg, a general insurrection compelled the bishop to yield within five days. In the North, on the border of Thuringia, the strong Bildhausen Peasant Camp was organized.

In the Odenwald, where Wendel Hipler, a noble and former chancellor of the Count of Hohenlohe, and Georg Metzler, an innkeeper at Ballenberg near Krautheim, were at the head of the revolutionary party, the storm broke out on March 26. The peasants marched from all directions towards the Tauber. Two thousand men from the Rottenburg camp joined. Georg Metzler took command, and having received all reinforcements, marched on April 4 to the monastery of Schoenthal on the Jaxt, where he was joined by the peasants of the Neckar valley. The latter, led by Jaecklein Rohrbach, an innkeeper at Boeckingen near Heilbronn, had proclaimed, on Judica Sunday, the insurrection in Flein, Southeim, etc., while, simultaneously, Wendel Hipler, with a number of conspirators, took Oehringen by surprise and drew the surrounding peasants into the movement. In Schoenthal, the two peasant columns, combined into the Gay Troop, accepted the Twelve Articles, and organised expeditions against the castles and monasteries. The Gay Troop was about 8,000 strong, and possessed cannon, as well as 3,000 guns. Florian Geyer, a Franconian knight, also joined the troop and formed the Black Host, a select division which had been recruited mainly from the Rottenburg and Oehringen infantry.

The Wuerttemberg magistrate in Neckarsulm, Count Ludwig von Helfenstein, opened hostilities. Without much ado, he ordered all peasants that fell into his hands to be executed. The Gay Troop marched against him. The peasants were embittered by the massacres as well as by news of the defeat of the Leipheim Troop, of Jakob Wehe's execution, and the Truchsess atrocities. Von Helfenstein, who had precipitously moved into Weinsberg, was there attacked. The castle was stormed by Florian Geyer. The city was won after a prolonged struggle, and Count Ludwig was taken prisoner, as were several knights. On the following day, April 17, Jaecklein Rohrbach, together with the most resolute members of the troop, held court over the prisoners, and ordered fourteen of them, with von Helfenstein at the head, to run the gauntlet, this being the most humiliating death he could invent for them. The capture of Weinsberg and the terroristic revenge of Jaecklein against von Helfenstein, did not fail to influence the nobility. Count von Loebenstein joined the Peasant Alliance. The Count von Hohenlohe, who had joined previously without offering any aid, immediately sent the desired cannon and powder.

The chiefs debated among themselves whether they should not make Goetz von Berlichingen their commander "since he could bring to them the nobility." The proposal found sympathy, but Florian Geyer, who saw in this mood of the peasants and their chiefs the beginning of reaction, seceded from the troop, and together with his Black Host, marched first through the Neckar Region, then the Wuerzburg territory, everywhere destroying castles and priests' nests.

The remainder of the troop marched first towards Heilbronn. In this powerful and free imperial city, the patriciate was confronted, as almost everywhere, by a middle-class and revolutionary opposition. The latter, in secret agreement with the peasants, opened the gates before G. Metzler and Jaecklein Rohrbach, on April 17, in the course of a general disturbance. The peasant chiefs with their people took possession of the city. They accepted membership in the brotherhood, and delivered 12,000 guilders in money and a squad of volunteers. Only the possessions of the clergy and the Teutonic Order were pillaged. On the 22d, the peasants moved away, leaving a small garrison. Heilbronn was designated as the centre of the various troops, the latter actually sending delegates and conferring over common actions and common demands of the peasantry. But the middle-class opposition and the honourables who had joined them after the peasant invasion, regained the upper hand in the city, preventing it from taking decisive steps and only waiting for the approach of the princes' troops in order to betray the peasants definitely.

The peasants marched toward the Odenwald. Goetz von Berlichingen who, a few days previous, had offered himself to the Grand Elector Palatine, then to the peasantry, then again to the

Grand Elector, was compelled on April 24 to join the Evangelist Fraternity, and to take over the supreme command of the Gay Bright Troop (in contrast to the Black Troop of Florian Geyer). At the same time, however, he was the prisoner of the peasants who mistrusted him and bound him to a council of chiefs without whom he could undertake nothing. Goetz and Metzler moved with a mass of peasants over Buchen to Armorbach, where they remained from April 30, until May 5, arousing the entire region of the Main. The nobility was everywhere compelled to join, and thus its castles were spared. Only the monasteries were burned and pillaged. The troops had obviously become demoralised. The most energetic men were away, either under Florian Geyer or under Jaecklein Rohrbach, who, after the capture of Heilbronn, also separated himself from the troops, apparently because he, judge of Count von Helfenstein, could no longer remain with a body which was in favour of reconciliation with the nobility. This insistence on an understanding with the nobility was in itself a sign of demoralisation. Later, Wendel Hipler proposed a very fitting reorganisation of the troops. He suggested that the Lansquenets, who offered themselves daily, should be drawn into the service, and that the troops should no longer be renewed monthly by assembling fresh contingents and dismissing old ones, but that those of them who had received more or less military training should be retained. The community assembly rejected both proposals. The peasants had become arrogant, viewing the entire war as nothing but a pillage. They wanted to be free to go home as soon as their pockets were full, but the competition of the Lansquenets promised them little. In Amorbach, it went so far that Hans Berlin, a member of the council of Heilbronn, induced the chiefs and the councils of the troops to accept the *Declaration of the Twelve Articles*, a document wherein the remaining sharp edges of the Twelve Articles were removed, and in which, a language of humble supplication was put into the mouths of the peasants. This was too much for the peasants, who rejected the Declaration under great tumult, and insisted on the retention of the original Articles.

In the meantime, a decisive change had taken place in the region of Wuerzburg. The bishop who, after the first uprising early in April, had withdrawn to the fortified Frauenberg near Wuerzburg, from there to send unsuccessful letters in all directions asking for aid, was finally compelled to make temporary concessions. On May 2, a Diet was opened with the peasants represented, but before any results could be achieved, letters were intercepted which proved the bishop's traitorous machinations. The Diet immediately dispersed, and hostilities broke out anew between the insurgent city inhabitants and the peasants on one hand, and the bishop's forces on the other. The bishop fled to Heidelberg on May 5, and on the following day Florian Geyer, with the Black Troop, appeared in Wuerzburg and with him the Franconian Tauber Troop which consisted of the peasants of Mergentheim, Rottenburg and Anspach. On May 7, Goetz von Berlichingen with his Gay Bright Troops came, and the siege of Frauenberg began.

In the vicinity of Limpurg and in the region of Ellwangen and Hall, another contingent was formed by the end of March and the beginning of April, that of Gaildorf or the Common Gay Troop. Its actions were very violent. It aroused the entire region, burned many monasteries and castles, including the castle of Hohenstaufen, compelled all the peasants to join it, and compelled all nobles, even the cup-bearers of Limpurg, to enter the Christian Alliance. Early in May it invaded Wuerttemberg, but was persuaded to withdraw. The separatism of the German system of small states stood then, as in 1848, in the way of a common action of the revolutionaries of the various state territories. The Gaildorf troop, limited to a small area, was naturally bound to disperse when all resistance within that area was broken. The members of this troop concluded an agreement with the city of Gmuend, and leaving only 500 under arms, they went home.

In the Palatinate, peasant troops were formed on either bank of the Rhine by the end of April. They destroyed many castles and monasteries, and on May 1 they took Neustadt on the Hardt. The Bruchrain peasants, who appeared in this region, had on the previous day forced Speyer to conclude an agreement. The Marshal of Zabern, with the few troops of the Elector, was powerless against them, and on May 10 the Elector was compelled to conclude an agreement with the peasants, guaranteeing them a redress of their grievances, to be effected by a Diet.

In Wuerttemberg the revolt had occurred early in separate localities. As early as February, the peasants of the Urach Alp formed a union against the priests and masters, and by the end of March the peasants of Blaubeuer, Urach, Muensingen, Balingen and Rosenfeld revolted. The Wuerttemberg region was invaded by the Gaildorf troop at Goeppingen, by Jaecklein Rohrbach at Brackenheim, and by the remnants of the vanquished Leipheim troop at Pfuelingen. All these newcomers aroused the rural population. There were also serious disturbances in other localities. On April 6, Pfuelingen capitulated before the peasants. The government of the Austrian Archduke was in a very difficult situation. It had no money and but few troops. The cities and castles were in a bad condition, lacking garrisons or munitions, and even Asperg was practically defenseless. The attempt of the government to call out city reserves against the peasants, decided its temporary defeat. On April 16 the reserves of the city of Bottwar refused to obey orders, marching, instead of to Stuttgart, to Wunnenstein near Bottwar, where they formed the nucleus of a camp of middle-class people and peasants, and added other numbers rapidly. On the same day the rebellion broke out in Zabergau. The monastery of Maulbronn was pillaged, and a number of monasteries and castles were ruined. The Gaeu peasants received reinforcements from the neighbouring Bruchrain.

The command of the Wunnenstein troop was taken by Matern Feuerbacher, a councillor of the city of Bottwar, one of the leaders of the middle-class opposition compromised enough to be compelled to join the peasants. In spite of his new affiliations, however, he remained very moderate, prohibiting the application of the Letter of Articles to the castles, and seeking everywhere to reconcile the peasants with the moderate middle-class. He prevented the amalgamation of the Wuerttemberg peasants with the Gay Bright Troop, and afterwards he also persuaded the Gaildorf troop to withdraw from Wuerttemberg. On April 19 he was deposed in consequence of his middle-class tendencies, but the next day he was again made commander. He was indispensable, and even when Jaecklein Rohrbach came, on April 22, with 200 of his associates to join the Wuerttemberg peasants, he could do nothing but leave Feuerbacher in his place of commander, confining himself to rigid supervision of his actions.

On April 18, the government attempted to negotiate with the peasants stationed at Wunnenstein. The peasants insisted upon acceptance of the Twelve Articles, but this the government's representatives refused to do. The troop now proceeded to act. On April 20, it reached Laufen, where, for the last time, it rejected the offers of the government delegates. On April 22, the troops, numbering 6,000, appeared in Bietighein, threatening Stuttgart. Most of the city council had fled, and a citizens' committee was placed at the head of the administration. The citizenry here was divided, as elsewhere, between the parties of the honourables, the middle-class opposition, and the revolutionary plebeians. On April 25, the latter opened the gates for the peasants, and Stuttgart was immediately garrisoned by them. Here the organisation of the Gay Christian Troop (as the Wuerttemberg insurgents called themselves) was perfected, and rules and regulations were established for remuneration, division of booty and alimentation. A detachment of Stuttgarters, under Theus Gerber, joined the troops.

On April 29, Feuerbacher with all his men marched against the Gaildorf troops, which had entered the Wuerttemberg region at Schorndorf. He drew the entire region into his alliance and thus persuaded the Gaildorf troops to withdraw. In this way, he prevented the revolutionary elements of his men under Rohrbach from combining with the reckless troops of Gaildorf and thus receiving a dangerous reinforcement. Having been informed of Truchsess' approach, he left Schorndorf to meet him, and on May 1 encamped near Kirchheim under Teck.

We have thus traced the origin and the development of the insurrection in that portion of Germany which must be considered the territory of the first group of peasant armies. Before we proceed to the other groups (Thuringia and Hesse, Alsace, Austria and the Alps) we must give an account of the military operations of Truchsess, in which he, alone at the beginning, later supported by various princes and cities, annihilated the first group of insurgents. We left Truchsess near Ulm, where he came by the end of March, having left an observation corps below Teck, under the command of Dietrich Spaet. Truchsess' corps which together with the Union reinforcements concentrated in Ulm counted hardly 10,000, among them 7,200 infantrymen, was the only army at his disposal capable of an offensive against the peasants. Reinforcements came to Ulm very slowly, due in part to the difficulties of recruiting in insurgent localities, in part to the lack of money in the hands of the government, and also to the fact that the few available troops were everywhere indispensable for garrisoning the fortresses and the castles. We have already observed what a small number of troops were at the disposal of the princes and cities that did not belong to the Suabian Union. Everything depended upon the successes which Georg Truchsess with his union army would score.

Truchsess turned first against the Baltringen troops which, in the meantime, had begun to destroy castles and monasteries in the vicinity of Ried. The peasants who, with the approach of the Union troops withdrew into Ried, were driven out of the marshes by an enveloping movement, crossed the Danube and ran into the ravines and forests of the Suabian Alps. In this region, where cannon and cavalry, the main source of strength of the Union army, were of little avail, Truchsess did not pursue them further. He marched instead against the Leipheim troops which numbered 5,000 men stationed at Leipheim, 4,000 in the valley of Mindel, and 6,000 at Illertissen, and was arousing the entire region, destroying monasteries and castles, and preparing to march against Ulm with its three columns. It seems that a certain demoralisation had set in among the peasants of this division, which had undermined their military morale, for Jakob

Wehe tried at the very beginning to negotiate with Truchsess. The latter, however, now backed by sufficient military power, declined negotiations, and on April 4 attacked the main troops at Leipheim and entirely disrupted them. Jakob Wehe and Ulrich Schoen, together with two other peasant leaders, were captured and beheaded. Leipheim capitulated, and after a few marches through the surrounding country, the entire region was subdued.

A new rebellion of the Lansquenets, caused by a demand for plunder and additional remuneration, again stopped Truchsess' activities until April 10, when he marched southwest against the Baltringen troop which in the meantime had invaded his estates, Waldburg, Zeil and Wolfegg, and besieged his castles. Here, also, he found the peasants disunited, and defeated them on April 11 and 12, one after the other, in various encounters which completely disrupted the Baltringen troops. Its remnants withdrew under the command of the priest Florian, and joined the Lake troops. Truchsess now turned against the latter. The Lake troops which in the meantime had made not only military marches but had also drawn the cities Buchhorn (Friedrichshafen) and Wollmatingen into the fraternity, held, on April 13, a big military council in the monastery of Salem, and decided to move against Truchsess. Alarm bells were sounded and 10,000 men, joined by the defeated remnants of the Baltringen troops, assembled in the camp of Bermatingen. On April 15 they stood their own in a combat with Truchsess, who did not wish to risk his army in a decisive battle, preferring to negotiate, the more so since he received news of the approach of the Allgaeu and Hegau troops. On April 17, in Weingarten, he concluded an agreement with the Lake and Baltringen peasants which seemed quite favourable to them, and which they accepted without suspicion. He also induced the delegates of the Upper and Lower Allgaeu peasants to accept the agreement, and then moved towards Wuerttemberg.

Truchsess' cunning saved him here from certain ruin. Had he not succeeded in fooling the weak, limited, for the most part demoralised peasants and their usually incapable, timid and venal leaders, he would have been closed in with his small army between four columns numbering at least from 25,000 to 30,000 men, and would have perished. It was the narrow-mindedness of his enemies, always inevitable among the peasant masses, that made it possible for him to dispose of them at the very moment when, with one blow, they could have ended the entire war, at least as far as Suabia and Franconia were concerned. The Lake peasants adhered to the agreement, which finally turned out to be their undoing, so rigidly that they later took up arms against their allies, the Hegau peasants. And although the Allgaeu peasants, involved in the betrayal by their leaders, soon renounced the agreement, Truchsess was then out of danger.

The Hegau peasants, though not included in the Weingarten agreement, gave a new example of the appalling narrow-mindedness and the stubborn provincialism which ruined the entire Peasant War. When, after unsuccessful negotiations with them, Truchsess moved towards Wuerttemberg, they followed him, continually pressing his flank, but it did not occur to them to unite with the Wuerttemberg Gay Christian Troop, because previously the peasants of Wuerttemberg and the Neckar valley refused to come to their assistance. When Truchsess had moved far enough from their home country, they returned peacefully and marched to Freiburg.

We left the Wuerttemberg peasants under the command of Mattern Feuerbacher at Kirchheim below Teck, from where the observation corps left by Truchsess had withdrawn towards Urach under the command of Dietrich Spaet. After an unsuccessful attempt to take Urach, Feuerbacher turned towards Nuertingen, sending letters to all neighbouring insurgent troops, calling reinforcements for the decisive battle. Considerable reinforcements actually came from the Wuerttemberg lowlands as well as from Gaeu. The Gaeu peasants had grouped themselves around the remnants of the Leipheim troop which had withdrawn to West Wuerttemberg, and they aroused the entire valleys of Neckar and Nagoldt up to Boeblingen and Leonberg. Those Gaeu peasants, on May 5, came in two strong columns to join Feuerbacher at Nuertingen. Truchsess met the united troops at Boeblingen. Their number, their cannon and their position perplexed him. As usual, he started negotiations and concluded an armistice with the peasants. But as soon as he had thus secured his position, he attacked them on May 12 *during the armistice*, and forced a decisive battle upon them. The peasants offered a long and brave resistance until finally Boeblingen was surrendered to Truchsess owing to the betrayal of the middle-class. The left wing of the peasants, deprived of its base of support, was forced back and encompassed. This decided the battle. The undisciplined peasants were thrown into disorder and, later, into a wild flight, those that were not killed or captured by the horsemen of the Union threw away their weapons and went home. The Bright Christian Troop, and with it the entire Wuerttemberg insurrection was gone. Theus Gerber fled to Esslingen, Feuerbacher fled to Switzerland, Jaecklein Rohrbach was captured and dragged in chains to Neckargartach, where Truchsess ordered him chained to a post, surrounded by firewood and roasted to death on a slow fire, while he, feasting with horsemen, gloated over this noble spectacle.

From Neckargartach, Truchsess gave aid to the operations of the Elector Palatine by invading Kraichgau. Having received word of Truchsess' successes, the Elector, who meanwhile had gathered troops, immediately broke his agreement with the peasants, attacked Bruchrain on May 23, captured and burned Malsch after vigorous resistance, pillaged a number of villages, and garrisoned Bruchsal. At the same time Truchsess attacked Eppingen and captured the chief of the local movement, Anton Eisenhut, whom the Elector immediately executed with a dozen other peasant leaders. Bruchrain and Kraichgau were thus subjugated and compelled to pay an indemnity of about 40,000 guilders. Both armies, that of Truchsess now reduced to 6,000 men in consequence of the preceding battles, and that of the Elector (6,500 men), united and moved towards the Odenwald.

Word of the Boeblingen defeat spread terror everywhere among the insurgents. The free imperial cities which had come under the heavy hand of the peasants, sighed in relief. The city of Heilbronn was the first to take steps towards reconciliation with the Suabian Union. Heilbronn was the seat of the peasants' main office and that of the delegates of the various troops who deliberated over the proposals to be made to the emperor and the empire in the name of all the insurgent peasants. In these negotiations which were to lay down general rules for all of Germany, it again became apparent that none of the existing estates, including the peasants, was developed sufficiently to be able to reconstruct the whole of Germany according to its own viewpoint. It became obvious that to accomplish this, the support of the peasantry and particularly of the middle-class must be gained. In consequence, Wendel Hipler took over the conduct of the negotiations. Of all the leaders of the movement, Wendel Hipler had the best understanding of the existing conditions. He was not a far-seeing revolutionary of Muenzer's type; he was not a representative of the peasants as were Metzler or Rohrbach; his many-sided experiences, his practical knowledge of the position of the various estates towards each other prevented him from representing one of the estates engaged in the movement in opposition to the other. Just as Muenzer, a representative of the beginnings of the proletariat then outside of the existing official organisation of society, was driven to the anticipation of communism, Wendel Hipler, the representative, as it were, of the average of all progressive elements of the nation, anticipated modern bourgeois society. The principles that he defended, the demands that he formulated, though not immediately possible, were the somewhat idealised, logical result of the dissolution of feudal society. In so far as the peasants agreed to propose laws for the whole empire, they were compelled to accept Hipler's principles and demands. Centralisation demanded by the peasants thus assumed, in Heilbronn, a definite form, which, however, was worlds away from the ideas of the peasants themselves on the subject. Centralisation, for instance, was more clearly defined in the demands for the establishment of uniform coins, measures and weights, for the abolition of internal customs, etc., in demands, that is to say, which were much more in the interests of the city

93

middle-class than in the interests of the peasants. Concessions made to the nobility were a certain approach to the modern system of redemption and aimed, finally, to transform feudal land ownership into bourgeois ownership. In a word, so far as the demands of the peasants were combined into a system of "imperial reform," they did not express the temporary demands of the peasants but became subordinate to the general interests of the middle-class as a whole.

While this reform of the empire was still being debated in Heilbronn, the author of the Declaration of the Twelve Articles, Hans Berlin, was already on his way to meet Truchsess, to negotiate in the name of the honourables, the middle-class and the citizenry on the surrender of the city. Reactionary movements within the city supported this betrayal, and Wendel Hipler was obliged to flee, as were the peasants. He went to Weinsberg where he attempted to assemble the remnants of the Wuerttemberg peasants and those few of the Gaildorf troops which could be mobilised. The approach of the Elector Palatine and of Truchsess, however, drove him out of there and he was compelled to go to Wuerzburg to cause the Gay Bright Troop to resume operations. In the meantime, the armies of the Union and the Elector subdued the Neckar region, compelled the peasants to take a new oath, burned many villages, and stabbed or hanged all fleeing peasants that fell into their hands. To avenge the execution of Helfenstein, Weinsberg was burned.

The troops that were assembled in front of Wuerzburg had in the meantime besieged Frauenberg. On May 15, before a gap was made by their fusillade, they bravely but unsuccessfully attempted to storm the fortress. Four hundred of the best men, mostly of Florian Geyer's host, remained in the ditches, dead or wounded. Two days later, May 17, Wendel Hipler appeared and ordered a military council. He proposed to leave at Frauenberg only 4,000 men and to place the main force, about 20,000 men, in a camp at Krautheim on the Jaxt, before the very eyes of Truchsess, so that all reinforcements might be assembled there. The plan was excellent. Only by keeping the masses together, and by a numerical superiority, could one hope to defeat the army of the princes which now numbered about 13,000 men. The demoralisation and discouragement of the peasants, however, had gone too far to make any energetic action possible. Goetz von Berlichingen, who soon afterwards openly appeared as a traitor, may have helped to hold the troop back. Thus Hipler's plan was never put into action; the troops were divided as ever, and only on May 23 did the Gay Bright Troop start action after the Franconians had promised to follow quickly. On May 26, the detachments of the Margrave of Anspach, located in Wuerzburg, were called, due to the word that the Margrave had opened hostilities against the peasants. The rest of the besieging army, with Florian Geyer's Black Troop, took position at Heidingsfeld not far from Wuerzburg.

The Gay Bright Troop arrived on May 24 in Krautheim in a condition far from good. Many peasants learned that in their absence their villages had taken the oath at Truchsess' behest, and this they used as a pretext to go home. The troops moved further to Neckarsulm, and on May 28 started negotiations with Truchsess, At the same time messengers were sent to the peasants of Franconia, Alsace and Black Forest-Hegau, with the demand to hurry reinforcements. From Neckarsulm Goetz marched towards Oehringen. The troops melted from day to day. Goetz von Berlichingen also disappeared during the march. He rode home, having previously negotiated with Truchsess through his old brother-in-arms, Dietrich Spaet, concerning his going over to the other side. In Oehringen, a false rumour of the enemy approaching threw the helpless and discouraged mass into a panic. The troop was rapidly disintegrating, and it was with difficulty that Metzler and Wendel Hipler succeeded in keeping together about 2,000 men, whom they again led towards Krautheim. In the meantime, the Franconian army, 5,000 strong, had come, but in consequence of a side march over Loewenstein towards Oehringen, ordered by Goetz apparently with treacherous intentions, it missed the Gay Troop and moved towards Neckarsulm. This small town, defended by a detachment of the Gay Bright Troop, was besieged by Truchsess. The Franconians arrived at night and saw the fires of the

Union army, but their leaders had not the courage to brave an attack. They retreated to Krautheim, where they at last found the remainder of the Gay Bright Troop. Receiving no aid, Neckarsulm surrendered on the 29th to the Union troops. Truchsess immediately ordered 13 peasants executed, and went to meet the troop, burning, pillaging and murdering all along the way through the valleys of Neckar, Kocher and Jaxt. Heaps of ruins and bodies of peasants hanging on trees marked his march.

At Krautheim the Union army met the peasants who, forced by a flank movement of Truchsess, had withdrawn towards Koenigshofen on the Tauber. Here they took their position, 8,000 in number, with 32 cannon. Truchsess approached them, hidden behind hills and forests. He sent out columns to envelop them, and on June 2, he attacked them with such a superiority of forces and energy that in spite of the stubborn resistance of several columns lasting into the night, they were defeated and dispersed. As everywhere, the horsemen of the Union, "the peasants' death," were mainly instrumental in annihilating the insurgent army, throwing themselves on the peasants, who were shaken by artillery gun fire and lance attacks, disrupting their ranks completely, and killing individual fighters. The kind of warfare conducted by Truchsess and his horsemen is manifested in the fate of 300 Koenigshof middle-class men united with the peasant army. During the battle, all but fifteen were killed, and of these remaining fifteen, four were subsequently decapitated.

Having thus completed his victory over the peasants of Odenwald, the Neckar valley and lower Franconia, Truchsess subdued the entire region by means of punitive expeditions, burning entire villages and causing numberless executions. From there he moved towards Wuerzburg. On his way he learned that the second Franconian troops under the command of Florian Geyer and Gregor von Burg-Bernsheim was stationed at Sulzdorf. He immediately moved against them.

Florian Geyer, who, after the unsuccessful attempt at storming Frauenberg, had devoted himself mainly to negotiations

with the princes and the cities, especially with Rottenburg and
Margrave Casimir of Anspach, urging them to join the peasant
fraternity, was suddenly recalled in consequence of word of the
Koenigshofen defeat. His troops were joined by those of Anspach under the command of Gregor von Burg-Bernsheim. The
latter troops had been only recently formed. Margrave Casimir
had managed, in true Hohenzollern style, to keep in check the
peasant revolt in his region, partly by promises and partly by
the threat of amassing troops. He maintained complete neutrality towards all outside troops as long as they did not include
Anspach subjects. He tried to direct the hatred of the peasants
mainly towards the church endowments, through the ultimate
confiscation of which he hoped to enrich himself. As soon as he
received word of the Boetlingen battle, he opened hostilities
against his rebellious peasants, pillaging and burning their villages, and hanging or otherwise killing many of them. The
peasants, however, quickly assembled, and under the command
of Gregor von Burg-Bernsheim defeated him at Windsheim,
May 29. While they were still pursuing him, the call of the
hard-pressed Odenwald peasants reached them, and they
turned towards Heidingsfeld and from there with Florian Geyer, again towards Wuerzburg (June 2). Still without word from
the Odenwald, they left 5,000 peasants there, and with the
remaining 4,000—many had run away—they followed the others. Reassured by false rumours of the outcome of the Koenigshofen battle, they were attacked by Truchsess at Sulzdorf and
completely defeated. The horsemen and servants of Truchsess
perpetrated, as usual, a terrible massacre. Florian Geyer kept
the remainder of his Black Troop, 600 in number, and battled
his way through the village of Ingolstadt. He placed 200 men in
the church and cemetery and 400 in the castle. He had been
pursued by the Elector Palatine's forces, of whom a column of
1,200 men captured the village and set fire to the church. Those
who did not perish in the flames were slaughtered. The Elector's troops then fired on the castle, made a gap in the ancient
wall, and attempted to storm it. Twice beaten back by the
peasants who stood hidden behind an internal wall, they shot

the wall to pieces, and attempted a third storming, which was successful. Half of Geyer's men were massacred; with the other 200 he managed to escape. Their hiding place, however, was discovered the following day (Whit-Monday). The Elector Palatine's soldiers surrounded the woods in which they lay hidden, and slaughtered all the men. Only seventeen prisoners were taken during those two days. Florian Geyer again fought his way through with a few of his most intrepid fighters and turned towards the Gaildorf peasants, who had again assembled in a body of about 7,000 men. Upon his arrival, he found them mostly dispersed, in consequence of crushing news from every side. He made a last attempt to assemble the dispersed peasants in the woods on June 9, but was attacked by the troops, and fell fighting.

Truchsess, who, immediately after the Koenigshofen victory, had sent word to the besieged Frauenberg, now marched towards Wuerzburg. The council came to a secret understanding with him so that, on the night of June 7, the Union army was in a position to surround the city where 5,000 peasants were stationed, and the following morning to march through the gates opened by the council, without even lifting a sword. By this betrayal of the Wuerzburg "honourables" the last troops of the Franconian peasants were disarmed and all the leaders arrested. Truchsess immediately ordered 81 of them decapitated. Here in Wuerzburg the various Franconian princes appeared, one after the other, among them the Bishop of Wuerzburg himself, the Bishop of Bamberg and the Margrave of Brandenburg-Anspach. The gracious lords distributed the rôles among themselves. Truchsess marched with the Bishop of Bamberg, who presently broke the agreement concluded with his peasants and offered his territory to the raging hordes of the Union army, who pillaged, massacred and burned. Margrave Casimir devastated his own land. Teiningen was burned, numerous villages were pillaged or made fuel for the flames. In every city the Margrave held a bloody court. In Neustadt, on the Aisch, he ordered eighteen rebels beheaded, in the Buergel March, forty-three suffered a similar fate. From there he went to Rottenburg where the honourables, in the meantime, had made a counter revolution and arrested Stephan von Menzingen. The Rottenburg lower middle-class and plebeians were now compelled to pay heavily for the fact that they behaved towards the peasants in such an equivocal way, refusing to help them to the very last moment and in their local narrow-minded egotism insisting on the suppression of the countryside crafts in favour of the city guilds, and only unwillingly renouncing the city revenues flowing from the feudal services of the peasants. The Margrave ordered sixteen of them executed, Menzingen among them. In a similar manner the Bishop of Wuerzburg marched through his region, pillaging, devastating and burning everywhere. On his triumphal march he ordered 256 rebels to be decapitated, and upon his return to Wuerzburg he crowned his work by decapitating thirteen more from among the Wuerzburg rebels.

In the region of Mainz the viceroy, Bishop Wilhelm von Strassburg, restored order without resistance. He ordered only four men executed. Rheingau, where the peasants had also been restless, but where, nevertheless, everybody had long before gone home, was subsequently invaded by Frowen von Hutten, a cousin of Ulrich, and finally "pacified" by the execution of twelve ringleaders. Frankfurt, which also had witnessed revolutionary movements of a considerable size, was held in check first by the conciliatory attitude of the council, then by recruited troops in the Rhenish Palatinate. Eight thousand peasants had assembled anew after the breach of agreement by the Elector, and had again burned monasteries and castles, but the Archbishop of Trier came to the aid of the Marshal of Zabern, and defeated them as early as May 23 at Pfedersheim. A series of atrocities (in Pfedersheim alone eighty-two were executed) and the capture of Weissenburg on July 7 terminated the insurrection here.

Of all the divisions of troops there remained only two to be vanquished, those of Hegau–Black Forest and of Allgaeu. Archduke Ferdinand had tried intrigues with both. In the same way as Margrave Casimir and other princes tried to utilise the insurrection to annex the church territories and principalities, so Ferdinand wished to utilise it to strengthen the power of the House of Austria. He had negotiated with the Allgaeu commander, Walter Bach, and with the Hegau commander, Hans Mueller, with the aim of inducing the peasants to declare their adherence to Austria, but, both chiefs being venal, their influence with the troops went only so far that the Allgaeu troop concluded an armistice with the Archbishop and observed neutrality towards Austria.

Retreating from the Wuerttemberg region, the peasants of Hegau destroyed a number of castles, and received reinforcements from the provinces of the Margraviate of Baden. On May 13 they marched towards Freiburg; on May 18 they bombarded it, and on May 23, the city having capitulated, they entered it with flying colours. From there they moved towards Stockach and Radolfzell, and waged a prolonged petty war against the garrisons of those cities. The latter, together with the nobility and other surrounding cities, appealed to the Lake peasants for help in accordance with the Weingarten agreement. The former rebels of the Lake Troop rose, 5,000 strong, against their former allies. So potent was the narrow-mindedness of the peasants who were confined to their local horizon, that only 600 refused to fight and expressed a desire to join the Hegau peasants, for which they were slaughtered. The Hegau peasants, themselves, persuaded by Hans Mueller of Bulgenbach, who had sold himself to the enemy, lifted their siege, and Hans Mueller having run away, most of them dispersed forthwith. The remaining ones entrenched themselves on the Hilzingen Steep, where, on July 16, they were beaten and annihilated by the troops that had in the meantime become free of other engagements. The Swiss cities negotiated an agreement with the Hegau peasants, which, however, did not prevent the other side from capturing and murdering Hans Mueller, his Laufenburg betrayal notwithstanding. In Breisgau, the city of Freiburg also deserted the peasant Union (July 17) and sent troops against it, but because of the weakness of the fighting forces of the princes, here as elsewhere, an agreement was reached (September 18), which also included Sundgau. The eight groups of the Black Forest and the Klettgau peasants, who were not yet disarmed, were again driven to an uprising by the tyranny of Count von Sulz, and were repulsed in October. On November 13, the Black Forest peasants were forced into an agreement, and on December 6, Walzhut, the last bulwark of the insurrection in the Upper Rhine, fell.

The Allgaeu peasants had, after the departure of Truchsess, renewed their campaign against the monasteries and castles and were using repressive measures in retaliation for the devastations caused by the Union army. They were confronted by few troops which braved only insignificant skirmishes, not being able to follow them into the woods. In June, a movement against the honourables started in Memmingen which had hitherto remained more or less neutral, and only the accidental nearness of some Union troops which came in time to the rescue of the nobility, made its suppression possible. Schapelar, the preacher and leader of the plebeian movement, fled to St. Gallen. The peasants appeared before the city and were about to start firing to break a gap, when they learned of the approach of Truchsess on his way from Wuerzburg. On June 27 they started against him, in two columns, over Babenhausen and Oberguenzburg. Archduke Ferdinand again attempted to win over the peasants to the House of Austria. Citing the armistice concluded with the peasants, he demanded of Truchsess to march no further against them. The Suabian Union, however, ordered Truchsess to attack them, but to refrain from pillaging and burning. Truchsess, however, was too clever to relinquish his primary and most effective means of battle, even were he in a position to keep in order the Lansquenets whom he had led between Lake Constance and the Main from one excess to another. The peasants took a stand behind the Iller and the Luibas, about 23,000 in number. Truchsess opposed them with 11,000. The positions of both armies were formidable. The cavalry could not operate on the territory that lay ahead, and if the Truchsess Lansquenets were superior to the peasants in organisation, military resources and discipline, the Allgaeu

101

peasants counted in their ranks a host of former soldiers and experienced commanders and possessed numerous well-manned cannon. On July 19, the armies of the Suabian Union opened a cannonade which was continued on every side of the 20th, but without result. On July 21, Georg von Frundsberg joined Truchsess with 300 Lansquenets. He knew many of the peasant commanders who had served under him in the Italian military expeditions and he entered into negotiations with them. Where military resources were insufficient, treason succeeded. Walter Bach and several other commanders and artillerymen sold themselves. They set fire to the powder store of the peasants and persuaded the troops to make an enveloping movement, but as soon as the peasants left their strong position they fell into the ambush placed by Truchsess in collusion with Bach and the other traitors. They were less capable of defending themselves since their traitorous commanders had left them under the pretext of reconnoitering and were already on their way to Switzerland. Thus two of the peasant camps were entirely disrupted. The third, under Knopf of Luibas, was still in a position to withdraw in order. It again took its position on the mountain of Kollen near Kampten, where it was surrounded by Truchsess. The latter did not dare to attack these peasants, but he cut them off from all supplies, and tried to demoralise them by burning about 200 villages in the vicinity. Hunger, and the sight of their burning homes, finally brought the peasants to surrender (July 25). More than twenty were immediately executed. Knopf of Luibas, the only leader of this troop who did not betray his banner, fled to Biegenz. There he was captured, however, and hanged, after a long imprisonment.

With this, the Peasant War in Suabia and Franconia came to an end.

VI

IMMEDIATELY after the outbreak of the first movement in Suabia, Thomas Muenzer again hurried to Thuringia, and since the end of February and the beginning of March, he established his quarters in the free imperial city of Muehlhausen, where his party was stronger than elsewhere. He held the threads of the entire movement in his hand. He knew what storm was about to break in Southern Germany, and he undertook to make Thuringia the centre of the movement for North Germany. He found very fertile soil. Thuringia, the main arena of the Reformation movement, was in the grip of great unrest. The economic misery of the downtrodden peasants, as well as the current revolutionary, religious and political doctrine, had also prepared the neighbouring provinces, Hesse, Saxony, and the region of the Harz, for the general uprising. In Muehlhausen itself, whole masses of the lower middle-class had been won over to the extreme Muenzer doctrine, and could hardly wait for the moment when they would assert themselves by a superiority of numbers against the haughty honourables. In order not to start before the proper moment, Muenzer was compelled to appear in the rôle of moderator, but his disciple, Pfeifer, who conducted the movement there, had committed himself to such an extent that he could not hold back the outbreak, and as early as March 17, 1525, before the general uprising in Southern Germany, Muehlhausen had its revolution. The old patrician council was overthrown, and the government was handed over to the newly-elected "eternal council," with Muenzer as president.

The worst thing that can befall a leader of an extreme party is

103

to be compelled to take over a government in an epoch when the movement is not yet ripe for the domination of the class which he represents and for the realisation of the measures which that domination would imply. What he *can* do depends not upon his will but upon the sharpness of the clash of interests between the various classes, and upon the degree of development of the material means of existence, the relations of production and means of communication upon which the clash of interests of the classes is based every time. What he *ought* to do, what his party demands of him, again depends not upon him, or upon the degree of development of the class struggle and its conditions. He is bound to his doctrines and the demands hitherto propounded which do not emanate from the interrelations of the social classes at a given moment, or from the more or less accidental level of relations of production and means of communication, but from his more or less penetrating insight into the general result of the social and political movement. Thus he necessarily finds himself in a dilemma. What he *can* do is in contrast to all his actions as hitherto practised, to all his principles and to the present interests of his party; what he *ought* to do cannot be achieved. In a word, he is compelled to represent not his party or his class, but the class for whom conditions are ripe for domination. In the interests of the movement itself, he is compelled to defend the interests of an alien class, and to feed his own class with phrases and promises, with the assertion that the interests of that alien class are their own interests. Whoever puts himself in this awkward position is irrevocably lost. We have seen examples of this in recent times. We need only be reminded of the position taken in the last French provisional government by the representatives of the proletariat, though they represented only a very low level of proletarian development. Whoever can still look forward to official positions after having become familiar with the experiences of the February government—not to speak of our own noble German provisional governments and imperial regencies—is either foolish beyond measure, or at best pays only lip service to the extreme revolutionary party.

Muenzer's position at the head of the "eternal council" of Muehlhausen was indeed much more precarious than that of any modern revolutionary regent. Not only the movement of his time, but the whole century, was not ripe for the realisation of the ideas for which he himself had only begun to grope. The class which he represented not only was not developed enough and incapable of subduing and transforming the whole of society, but it was just beginning to come into existence. The social transformation that he pictured in his fantasy was so little grounded in the then existing economic conditions that the latter were a preparation for a social system diametrically opposed to that of which he dreamt. Nevertheless, he was bound to his preachings of Christian equality and evangelical community of possessions. He was at least compelled to make an attempt at their realisation. Community of all possessions, universal and equal labour duty, and the abolition of all authority were proclaimed. In reality, Muehlhausen remained a republican imperial city with a somewhat democratic constitution, with a senate elected by universal suffrage and under the control of a forum, and with the hastily improvised feeding of the poor. The social change, which so horrified the Protestant middle-class contemporaries, in reality never went beyond a feeble and unconscious attempt prematurely to establish the bourgeois society of a later period.

Muenzer, himself, seems to have realised the wide abyss between his theories and surrounding realities. This abyss must have been felt the more keenly, the more distorted the views of this genius of necessity appeared, reflected in the heads of the mass of his followers. He threw himself into widening and organising the movement with a zeal rare even for him. He wrote letters and sent out emissaries in all directions. His letters and sermons breathed a revolutionary fanaticism which was amazing in comparison with his former writings. Gone completely was the naïve youthful humour of Muenzer's revolutionary pamphlets. The quiet instructive language of the thinker, which had been so characteristic of him, appeared no more. Muenzer was now entirely a prophet of the revolution. Incessantly he fanned the flame of hatred against the ruling classes. He spurred the wildest passions, using forceful terms of expression the like of which religious and nationalist delirium had put into the mouths of the Old Testament prophets. The style up to which he worked himself reveals the level of education of that public which he was to affect. The example of Muehlhausen and the propaganda of Muenzer had a quick and far-reaching effect. In Thuringia, Eichsfeld, Harz, in the duchies of Saxony, in Hesse and Fulda, in Upper Franconia and in Vogtland, the peasants arose, assembled in armies, and burned castles and monasteries. Muenzer was more or less recognised as the leader of the entire movement, and Muehlhausen remained the central point, while in Erfurt a purely middle-class movement became victorious, and the ruling party there constantly maintained an undecided attitude towards the peasants.

In Thuringia, the princes were at the beginning just as helpless and powerless in relation to the peasants as they had been in Franconia and Suabia. Only in the last days of April, did the Landgrave of Hesse succeed in assembling a corps. It was that same Landgrave Philipp, whose piety is being praised so much by the Protestant and bourgeois histories of the Reformation, and of whose infamies towards the peasants we will presently have a word to say. By a series of quick movements and by decisive action, Landgrave Philipp subdued the major part of his land. He called new contingents, and then turned towards the region of the Abbot of Fulda, who hitherto was his lord. On May 3, he defeated the Fulda peasant troop at Frauenberg, subdued the entire land, and seized the opportunity not only to free himself from the sovereignty of the Abbot, but to make the Abbey of Fulda a vassalage of Hesse, naturally pending its subsequent secularisation. He then took Eisenach and Langensalza, and jointly with the Saxon troops, moved towards the headquarters of the rebellious Muehlhausen. Muenzer assembled his forces at Frankenhausen 8,000 men and several cannons. The Thuringian troops were far from possessing that fighting power which the Suabian and Franconian troops developed in their struggle with Truchsess. The men were poorly armed and badly disciplined. They counted few ex-soldiers among them, and sorely lacked leadership. It appears that Muenzer possessed no military knowledge whatsoever. Nevertheless, the princes found it proper to use here the same tactics that so often helped Truchsess to victory—breach of faith. On May 16, they entered negotiations, concluded an armistice, but attacked the peasants before the time of the armistice had elapsed.

Muenzer stood with his people on the mountain which is still called Mount Battle (Schlachtberg), entrenched behind a barricade of wagons. The discouragement among the troops was rapidly increasing. The princes had promised them amnesty should they deliver Muenzer alive. Muenzer assembled his people in a circle, to debate the princes' proposals. A knight and a priest expressed themselves in favour of capitulation. Muenzer had them both brought inside the circle, and decapitated. This act of terrorist energy, jubilantly met by the outspoken revolutionaries, caused a certain halt among the troops, but most of the men would have gone away without resistance had it not been noticed that the princes' Lansquenets, who had encircled the entire mountain, were approaching in close columns, in spite of the armistice. A front was hurriedly formed behind the wagons, but already the cannon balls and guns were pounding the half-defenseless peasants, unused to battle, and the Lansquenets reached the barricade. After a brief resistance, the line of the wagons was broken, the peasants' cannon captured, and the peasants dispersed. They fled in wild disorder, and fell into the hands of the enveloping columns and the cavalry, who perpetrated an appalling massacre among them. Out of 8,000 peasants, over 5,000 were slaughtered. The survivors arrived at Frankenhaus, and simultaneously with them, the princes' cavalry. The city was taken. Muenzer, wounded in the head, was discovered in a house and captured. On May 25, Muehlhausen also surrendered. Pfeifer, who had remained there, ran away, but was captured in the region of Eisenach.

Muenzer was put on the rack in the presence of the princes, and then decapitated. He went to his death with the same courage with which he had lived. He was barely twenty-eight when he was executed. Pfeifer, with many others, was also executed. In Fulda, that holy man, Philipp of Hesse, had opened his bloody court. He and the Prince of Hesse ordered many others to be killed by the sword—in Eisenach, twenty-four; in Langensalza, forty-one; after the battle of Frankenhaus, 300; in Muehlhausen, over 100; at Germar, twenty-six; at Tungeda, fifty, at Sangenhausen, twelve; in Leipzig, eight, not to speak of mutilations and the more moderate measures of pillaging and burning villages and cities.

Muehlhausen was compelled to give up its liberty under the empire, and was incorporated into the Saxon lands, just as the Abbey of Fulda was incorporated in the Landgraviate of Hesse.

The prince now moved through the forest of Thuringia, where Franconian peasants of the Bildhaus camp had united with the Thuringians, and burned many castles. A battle took place before Meiningen. The peasants were beaten and withdrew towards the city, which closed its gates to them, and threatened to attack them from the rear. The troops, thus placed in a quandary by the betrayal of their allies, capitulated before the prince, and dispersed, while negotiations were still under way. The camp of Bildhaus had long dispersed, and with this, the remnants of the insurgents of Saxony, Hesse, Thuringia, and Upper Franconia, were annihilated.

In Alsace the rebellion broke out after the movement had started on the right side of the Rhine. The peasants of the bishopric of Strassbourg arose as late as the middle of April. Soon after, there was an upheaval of the peasants of upper Alsace and Sundgau. On April 18, a contingent of Lower Alsace peasants pillaged the monastery of Altdorf. Other troops were formed near Ebersheim and Barr, as well as in the Urbis valley. These were soon concentrated into the large Lower Alsace division and proceeded in an organised way to take cities and towns and to destroy monasteries. One out of every three men was called to the colours. The Twelve Articles of this group were considerably more radical than those of the Suabian and Franconian groups.

While one column of the Lower Alsace peasants first concentrated near St. Hippolite early in May, attempting to take the city but without success, and then, through an understanding with the citizens, came into possession of Barken on May 10, of Rappoldtsweiler on May 13, and Reichenweier on May 14, a second column under Erasmus Gerber marched to attack Strassbourg by surprise. The attempt was unsuccessful, and the column now turned towards the Vosges, destroyed the monastery of Mauersmuenster, and besieged Zabern, taking it on May 13. From here it moved towards the frontier of Lorraine and aroused the section of the duchy adjoining the frontier, at the same time fortifying the mountain passes. Two columns were formed at Herbolzheim on the Saar, and at Neuburg, at Saargemund, 4,000 German-Lorraine peasants entrenched themselves. Finally, two advanced troops, the Kolben in the Vosges at Stuerzelbrunn, and the Kleeburg at Weissenburg, covered the front and the right flank, while the left flank was adjoining those of Upper Alsace.

The latter, in motion since April 20, had forced the city of Sulz into the peasant fraternity on May 10, Gebweiler, on May 12, and Sennheim and vicinity, May 15. The Austrian government and the surrounding imperial cities immediately united against them, but they were too weak to offer serious resistance, not to speak of attack. Thus, in the middle of May, the whole of Alsace, with the exception of only a few cities, came into the hands of the insurgents.

But already the army was approaching which was destined to break the ungodly attack of the Alsace peasants. It was the French who effected here the restoration of the nobility. Already, on May 16, Duke Anton of Lorraine marched out with an army of 30,000, among them the flower of the French nobility, as well as Spanish, Piedmontese, Lombardic, Greek and Albanian auxiliary troops. On May 16 he met 4,000 peasants at Luetzelstein whom he defeated without effort, and on the 17th he forced Zabern, which was besieged by the peasants, to surrender. But even while the Lorrainers were entering the city and the peasants were being disarmed, the conditions of the surrender were broken. The defenseless peasants were attacked by the Lansquenets and most of them were slaughtered. The remaining Lower Alsace columns disbanded, and Duke Anton went to meet the Upper Alsatians. The latter, who had refused to join the Lower Alsatians at Zabern, were now attacked at Scherweiler by the entire force of the Lorrainers. They resisted with great bravery, but the enormous numerical superiority—30,000 as against 7,000—and the betrayal of a number of knights, especially that of the magistrate of Reichenweier, made all daring futile. They were totally beaten and dispersed. The Duke subdued the whole of Alsace with the usual atrocities. Only Sundgau was spared. By threatening to call him into the land, the Austrian government forced the peasants to conclude the Ensisheim agreement early in June. The government soon broke the agreement, however, ordering numbers of preachers and leaders of the movement to be hanged. The peasants made a new insurrection which ended with the inclusion of the Sundgau peasants into the Offenburg agreement (September 18).

There now remains only the report of the Peasant War in the Alpine regions of Austria. These regions, as well as the adjoining Archbishopric of Salzburg were in continuous opposition to the government and the nobility ever since the Stara Prawa, and the Reformation doctrines found there a fertile soil. Religious persecutions and wilful taxation brought the rebellion to a crisis.

The city of Salzburg, supported by the peasants and the pitmen, had been in controversy with the Archbishop since 1522 over city privileges and the freedom of religious practice. By the end of 1523, the Archbishop attacked the city with recruited Lansquenets, terrorised it by a cannonade from the castle, and persecuted the heretical preachers. At the same time he imposed new crushing taxes, and thereby irritated the population to the utmost. In the spring of 1525, simultaneously with the Suabian-Franconian and Thuringian uprisings, the peasants and pitmen of the entire country suddenly arose, organised themselves under the commanders Brossler and Weitmoser, freed the city and besieged the castle of Salzburg. Like the West

German peasants, they organised a Christian alliance and formulated their demands into fourteen articles.

In Styria, in Upper Austria, in Carinthia and Carniola, where new extortionate taxes, duties and edicts had severely injured the interests closest to the people, the peasants arose in the Spring of 1525. They took a number of castles and at Grys, defeated the conqueror of the Stara Prawa, the old field commander Dietrichstein. Although the government succeeded in placating some of the insurgents with false promises, the bulk of them remained together and united with the Salzburg peasants, so that the entire region of Salzburg and the major part of Upper Austria, Styria, Carinthia and Carniola were in the hands of the peasants and pitmen.

In the Tyrol, the Reformation doctrines had also found adherence. Here even more than in the other Alpine regions of Austria, Muenzer's emissaries had been successfully active. Archbishop Ferdinand persecuted the preachers of the new doctrines here as elsewhere, and impinged the rights of the population by arbitrary financial regulations. In consequence, an uprising took place in the Spring of 1525. The insurgents, whose commander was a Muenzer man named Geismaier, the only noted military talent among all the peasant chiefs, took a great number of castles, and proceeded energetically against the priests, particularly in the south and the region of Etsch. The Vorarlberg peasants also arose and joined the Allgaeu peasants.

The Archbishop, pressed from every side, now began to make concession after concession to the rebels whom a short time before he had wished to annihilate by means of burning, scourging, pillaging and murdering. He summoned the Diets of the hereditary lands, and pending their assembling, concluded an armistice with the peasants. In the meantime he was strenuously arming, in order, as soon as possible, to be able to speak to the ungodly ones in a different language.

Naturally, the armistice was not kept long. Dietrichstein, having run short of cash, began to levy contributions in the duchies; his Slavic and Magyar troops allowed themselves, besides, the most shameful atrocities against the population. This brought the Styrians to new rebellion. The peasants attacked Dietrichstein at Schladming during the night of July 3d and slaughtered everybody who did not speak German. Dietrichstein himself was captured. On the morning of July 4, the peasants organised a jury to try the captives, and forty Czech and Croatian noble prisoners were sentenced to death. This was effective. The Archbishop immediately consented to all the demands of the estates of the five duchies (Upper and Lower Austria, Styria, Carinthia and Carniola).

In Tyrol, the demands of the Diet were also granted, and thereby the North was quieted. The South, however, insisting on its original demands as against the much more moderate decisions of the Diet, remained under arms. Only in December was the Archbishop in a position to restore order by force. He did not fail to execute a great number of instigators and leaders of the upheaval who fell into his hands.

Now 10,000 Bavarians moved against Salzburg, under Georg of Frundsberg. This imposing military power, as well as the quarrels that had broken out among the peasants, induced the Salzburg peasants to conclude an agreement with the Archbishop, which came into being September 1, and was also accepted by the Archduke. In spite of this, the two princes, who had meanwhile considerably strengthened their troops, soon broke the agreement and thereby drove the Salzburg peasants to a new uprising. The insurgents held their own throughout the winter. In the Spring, Geismaier came to them to open a splendid campaign against the troops which were approaching from every side. In a series of brilliant battles in May and June, 1526, he defeated the Bavarian, Austrian and Suabian Union troops and the Lansquenets of the Archbishop of Salzburg, one after another, and for a long time he prevented the various corps from uniting. He also found time to besiege Radstadt. Finally, surrounded by overwhelming forces, he was compelled to withdraw. He battled his way through and led the remnants of his corps through the Austrian Alps into Venetian territory. The republic of Venice and Switzerland offered the indefatigable peasant chief starting points for new conspiracies. For a whole year he was still attempting to involve them in a war against Austria, which would have offered him an occasion for a new peasant uprising. The hand of the murderer, however, reached him in the course of these negotiations. Archbishop Ferdinand and the Archbishop of Salzburg could not rest as long as Geismaier was alive. They therefore paid a bandit who, in 1527, succeeded in removing the dangerous rebel from among the living.

VII

AFTER Geismaier's withdrawal into Venetian territory, the epilogue of the Peasant War was ended. The peasants were everywhere brought again under the sway of their ecclesiastical, noble or patrician masters. The agreements that were concluded with them here and there were broken, and heavy burdens were augmented by the enormous indemnities imposed by the victors on the vanquished. The magnificent attempt of the German people ended in ignominious defeat and, for a time, in greater oppression. In the long run, however, the situation of the peasants did not become worse. Whatever the nobility, princes and priests could wring out of the peasants had been wrung out even before the war. The German peasant of that time had this in common with the modern proletarian, that his share in the products of the work was limited to a subsistence minimum necessary for his maintenance and for the propagation of the race. It is true that peasants of some little wealth were ruined. Hosts of bondsmen were forced into serfdom; whole stretches of community lands were confiscated; a great number of peasants were driven into vagabondage or forced to become city plebeians by the destruction of their domiciles and the devastation of their fields in addition to the general disorder. Wars and devastations, however, were every-day phenomena at that time, and in general, the peasant class was on too low a level to have its situation made worse for a long time through increased taxes. The subsequent religious wars and finally the Thirty Years' War with its constantly repeated mass devastations and depopulations pounded the peasants much more painfully than did the Peasant War. It was notably the Thirty Years' War which annihilated the most important parts of the productive forces in agriculture, through which, as well as through the simultaneous destruction of many cities, it lowered the living standards of the peasants, plebeians and the ruined city inhabitants to the level of Irish misery in its worst form.

The class that suffered most from the Peasant War was the *clergy*. Its monasteries and endowments were burned down; its valuables plundered, sold into foreign countries, or melted; its stores of goods consumed. They had been least of all capable of offering resistance, and at the same time the weight of the people's old hatred fell heaviest upon them. The other estates, princes, nobility and the middle-class, even experienced a secret joy at the sufferings of the hated prelates. The Peasant War had made popular the secularisation of the church estates in favour of the peasants. The lay princes, and to a certain degree the cities, determined to bring about secularisation in their own interests, and soon the possessions of the prelates in Protestant countries were in the hands of either the princes or the honourables. The power and authority of the ecclesiastical princes were also infringed upon, and the lay princes understood how to exploit the people's hatred also in this direction. Thus we have seen how the Abbot of Fulda was relegated from a feudal lord of Philipp of Hesse to the position of his vassal. Thus the city of Kempten forced the ecclesiastical prince to sell to it for a trifle a series of precious privileges which he enjoyed in the city.

The *nobility* had also suffered considerably. Most of its castles were destroyed, and a number of its most respected families were ruined and could find means of subsistence only in the service of the princes. Its powerlessness in relation to the peasants was proven. It had been beaten everywhere and forced to surrender. Only the armies of the princes had saved it. The nobility was bound more and more to lose its significance as a free estate under the empire and to fall under the dominion of the princes.

Nor did the *cities* generally gain any advantages from the Peasant War. The rule of the honourables was almost everywhere reestablished with new force, and the opposition of the middle-class remained broken for a long time. Old patrician routine thus dragged on, hampering commerce and industry in every way, up to the French Revolution. Moreover, the cities were made responsible by the princes for the momentary successes which the middle-class or plebeian parties had achieved within their confines during the struggle. Cities which had previously belonged to the princes were forced to pay heavy indemnities, robbed of their privileges, and made subject to the avaricious wilfulness of the princes (Frankenhausen, Arnstadt, Schmalkalden, Wurzburg, etc.), cities of the empire were incorporated into territories of the princes (Muehlhausen), or they were at least placed under moral dependence on the princes of the adjoining territory, as was the case with many imperial cities in Franconia.

The sole gainers under these conditions were the *princes*. We have seen at the beginning of our exposition that low development of industry, commerce and agriculture made the centralisation of the Germans into a *nation* impossible, that it allowed only local and provincial centralisation, and that the princes, representing centralisation within disruption, were the only class to profit from every change in the existing social and political conditions. The state of development of Germany in those days was so low and at the same time so different in various provinces, that along with lay principalities there could still exist ecclesiastical sovereignties, city republics, and sovereign counts and barons. Simultaneously, however, this development was continually, though slowly and feebly, pressing towards *provincial* centralisation, towards subjugating all imperial estates under the princes. It is due to this that only the princes could gain by the ending of the Peasant War. This happened in reality. They gained not only relatively, through the weakening of their opponents, the clergy, the nobility and the cities, but also absolutely through the prizes of war which they collected. The church estates were secularised in their favour; part of the nobility, fully or partly ruined, was obliged gradually to place itself in their vassalage; the indemnities of the cities and peasantry swelled their treasuries, which, with the abolition of so many city privileges, had now obtained a much more extended field for financial operations.

The decentralisation of Germany, the widening and strengthening of which was the chief result of the war, was at the same time the cause of its failure.

We have seen that Germany was split not only into numberless independent provinces almost totally foreign to each other, but that in every one of these provinces the nation was divided into various strata of estates and parts of estates. Besides princes and priests we find nobility and peasants in the countryside; patricians, middle-class and plebeians in the cities. At best, these classes were indifferent to each other's interests if not in actual conflict. Above all these complicated interests there still were the interests of the empire and the pope. We have seen that, with great difficulty, imperfectly, and differing in various localities, these various interests finally formed three great groups. We have seen that in spite of this grouping, achieved with so much labour, every estate opposed the line indicated by circumstances for the national development, every estate conducting the movement of its own accord, coming into conflict not only with the conservatives but also with the rest of the opposition estates. Failure was, therefore, inevitable. This was the fate of the nobility in Sickingen's uprising, the fate of the peasants in the Peasant War, of the middle-class in their tame Reformation. This was the fate even of the peasants and plebeians who in most localities of Germany could not unite for common action and stood in each other's way. We have also seen the causes of this split in the class struggle and the resultant defeat of the middle-class movement.

How local and provincial decentralisation and the resultant local and provincial narrow-mindedness ruined the whole movement, how neither middle-class nor peasantry nor plebeians could unite for concerted national action; how the peasants of every province acted only for themselves, as a rule refusing aid to the insurgent peasants of the neighbouring region, and therefore being annihilated in individual battles one after another by armies which in most cases counted hardly one-tenth of the total number of the insurgent masses,—all this must be quite clear to the reader from this presentation. The armistices and the agreements concluded by individual groups with their enemies also constituted acts of betrayal of the common cause, and the grouping of the various troops not according to the greater or smaller community of their own actions, the only possible grouping, but according to the community of the special adversary to whom they succumbed, is striking proof of the degree of the mutual alienation of the peasants in various provinces.

The analogy with the movement of 1848–50 is here also apparent. In 1848 as in the Peasant War, the interests of the opposition classes clashed with each other and each acted of its own accord. The bourgeoisie, developed sufficiently not to tolerate any longer the feudal and bureaucratic absolutism, was not powerful enough to subordinate the claims of other classes to its own interests. The proletariat, too weak to be able to count on skipping the bourgeois period and immediately conquering power for itself, had, still under absolutism, tasted too well the sweetness of bourgeois government, and was generally far too developed to identify for one moment its own emancipation with the emancipation of the bourgeoisie. The mass of the nation, small bourgeois artisans and peasants, were left in the lurch by their nearest and natural allies, the bourgeoisie, because they were too revolutionary, and partly by the proletariat because they were not sufficiently advanced. Divided in itself, this mass of the nation achieved nothing, while opposing their fellow opponents on the right and the left. As to provincial narrow-mindedness, it could hardly have been greater in 1525 among the peasants than it was among the classes participating in the movement of 1848. The hundred local revolutions as well as the hundred local reactions following them and completed without hindrance, the retention of the split into numerous small states—all this speaks loud enough indeed. *He who, after the two German revolutions, of 1525 and 1548, and their results, still dreams of a federated republic, belongs in a house for the insane.*

Still, the two revolutions, that of the Sixteenth Century and that of 1848–50, are, in spite of all analogies, materially different from each other. The revolution of 1848 bespeaks, if not the progress of Germany, the progress of Europe.

Who profited by the revolution of 1525? The princes. Who profited by the revolution of 1848? The *big* princes, Austria and Prussia. Behind the princes of 1525 there stood the lower middle-class of the cities, held chained by means of taxation. Behind the big provinces of 1850, there stood the modern big bourgeoisie, quickly subjugating them by means of the State debt. Behind the big bourgeoisie stand the proletarians.

The revolution of 1525 was a local German affair. The English, French, Bohemians and Hungarians had already gone through their peasant wars when the Germans began theirs. If Germany was decentralised, Europe was so to a much greater extent. The revolution of 1848 was not a local German affair, it was one phase of a great European movement. The moving forces throughout the period of its duration were not confined to the narrow limits of one individual country, not even to the limits of one-quarter of the globe. In fact, the countries which were the arena of the revolution were least active in producing it. They were more or less unconscious raw materials without a will of their own. They were moulded in the course of a movement in which the entire world participated, a movement which under existing social conditions may appear to us as an alien power, but which, in the end, is nothing but our own. This is why the revolution of 1848–50 could not end in the way that the revolution of 1525 ended.

GERMANY:
REVOLUTION AND COUNTER-REVOLUTION

I

THE first act of the revolutionary drama on the continent of Europe has closed. The "powers that were" before the hurricane of 1848 are again the "powers that be," and the more or less popular rulers of a day, provisional governors, triumvirs, dictators, with their tail of representatives, civil commissioners, military commissioners, prefects, judges, generals, officers, and soldiers, are thrown upon foreign shores, and "transported beyond the seas" to England or America, there to form new governments *in partibus infidelium,* European committees, central committees, national committees, and to announce their advent with proclamations quite as solemn as those of any less imaginary potentates.

A more signal defeat than that undergone by the continental revolutionary party—or rather parties—upon all point of the line of battle, cannot be imagined. But what of that? Has not the struggle of the British middle classes for their social and political supremacy embraced forty-eight, that of the French middle classes forty, years of unexampled struggles? And was their triumph ever nearer than at the very moment when restored monarchy thought itself more firmly settled than ever? The times of that superstition which attributed revolutions to the ill will of a few agitators have long passed away. Everyone knows nowadays that wherever there is a revolutionary convulsion, there must be some social want in the background, which is prevented, by outworn institutions, from satisfying itself. The want may not yet be felt as strongly, as generally, as might

123

ensure immediate success; but every attempt at forcible repression will only bring it forth stronger and stronger, until it bursts its fetters. If, then, we have been beaten, we have nothing else to do but to begin again from the beginning. And, fortunately, the probably very short interval of rest which is allowed us between the close of the first and the beginning of the second act of the movement, gives us time for a very necessary piece of work: the study of the causes that necessitated both the later outbreak and its defeat; causes that are not to be sought for in the accidental efforts, talents, faults, errors, or treacheries of some of the leaders, but in the general social state and conditions of existence of each of the convulsed nations. That the sudden movements of February and March 1848 were not the work of single individuals, but spontaneous, irresistible manifestations of national wants and necessities, more or less clearly understood, but very distinctly felt by numerous classes in every country, is a fact recognised everywhere; but when you inquire into the causes of the counter-revolutionary successes, there you are met on every hand with the ready reply that it was Mr. This or Citizen That who "betrayed" the people. Which reply may be very true or not, according to circumstances, but under no circumstances does it explain anything—not even show how it came to pass that the "people" allowed themselves to be thus betrayed. And what a poor chance stands a political party whose entire stock-in-trade consists in a knowledge of the solitary fact that Citizen So-and-so is not to be trusted.

The inquiry into, and the exposition of, the causes, both of the revolutionary convulsion and its suppression, are, besides, of paramount importance from an historical point of view. All these petty, personal quarrels and recriminations—all these contradictory assertions that it was Marrast, or Ledru-Rollin, or Louis Blanc, or any other member of the Provisional Government, or the whole of them, that steered the Revolution amidst the rocks upon which it foundered—of what interest can they be, what light can they afford, to the American or Englishman who observed all these various movements from a distance too great to allow of his distinguishing any of the details of operations? No man in his senses will ever believe that eleven men, mostly of very indifferent capacity either for good or evil, were able in three months to ruin a nation of thirty-six millions, unless those thirty-six millions saw as little of their way before them as the eleven did. But how it came to pass that thirty-six millions were at once called upon to decide for themselves which way to go, although partly groping in dim twilight, and how then they got lost and their old leaders were for a moment allowed to return to their leadership, that is just the question.

If, then, we try to lay before the readers of the *Tribune* the causes which, while they necessitated the German Revolution of 1848, led quite as inevitably to its momentary repression in 1849 and 1850, we shall not be expected to give a complete history of events as they passed in that country. Later events, and the judgment of coming generations, will decide what portion of that confused mass of seemingly accidental, incoherent, and incongruous facts is to form a part of the world's history. The time for such a task has not yet arrived; we must confine ourselves to the limits of the possible, and be satisfied, if we can find rational causes, based upon undeniable facts, to explain the chief events, the principal vicissitudes of that movement, and to give us a clue as to the direction which the next, and perhaps not very distant, outbreak will impart to the German people.

And firstly, what was the state of Germany at the outbreak of the Revolution?

The composition of the different classes of the people which form the groundwork of every political organisation was, in Germany, more complicated than in any other country. While in England and France feudalism was entirely destroyed, or, at least, reduced, as in the former country, to a few insignificant forms, by a powerful and wealthy middle class, concentrated in large towns, and particularly in the capital, the feudal nobility in Germany had retained a great portion of their ancient privileges. The feudal system of tenure was prevalent almost everywhere. The lords of the land had even retained the jurisdiction over their tenants. Deprived of their political privileges, of the right to control the princes, they had preserved almost all their mediaeval supremacy over the peasantry of their demesnes, as well as their exemption from taxes. Feudalism was more flourishing in some localities than in others, but nowhere except on the left bank of the Rhine was it entirely destroyed. This feudal nobility, then extremely numerous and partly very wealthy, was considered, officially, the first "Order" in the country. It furnished the higher Government officials, it almost exclusively officered the army.

The bourgeoisie of Germany was by far not as wealthy and concentrated as that of France or England. The ancient manufactures of Germany had been destroyed by the introduction of steam, and the rapidly extending supremacy of English manufactures; the more modern manufactures, started under the Napoleonic continental system, established in other parts of the country, did not compensate for the loss of the old ones, nor suffice to create a manufacturing interest strong enough to force its wants upon the notice of Governments jealous of every extension of non-noble wealth and power. If France carried her silk manufactures victorious through fifty years of revolutions and wars, Germany, during the same time, all but lost her ancient linen trade. The manufacturing districts, besides, were few and far between; situated far inland, and using, mostly, foreign, Dutch, or Belgian ports for their imports and exports, they had little or no interest in common with the large seaport towns on the North Sea and the Baltic; they were, above all, unable to create large manufacturing and trading centres, such as Paris and Lyons, London and Manchester. The causes of this backwardness of German manufactures were manifold, but two will suffice to account for it: the unfavourable geographical situation of the country, at a distance from the Atlantic, which had become the great highway for the world's trade, and the continuous wars in which Germany was involved, and which were fought on her soil, from the sixteenth century to the present day. It was this want of numbers, and particularly of anything like concentrated numbers, which prevented the German middle classes from attaining that political supremacy which the English bourgeoisie has enjoyed ever since 1688, and which the French conquered in 1789. And yet, ever since 1815, the wealth, and with the wealth the political importance of the middle class in Germany, was continually growing. Governments were, although reluctantly, compelled to bow, at least to its more immediate material interests. It may even be truly said that from 1815 to 1830, and from 1832 to 1840, every particle of political influence, which, having been allowed to the middle class in the constitutions of the smaller States, was again wrested from them during the above two periods of political reaction, that every such particle was compensated for by some more practical advantage allowed to them. Every political defeat of the middle class drew after it a victory on the field of commercial legislation. And, certainly, the Prussian Protective Tariff of 1818, and the formation of the Zollverein, were worth a good deal more to the traders and manufacturers of Germany than the equivocal right of expressing in the chambers of some diminutive dukedom their want of confidence in ministers who laughed at their votes. Thus, with growing wealth and extending trade, the bourgeoisie soon arrived at a stage where it found the development of its most important interests checked by the political constitution of the country; by its random division among thirty-six princes with conflicting tendencies and caprices; by the feudal fetters upon agriculture and the trade connected with it; by the prying superintendence to which an ignorant and presumptious bureaucracy subjected all its transactions. At the same time the extension and consolidation of the Zollverein, the general introduction of steam communication, the growing competition in the home trade, brought the commercial classes of the different States and Provinces closer together, equalised their interests, centralised their strength. The natural consequence was the passing of the whole mass of them into the camp of the Liberal Opposition, and the gaining of the first serious struggle of the German middle class for political power. This change may be dated from 1840, from the moment when the bourgeoisie of Prussia assumed the lead of the middle-class movement of Germany. We shall hereafter revert to this Liberal Opposition movement of 1840–47.

The great mass of the nation, which neither belonged to the nobility nor to the bourgeoisie, consisted in the towns of the small trading and shopkeeping class and the working people, and in the country of the peasantry.

The small trading and shopkeeping class is exceedingly numerous in Germany, in consequence of the stinted development which the large capitalists and manufacturers as a class have had in that country. In the larger towns it forms almost the majority of the inhabitants; in the smaller ones it entirely predominates, from the absence of wealthier competitors or influence. This class, a most important one in every body politic, and in all modern revolutions, is still more important in Germany, where, during the recent struggles, it generally played the decisive part. Its intermediate position between the class of larger capitalists, traders, and manufacturers, the bourgeoisie properly so-called, and the proletarian or industrial class, determines its character. Aspiring to the position of the first, the least adverse turn of fortune hurls the individuals of this class down into the ranks of the second. In monarchical and feudal countries the custom of the court and aristocracy becomes necessary to its existence; the loss of this custom might ruin a great part of it. In the smaller towns a military garrison, a county government, a court of law with its followers, form very often the base of its prosperity; withdraw these, and down go the shopkeepers, the tailors, the shoemakers, the joiners. Thus eternally tossed about between the hope of entering the ranks of the wealthier class, and the fear of being reduced to the state of proletarians or even paupers; between the hope of promoting their interests by conquering a share in the direction of public affairs, and the dread of rousing, by ill-timed opposition, the ire of a Government which disposes of their very existence, because it has the power of removing their best customers; possessed of small means, the insecurity of the possession of which is in the inverse ratio of the amount,—this class is extremely vacillating in its views. Humble and crouchingly submissive under a powerful feudal or monarchical Government, it turns to the side of Liberalism when the middle class is in the ascendant; it becomes seized with violent democratic fits as soon as the middle class has secured its own supremacy, but falls back into the abject despondency of fear as soon as the class below itself, the proletarians, attempts an independent movement. We shall by and by see this class, in Germany, pass alternately from one of these stages to the other.

The working class in Germany is, in its social and political development, as far behind that of England and France as the German bourgeoisie is behind the bourgeoisie of those countries. Like master, like man. The evolution of the conditions of existence for a numerous, strong, concentrated, and intelligent proletarian class goes hand in hand with the development of the conditions of existence for a numerous, wealthy, concentrated, and powerful middle class. The working-class movement itself never is independent, never is of an exclusively proletarian character until all the different factions of the middle class, and particularly its most progressive faction, the large manufacturers, have conquered political power, and remodelled the State according to their wants. It is then that the inevitable conflict between the employer and the employed becomes imminent, and cannot be adjourned any longer; that the working class can no longer be put off with delusive hopes and promises never to be realised; that the great problem of the nineteenth century, the abolition of the proletariat, is at last brought forward fairly and in its proper light. Now, in Germany the mass of the working class were employed, not by those modern manufacturing lords of which Great Britain furnishes such splendid specimens, but by small tradesmen, whose entire manufacturing system is a mere relic of the Middle Ages. And as there is an enormous difference between the great cotton lord and the petty cobbler or master tailor, so there is a corresponding distance from the wide-awake factory operative of modern manufacturing Babylons to the bashful journeyman tailor or cabinet-maker of a small country town, who lives in circumstances and works after a plan very little different from those of the like sort of men some five hundred years ago. This general absence of modern conditions of life, of modern modes of industrial production, of course, was accompanied by a pretty equally general absence of modern ideas, and it is, therefore, not to be wondered at if, at the outbreak of the Revolution, a large part of the working classes should cry out for the immediate re-establishment of guilds and Mediaeval privileged trades corporations. Yet from the manufacturing districts, where the modern system of production predominated, and in consequence of the facilities of intercommunication and mental development afforded by the migratory life of a large number of the working men, a strong nucleus formed itself, whose ideas about the emancipation of their class were far clearer and more in accordance with existing facts and historical necessities; but they were a mere minority. If the active movement of the middle classes may be dated from 1840, that of the working class commences its advent by the insurrections of the Silesian and Bohemian factory operatives in 1844, and we shall soon have occasion to pass in review the different stages through which this movement passed.

Lastly, there was the great class of the small farmers, the peasantry, which, with its appendix of farm labourers, constitutes a considerable majority of the entire nation. But this class again subdivided itself into different factions. There were, firstly, the more wealthy farmers, what is called in Germany *Gross* and *Mittel-Bauern*, proprietors of more or less extensive farms and each of them commanding the services of several agricultural labourers. This class, placed between the large untaxed feudal landowners, and the smaller peasantry and farm labourers, for obvious reasons found in an alliance with the antifeudal middle class of the towns its most natural political course. Then there were, secondly, the small freeholders, predominating in the Rhine country, where feudalism had succumbed before the mighty strokes of the great French Revolution. Similar independent small freeholders also existed here and there in other provinces, where they had succeeded in buying off the feudal charges formerly due upon their lands. This class, however, was a class of freeholders by name only, their property being generally mortgaged to such an extent, and under such onerous conditions, that not the peasant, but the usurer who had advanced the money, was the real landowner. Thirdly, the feudal tenants, who could not be easily turned out of their holdings, but who had to pay a perpetual rent, or to perform in perpetuity a certain amount of labour in favour of the lord of the manor. Lastly, the agricultural labourers, whose condition, in many large farming concerns, was exactly that of the same class in England, and who in all cases lived and died poor, ill-fed, and the slaves of their employers. These three latter classes of the agricultural population, the small freeholders, the feudal tenants, and the agricultural labourers, never troubled their heads much about politics before the Revolution, but it is evident that this event must have opened to them a new career, full of brilliant prospects. To every one of them the Revolution offered advantages, and the movement once fairly engaged in, it was to be expected that each, in their turn, would join it. But at the same time it is quite as evident, and equally borne out by the history of all modern countries, that the agricultural population, in consequence of its dispersion over a great space, and of the difficulty of bringing about an agreement among any considerable portion of it, never can attempt a successful independent movement; they require the initiatory impulse of the more concentrated, more enlightened, more easily moved people of the towns.

The preceding short sketch of the most important of the classes, which in their aggregate formed the German nation at the outbreak of the recent movements, will already be sufficient to explain a great part of the incoherence, incongruence, and apparent contradiction which prevailed in that movement. When interests so varied, so conflicting, so strangely crossing each other, are brought into violent collision; when these contending interests in every district, every province, are mixed in different proportions; when, above all, there is no great centre in the country, no London, no Paris, the decisions of which, by their weight, may supersede the necessity of fighting out the same quarrel over and over again in every single locality; what else is to be expected but that the contest will dissolve itself into a mass of unconnected struggles, in which an enormous quantity of blood, energy, and capital is spent, but which for all that remain without any decisive results?

The political dismemberment of Germany into three dozen of more or less important principalities is equally explained by this confusion and multiplicity of the elements which compose the nation, and which again vary in every locality. Where there are no common interests there can be no unity of purpose, much less of action. The German Confederation, it is true, was declared everlastingly indissoluble; yet the Confederation, and its organ, the Diet, never represented German unity. The very highest pitch to which centralisation was ever carried in Germany was the establishment of the Zollverein; by this the States on the North Sea were also forced into a Customs Union of their own, Austria remaining wrapped up in their separate prohibitive tariff. Germany had the satisfaction to be, for all practical purposes, divided between three independent powers only, instead of between thirty-six. Of course the paramount supremacy of the Russian Czar, as established in 1814, underwent no change on this account.

Having drawn these preliminary conclusions from our premisses, we shall see, in our next, how the aforesaid various classes of the German people were set into movement one after the other, and what character the movement assumed on the outbreak of the French Revolution of 1848.

New York Daily Tribune, October 25th, 1851

132

II

THE political movement of the middle class or bourgeoisie, in Germany, may be dated from 1840. It had been preceded by symptoms showing that the moneyed and industrial class of that country was ripening into a state which would no longer allow it to continue apathetic and passive under the pressure of a half-feudal, half-bureaucratic Monarchism. The smaller princes of Germany, partly to insure to themselves a greater independence against the supremacy of Austria and Prussia, or against the influence of the nobility of their own States, partly in order to consolidate into a whole the disconnected provinces united under their rule by the Congress of Vienna, one after the other granted constitutions of a more or less liberal character. They could do so without any danger to themselves; for if the Diet of the Confederation, this mere puppet of Austria and Prussia, was to encroach upon their independence as sovereigns, they knew that in resisting its dictates they would be backed by public opinion and the Chambers; and if, on the contrary, these Chambers grew too strong, they could readily command the power of the Diet to break down all opposition. The Bavarian, Würtemberg, Baden or Hanoverian Constitutional institutions could not, under such circumstances, give rise to any serious struggle for political power, and, therefore, the great bulk of the German middle class kept very generally aloof from the petty squabbles raised in the Legislatures of the small States, well knowing that without a fundamental change in the policy and constitution of the two great powers of Germany, no secondary efforts and

133

victories would be of any avail. But, at the same time, a race of Liberal lawyers, professional oppositionists, sprung up in these small assemblies: the Rottecks, the Welckers, the Roemers, the Jordans, the Stüves, the Eisenmanns, those great "popular men" (*Volksmänner*) who, after a more or less noisy, but always unsuccessful, opposition of twenty years, were carried to the summit of power by the revolutionary springtide of 1848, and who, after having there shown their utter impotency and insignificance, were hurled down again in a moment. These first specimens upon German soil of the trader in politics and opposition, by their speeches and writings made familiar to the German ear the language of Constitutionalism, and by their very existence foreboded the approach of a time when the middle class would seize upon and restore to their proper meaning political phrases which these talkative attorneys and professors were in the habit of using without knowing much about the sense originally attached to them.

German literature, too, laboured under the influence of the political excitement into which all Europe had been thrown by the events of 1830. A crude Constitutionalism, or a still cruder Republicanism, were preached by almost all writers of the time. It became more and more the habit, particularly of the inferior sorts of literati, to make up for the want of cleverness in their productions, by political allusions which were sure to attract attention. Poetry, novels, reviews, the drama, every literary production teemed with what was called "tendency," that is with more or less timed exhibitions of an anti-governmental spirit. In order to complete the confusion of ideas reigning after 1830 in Germany, with these elements of political opposition there were mixed up ill-digested university-recollections of German philosophy, and misunderstood gleanings from French Socialism, particularly Saint-Simonism; and the clique of writers who expatiated upon this heterogeneous conglomerate of ideas, presumptuously called themselves "Young Germany," or "the Modern School." They have since repented their youthful sins, but not improved their style of writing.

Lastly, German philosophy, that most complicated, but at the same time most sure, thermometer of the development of the German mind, had declared for the middle class, when Hegel in his *Philosophy of Law* pronounced Constitutional Monarchy to be the final and most perfect form of government. In other words, he proclaimed the approaching advent of the middle classes of the country to political power. His school, after his death, did not stop here. While the more advanced section of his followers, on one hand, subjected every religious belief to the ordeal of a rigorous criticism, and shook to its foundation the ancient fabric of Christianity, they at the same time brought forward bolder political principles than hitherto it had been the fate of German ears to hear expounded, and attempted to restore to glory the memory of the heroes of the first French Revolution. The abstruse philosophical language in which these ideas were clothed, if it obscured the mind of both the writer and the reader, equally blinded the eyes of the censor, and thus it was that the "young Hegelian" writers enjoyed a liberty of the Press unknown in every other branch of literature.

Thus it was evident that public opinion was undergoing a great change in Germany. By degrees the vast majority of those classes whose education or position in life enabled them, under an Absolute Monarchy, to gain some political information, and to form anything like an independent political opinion, united into one mighty phalanx of opposition against the existing system. And in passing judgment upon the slowness of political development in Germany no one ought to omit taking into account the difficulty of obtaining correct information upon any subject in a country where all sources of information were under the control of the Government, where from the Ragged School and the Sunday School to the Newspaper and University nothing was said, taught, printed, or published but what had previously obtained its approbation. Look at Vienna, for instance. The people of Vienna, in industry and manufactures, second to none perhaps in Germany; in spirit, courage, and revolutionary energy, proving themselves far superior to all, were yet more ignorant as to their real interests, and committed more blunders during the Revolution than any others, and this

135

was due in a very great measure to the most absolute ignorance with regard to the very commonest political subjects in
which Metternich's Government had succeeded in keeping
them.

It needs no further explanation why, under such a system,
political information was an almost exclusive monopoly of such
classes of society as could afford to pay for its being smuggled
into the country, and more particularly of those whose interests
were most seriously attacked by the existing state of things,
namely, the manufacturing and commercial classes. They,
therefore, were the first to unite in a mass against the continu-
ance of a more or less disguised Absolutism, and from their
passing into the ranks of the opposition must be dated the
beginning of the real revolutionary movement in Germany.

The oppositional pronunciamento of the German bourgeoisie
may be dated from 1840, from the death of the late King of
Prussia, the last surviving founder of the Holy Alliance of 1815.
The new King was known to be no supporter of the predominantly bureaucratic and military monarchy of his father. What
the French middle class had expected from the advent of Louis
XVI, the German bourgeoisie hoped, in some measure, from
Frederick William IV of Prussia. It was agreed upon all hands
that the old system was exploded, worn out, and must be given
up; and what had been borne in silence under the old King now
was loudly proclaimed to be intolerable.

But if Louis XVI, "Louis le Désiré," had been a plain, unpre-
tending simpleton, half conscious of his own nullity, without
any fixed opinions, ruled principally by the habits contracted
during his education, "Frederick William le Désiré" was something quite different. While he certainly surpassed his French
original in weakness of character, he was neither without pre-
tensions nor without opinions. He had made himself acquainted, in an amateur sort of way, with the rudiments of most
sciences, and thought himself, therefore, learned enough to
consider final his judgment upon every subject. He made sure
he was a first-rate orator, and there was certainly no commercial
traveller in Berlin who could beat him either in prolixity of

pretended wit, or in fluency of elocution. And, above all, he had
his opinions. He hated and despised the bureaucratic element
of the Prussian Monarchy, but only because all his sympathies
were with the feudal element. Himself one of the founders of,
and chief contributors to, the *Berlin Political Weekly Paper,* the
so-called Historical School (a school living upon the ideas of
Bonald, De Maistre, and other writers of the first generation of
French Legitimists), he aimed at a restoration, as complete as
possible, of the predominant social position of the nobility. The
King, first nobleman of his realm, surrounded in the first instance by a splendid court of mighty vassals, princes, dukes,
and counts; in the second instance, by a numerous and wealthy
lower nobility; ruling according to his discretion over his loyal
burgesses and peasants, and thus being himself the chief of a
complete hierarchy of social ranks or castes, each of which was
to enjoy its particular privileges, and to be separated from the
others by the almost insurmountable barrier of birth, or of a
fixed, inalterable social position; the whole of these castes, or
"estates of the realm" balancing each other at the same time so
nicely in power and influence that a complete independence of
action should remain to the King—such was the beau-ideal
which Frederick William IV undertook to realise, and which he
is again trying to realise at the present moment.

It took some time before the Prussian bourgeoisie, not very
well versed in theoretical questions, found out the real purport
of their King's tendency. But what they very soon found out
was the fact that he was bent upon things quite the reverse of
what they wanted. Hardly did the new King find his "gift of the
gab" unfettered by his father's death than he set about proclaiming his intentions in speeches without number; and every
speech, every act of his, went far to estrange from him the
sympathies of the middle class, He would not have cared much
for that, if it had not been for some stern and startling realities
which interrupted his poetic dreams, Alas, that romanticism is
not very quick at accounts, and that feudalism, ever since Don
Quixote, reckons without its host! Frederick William IV partook
too much of that contempt of ready cash which ever has been

the noblest inheritance of the sons of the Crusaders. He found at his accession a costly, although parsimoniously arranged system of government, and a moderately filled State Treasury. In two years every trace of a surplus was spent in court festivals, royal progresses, largesses, subventions to needy, seedy, and greedy noblemen, etc., and the regular taxes were no longer sufficient for the exigencies of either Court or Government. And thus His Majesty found himself very soon placed between a glaring deficit on one side, and a law of 1820 on the other, by which any new loan, or any increase of the then existing taxation was made illegal without the assent of "the future Representation of the People." This representation did not exist; the new King was less inclined than even his father to create it; and if he had been, he knew that public opinion had wonderfully changed since his accession.

Indeed, the middle classes, who had partly expected that the new King would at once grant a Constitution, proclaim the Liberty of the Press, Trial by Jury, etc., etc.—in short, himself take the lead of that peaceful revolution which they wanted in order to obtain political supremacy—the middle classes had found out their error, and had turned ferociously against the King. In the Rhine Provinces, and more or less generally all over Prussia, they were so exasperated that they, being short themselves of men able to represent them in the Press, went to the length of an alliance with the extreme philosophical party, of which we have spoken above. The fruit of this alliance was the *Rhenish Gazette* of Cologne, a paper which was suppressed after fifteen months' existence, but from which may be dated the existence of the Newspaper Press in Germany. This was in 1842.

The poor King, whose commercial difficulties were the keenest satire upon his Mediaeval propensities, very soon found out that he could not continue to reign without making some slight concession to the popular outcry for that "Representation of the People," which, as the last remnant of the long-forgotten promises of 1813 and 1815, had been embodied in the law of 1820. He found the least objectionable mode of satisfying this untoward law in calling together the Standing Committees of the Provincial Diets. The Provincial Diets had been instituted in 1823. They consisted for every one of the eight provinces of the kingdom: (1) Of the higher nobility, the formerly sovereign families of the German Empire, the heads of which were members of the Diet by birthright. (2) Of the representatives of the knights, or lower nobility. (3) Of representatives of towns. (4) Of deputies of the peasantry, or small farming class. The whole was arranged in such a manner that in every province the two sections of the nobility always had a majority of the Diet. Every one of these eight Provincial Diets elected a Committee, and these eight Committees were now called to Berlin in order to form a Representative Assembly for the purpose of voting the much-desired loan. It was stated that the Treasury was full, and that the loan was required, not for current wants, but for the construction of a State railway. But the united Committees gave the King a flat refusal, declaring themselves incompetent to act as the representatives of the people, and called upon His Majesty to fulfil the promise of a Representative Constitution which his father had given, when he wanted the aid of the people against Napoleon.

The sitting of the united Committees proved that the spirit of opposition was no longer confined to the bourgeoisie. A part of the peasantry had joined them, and many nobles, being themselves large farmers on their own properties, and dealers in corn, wool, spirits, and flax, requiring the same guarantees against absolutism, bureaucracy, and feudal restoration, had equally pronounced against the Government, and for a Representative Constitution. The King's plan had signally failed; he had got no money, and had increased the power of the opposition. The subsequent sitting of the Provincial Diets themselves was still more unfortunate for the King. All of them asked for reforms, for the fulfilment of the promises of 1813 and 1815, for a Constitution and a Free Press; the resolutions to this effect of some of them were rather disrespectfully worded, and the ill-humoured replies of the exasperated King made the evil still greater.

In the meantime, the financial difficulties of the Government went on increasing. For a time, abatements made upon the moneys appropriated for the different public services, fraudulent transactions with the "Seehandlung," a commercial establishment speculating and trading for account and risk of the State, and long since acting as its money-broker, had sufficed to keep up appearances; increased issues of State paper-money had furnished some resources; and the secret, upon the whole, had been pretty well kept. But all these contrivances were soon exhausted. There was another plan tried: the establishment of a bank, the capital of which was to be furnished partly by the State and partly by private shareholders; the chief direction to belong to the State, in such a manner as to enable the Government to draw upon the funds of this bank to a large amount, and thus to repeat the same fraudulent transactions that would no longer do with the "Seehandlung." But, as a matter of course, there were no capitalists to be found who would hand over their money upon such conditions; the statutes of the bank had to be altered, and the property of the shareholders guaranteed from the encroachments of the Treasury, before any shares were subscribed for. Thus, this plan having failed, there remained nothing but to try a loan, if capitalists could be found who would lend their cash without requiring the permission and guarantee of that mysterious "future Representation of the People." Rothschild was applied to, and he declared that if the loan was to be guaranteed by this "Representation of the People," he would undertake the thing at a moment's notice—if not, he could not have anything to do with the transaction.

Thus every hope of obtaining money had vanished, and there was no possibility of escaping the fatal "Representation of the People." Rothschild's refusal was known in autumn, 1846, and in February of the next year the King called together all the eight Provincial Diets to Berlin, forming them into one "United Diet." This Diet was to do the work required, in case of need, by the law of 1820; it was to vote loans and increase taxes, but beyond that it was to have no rights. Its voice upon general legislation was to be merely consultative; it was to assemble, not at fixed periods, but whenever it pleased the King; it was to discuss nothing but what the Government pleased to lay before it. Of course, the members were very little satisfied with the part they were expected to perform. They repeated the wishes they had enounced when they met in the provincial assemblies; the relations between them and the Government soon became acrimonious, and when the loan, which was again stated to be required for railway construction, was demanded from them, they again refused to grant it.

This vote very soon brought their sitting to a close. The King, more and more exasperated, dismissed them with a reprimand, but still remained without money. And, indeed, he had every reason to be alarmed at his position, seeing that the Liberal League, headed by the middle classes, comprising a large part of the lower nobility, and all the manifold discontents that had been accumulated in the different sections of the lower orders—that this Liberal League was determined to have what it wanted. In vain the King had declared, in the opening speech, that he would never, never grant a Constitution in the modern sense of the word; the Liberal League insisted upon such a modern, anti-feudal, Representative Constitution, with all its sequels, Liberty of the Press, Trial by Jury, etc.; and before they got it, not a farthing of money would they grant. There was one thing evident: that things could not go on long in this manner, and that either one of the parties must give way, or that a rupture—a bloody struggle—must ensue. And the middle classes knew that they were on the eve of a revolution, and they prepared themselves for it. They sought to obtain by every possible means the support of the working class of the towns, and of the peasantry in the agricultural districts, and it is well known that there was, in the latter end of 1847, hardly a single prominent political character among the bourgeoisie who did not proclaim himself a "Socialist," in order to insure to himself the sympathy of the proletarian class. We shall see these "Socialists" at work by and by.

This eagerness of the leading bourgeoisie to adopt, at least, the outward show of Socialism, was caused by a great change that had come over the working classes of Germany. There had been ever since 1840 a fraction of German workmen, who, travelling in France and Switzerland, had more or less imbibed the crude Socialist or Communist notions then current among the French workmen. The increasing attention paid to similar ideas in France ever since 1840 made Socialism and Communism fashionable in Germany also, and as far back as 1843, all newspapers teemed with discussions of social questions. A school of Socialists very soon formed itself in Germany, distinguished more for the obscurity than for the novelty of its ideas; its principal efforts consisted in the translation of French Fourierist, Saint-Simonian, and other doctrines into the abstruse language of German philosophy. The German Communist school, entirely different from this sect, was formed about the same time.

In 1844, there occurred the Silesian weavers' riots, followed by the insurrection of the calico printers of Prague. These riots, cruelly suppressed, riots of working men not against the Government, but against their employers, created a deep sensation, and gave a new stimulus to Socialist and Communist propaganda amongst the working people. So did the bread riots during the year of famine, 1847. In short, in the same manner as Constitutional Opposition rallied around its banner the great bulk of the propertied classes (with the exception of the large feudal land-holders), so the working classes of the larger towns looked for their emancipation to the Socialist and Communist doctrines, although, under the then existing Press laws, they could be made to know only very little about them. They could not be expected to have any very definite ideas as to what they wanted; they only knew that the programme of the Constitutional bourgeoisie did not contain all they wanted, and that their wants were no wise contained in the Constitutional circle of ideas.

There was then no separate Republican party in Germany. People were either Constitutional Monarchists, or more or less clearly defined Socialists or Communists.

With such elements the lightest collision must have brought

about a great revolution. While the higher nobility and the older civil and military officers were the only safe supports of the existing system; while the lower nobility, the trading middle classes, the universities, the schoolmasters of every degree, and even part of the lower ranks of the bureaucracy and military officers were all leagued against the Government; while behind these there stood the dissatisfied masses of the peasantry, and of the proletarians of the large towns, supporting, for the time being, the Liberal Opposition, but already muttering strange words about taking things into their own hands; while the bourgeoisie was ready to hurl down the Government, and the proletarians were preparing to hurl down the bourgeoisie in its turn; this Government went on obstinately in a course which must bring about a collision. Germany was, in the beginning of 1848, on the eve of a revolution, and this revolution was sure to come, even had the French Revolution of February not hastened it.

What the effects of this Parisian Revolution were upon Germany we shall see in our next.

New York Daily Tribune, October 28th, 1851

III

In our last we confined ourselves almost exclusively to that State which, during the years 1840 to 1848, was by far the most important in the German movement, namely, to Prussia. It is, however, time to pass a rapid glance over the other States of Germany during the same period.

As to the petty States, they had, ever since the revolutionary movements of 1830, completely passed under the dictatorship of the Diet, that is of Austria and Prussia. The several Constitutions, established as much as a means of defence against the dictates of the larger States, as to insure popularity to their princely authors, and unity to heterogeneous Assemblies of Provinces, formed by the Congress of Vienna, without any leading principle whatever—these Constitutions, illusory as they were, had yet proved dangerous to the authority of the petty princes themselves during the exciting times of 1830 and 1831. They were all but destroyed; whatever of them was allowed to remain was less than a shadow, and it required the loquacious self-complacency of a Welcker, a Rotteck, a Dahlmann, to imagine that any results could possibly flow from the humble opposition, mingled with degrading flattery, which they were allowed to show off in the impotent Chambers of these petty States.

The more energetic portion of the middle class in these smaller States, very soon after 1840, abandoned all the hopes they had formerly based upon the development of Parliamen-

144

tary government in these dependencies of Austria and Prussia. No sooner had the Prussian bourgeoisie and the classes allied to it shown a serious resolution to struggle for Parliamentary government in Prussia, than they were allowed to take the lead of the Constitutional movement over all non-Austrian Germany. It is a fact which now will not any longer be contested, that the nucleus of those Constitutionalists of Central Germany, who afterwards seceded from the Frankfort National Assembly, and who, from the place of their separate meetings, were called the Gotha party, long before 1848 contemplated a plan which, with little modification, they in 1849 proposed to the representatives of all Germany. They intended a complete exclusion of Austria from the German Confederation, the establishment of a new Confederation, with a new fundamental law, and with a Federal Parliament, under the protection of Prussia, and the incorporation of the more insignificant States into the larger ones. All this was to be carried out the moment Prussia entered into the ranks of Constitutional Monarchy, established the Liberty of the Press, assumed a policy independent from that of Russia and Austria, and thus enabled the Constitutionalists of the lesser States to obtain a real control over their respective Governments. The inventor of this scheme was Professor Gervinus, of Heidelberg (Baden). Thus the emancipation of the Prussian bourgeoisie was to be the signal for that of the middle classes of Germany generally, and for an alliance, offensive and defensive, of both against Russia and Austria, for Austria was, as we shall see presently, considered as an entirely barbarian country, of which very little was known, and that little not to the credit of its population; Austria, therefore, was not considered as an essential part of Germany.

As to the other classes of society, in the smaller States they followed, more or less rapidly, in the wake of their equals in Prussia. The shopkeeping class got more and more dissatisfied with their respective Governments, with the increase of taxation, with the curtailments of those political sham-privileges of which they used to boast when comparing themselves to the "slaves of despotism" in Austria and Prussia; but as yet they had nothing definite in their opposition which might stamp them as an independent party, distinct from the Constitutionalism of the higher bourgeoisie. The dissatisfaction among the peasantry was equally growing, but it is well known that this section of the people, in quiet and peaceful times, will never assert its interests and assume its position as an independent class, except in countries where universal suffrage is established. The working classes in the trades and manufactures of the towns commenced to be infected with the "poison" of Socialism and Communism, but there being few towns of any importance out of Prussia, and still fewer manufacturing districts, the movement of this class, owing to the want of centres of action and propaganda, was extremely slow in the smaller States.

Both in Prussia and in the smaller States the difficulty of giving vent to political opposition created a sort of religious opposition in the parallel movements of German Catholicism and Free Congregationalism. History affords us numerous examples where, in countries which enjoy the blessings of a State Church, and where political discussion is fettered, the profane and dangerous opposition against the worldly power is hid under the more sanctified and apparently more disinterested struggle against spiritual despotism. Many a Government that will not allow of any of its acts being discussed, will hesitate before it creates martyrs and excites the religious fanaticism of the masses. Thus in Germany, in 1845, in every State, either the Roman Catholic or the Protestant religion, or both, were considered part and parcel of the law of the land. In every State, too, the clergy of either of those denominations, or of both, formed an essential part of the bureaucratic establishment of the Government. To attack Protestant or Catholic orthodoxy, to attack priestcraft, was then to make an underhand attack upon the Government itself. As to the German Catholics, their very existence was an attack upon the Catholic Governments of Germany, particularly Austria and Bavaria; and as such it was taken by those Governments. The Free Congregationalists, Protestant Dissenters, somewhat resembling the English and American Unitarians, openly professed their opposition to the clerical and

rigidly orthodox tendency of the King of Prussia and his favourite Minister for the Educational and Clerical Department, Mr.
Eickhorn. The two new sects, rapidly extending for a moment,
the first in Catholic, the second in Protestant countries, had no
other distinction but their different origin; as to their tenets,
they perfectly agreed upon this most important point—that all
definite dogmas were nugatory. This want of any definition was
their very essence; they pretended to build that great temple
under the roof of which all Germans might unite; they thus
represented, in a religious form, another political idea of the
day—that of German unity, and yet they could never agree
among themselves.

The idea of German unity, which the above-mentioned sects
sought to realise, at least, upon religious ground, by inventing a
common religion for all Germans, manufactured expressly for
their use, habits, and taste—this idea was, indeed, very widely
spread, particularly in the smaller States. Ever since the dissolution of the German Empire by Napoleon, the cry for a union of
all the *disjecta membra* of the German body had been the most
general expression of discontent with the established order of
things, and most so in the smaller States, were the costliness of a
court, an administration, an army, in short, the dead weight of
taxation, increased in a direct ratio with the smallness and
impotency of the State. But what this German unity was to be
when carried out was a question upon which parties disagreed.
The bourgeoisie, which wanted no serious revolutionary convulsions, were satisfied with what we have seen they considered
"practicable," namely, a union of all Germany, exclusive of
Austria, under the supremacy of a Constitutional Government
of Prussia; and surely, without conjuring dangerous storms,
nothing more could, at that time, be done. The shopkeeping
class and the peasantry, as far as these latter troubled themselves about such things, never arrived at any definition of that
German unity they so loudly clamoured after; a few dreamers,
mostly feudalist reactionists, hoped for the re-establishment of
the German Empire; some few ignorant, soi-disant Radicals,
admiring Swiss institutions, of which they had not yet made

that practical experience which afterwards most ludicrously undeceived them, pronounced for a Federated Republic; and it was only the most extreme party which, at that time, dared pronounce for a German Republic, one and indivisible. Thus, German unity was in itself a question big with disunion, discord, and, in the case of certain eventualities, even civil war.

To resume, then; this was the state of Prussia, and the smaller States of Germany, at the end of 1847. The middle class, feeling their power, and resolved not to endure much longer the fetters with which a feudal and bureaucratic despotism enchained their commercial transactions, their industrial productivity, their common action as a class; a portion of the landed nobility so far changed into producers of mere marketable commodities, as to have the same interests and to make common cause with the middle class; the smaller trading class, dissatisfied, grumbling at the taxes, at the impediments thrown in the way of their business, but without any definite plan for such reforms as should secure their position in the social and political body; the peasantry, oppressed here by feudal exactions, there by money-lenders, usurers, and lawyers; the working people of the towns infected with the general discontent, equally hating the Government and the large industrial capitalists, and catching the contagion of Socialist and Communist ideas; in short, a heterogeneous mass of opposition, springing from various interests, but more or less led on by the bourgeoisie, in the first ranks of which again marched the bourgeoisie of Prussia, and particularly of the Rhine Province. On the other hand, Governments disagreeing upon many points, distrustful of each other, and particularly of that of Prussia, upon which yet they had to rely for protection; in Prussia a Government forsaken by public opinion, forsaken by even a portion of the nobility, leaning upon an army and a bureaucracy which every day got more infected by the ideas, and subjected to the influence, of the oppositional bourgeoisie—a Government, besides all this, penniless in the most literal meaning of the word, and which could not procure a single cent to cover its increasing deficit, but by surrendering at discretion to the opposition of the bourgeoisie.

Germany: Revolution and Counter-Revolution

Was there ever a more splendid position for the middle class of any country, while it struggled for power against the established Government?

New York Daily Tribune, November 6th, 1851

IV

London, September 1851

WE have now to consider Austria; that country which, up to March 1848, was sealed up to the eyes of foreign nations almost as much as China before the late war with England.

As a matter of course, we can here take into consideration nothing but German Austria. The affairs of the Polish, Hungarian, or Italian Austrians do not belong to our subject, and as far as they, since 1848, have influenced the fate of the German Austrians, they will have to be taken into account hereafter.

The Government of Prince Metternich turned upon two hinges; firstly, to keep every one of the different nations subjected to the Austrian rule, in check, by all other nations similarly conditioned; secondly, and this always has been the fundamental principle of absolute monarchies, to rely for support upon two classes, the feudal landlords and the large stock-jobbing capitalists; and to balance, at the same time, the influence and power of either of these classes by that of the other, so as to leave full independence of action to the Government. The landed nobility, whose entire income consisted in feudal revenues of all sorts, could not but support a Government which proved their only protection against that downtrodden class of serfs upon whose spoils they lived; and whenever the less wealthy portion of them, as in Galicia, in 1846, rose in opposition against the Government, Metternich in an instant let loose upon them these very serfs, who at any rate profited by the occasion to wreak a terrible vengeance upon their more immediate oppressors. On the other hand, the large capitalists of the Exchange were chained to Metternich's Government by the vast share they had in the public funds of the country. Austria, restored to her full power in 1815, restoring, and maintaining in Italy Absolute Monarchy ever since 1820, freed from part of her liabilities by the bankruptcy of 1810, had, after the peace, very soon re-established her credit in the great European money markets; and in proportion as her credit grew, she had drawn against it. Thus all the large European money-dealers had engaged considerable portions of their capital in the Austrian funds; they all of them were interested in upholding the credit of that country, and as Austrian public credit, in order to be upheld, ever required new loans, they were obliged from time to time to advance new capital in order to keep up the credit of the securities for that which they already had advanced. The long peace after 1815, and the apparent impossibility of a thousand years' old empire, like Austria, being upset, increased the credit of Metternich's Government in a wonderful ratio, and made it even independent of the goodwill of the Vienna bankers and stock-jobbers; for as long as Metternich could obtain plenty of money at Frankfort and Amsterdam, he had, of course, the satisfaction of seeing the Austrian capitalists at his feet. They were, besides, in every other respect at his mercy; the large profits which bankers, stockjobbers, and Government contractors always contrive to draw out of an absolute monarchy, were compensated for by the almost unlimited power which the Government possessed over their persons and fortunes; and not the smallest shadow of an opposition was, therefore, to be expected from this quarter. Thus Metternich was sure of the support of the two most powerful and influential classes of the empire, and he possessed besides an army and a bureaucracy, which for all purposes of absolutism could not be better constituted. The civil and military officers in the Austrian service form a race of their own; their fathers have been in the service of the Kaiser, and so will their sons be; they belong to none of the multifarious nationalities congregated under the wing of the double-headed eagle; they are, and ever have been, removed from one end of the empire to the other, from Poland to Italy, from Germany to Transylvania; Hungarian, Pole, German, Roumanian, Italian, Croat, every individual not stamped with "imperial and royal authority," etc., bearing a separate national character, is equally despised by them; they have no nationality, or rather, they alone make up the really Austrian nation. It is evident what a pliable, and at the same time powerful instrument, in the hands of an intelligent and energetic chief, such a civil and military hierarchy must be.

As to the other classes of the population, Metternich, in the true spirit of a statesman of the *ancien régime,* cared little for their support. He had, with regard to them, but one policy: to draw as much as possible out of them in the shape of taxation, and at the same time to keep them quiet. The trading and manufacturing middle class was but of slow growth in Austria. The trade of the Danube was comparatively unimportant; the country possessed but one port, Trieste, and the trade of the port was very limited. As to the manufacturers, they enjoyed considerable protection, amounting even in most cases to the complete exclusion of all foreign competition; but this advantage had been granted to them principally with a view to increase their tax-paying capabilities, and was in a high degree counterpoised by internal restrictions on manufactures, privileges on guilds, and other feudal corporations, which were scrupulously upheld as long as they did not impede the purposes and views of the Government. The petty tradesmen were encased in the narrow bounds of these Mediaeval guilds, which kept the different trades in a perpetual war of privilege against each other, and at the same time, by all but excluding individuals of the working class from the possibility of raising themselves in the social scale, gave a sort of hereditary stability to the members of those involuntary associations. Lastly, the peasant and the working man were treated as mere taxable matter, and the only care that was taken of them was to keep them as much as possible in the same conditions of life in which they then existed, and in which their fathers had existed before them. For this purpose every old, established, hereditary authority was upheld in the same manner as that of the State; the authority of the landlord over the petty tenant farmer, that of the manufacturer over the operative, of the small master over the journeyman and apprentice, of the father over the son, was everywhere rigidly maintained by the Government, and every branch of disobedience punished the same as a transgression of the law, by that universal instrument of Austrian justice—the stick.

Finally, to wind up into one comprehensive system all these attempts at creating an artificial stability, the intellectual food allowed to the nation was selected with the minutest caution, and dealt out as sparingly as possible. Education was everywhere in the hands of the Catholic priesthood, whose chiefs, in the same manner as the large feudal landowners, were deeply interested in the conservation of the existing system. The universities were organised in a manner which allowed them to produce nothing but special men, that might or might not obtain great proficiency in sundry particular branches of knowledge, but which, at all events, excluded that universal liberal education which other universities are expected to impart. There was absolutely no newspaper press, except in Hungary, and the Hungarian papers were prohibited in all other parts of the monarchy. As to general literature, its range had not widened for a century; it had narrowed again after the death of Joseph II. And all around the frontier, wherever the Austrian States touched upon a civilised country, a cordon of literary censors was established in connection with the cordon of customhouse officials, preventing any foreign book or newspaper from passing into Austria before its contents had been twice or three times thoroughly sifted, and found pure of even the slightest contamination of the malignant spirit of the age.

For about thirty years after 1815 this system worked with wonderful success. Austria remained almost unknown to Europe, and Europe was quite as little known in Austria. The social state of every class of the population, and of the population as a whole, appeared not to have undergone the slightest change. Whatever rancour there might exist from class to class

—and the existence of this rancour was for Metternich a principal condition of government, which he even fostered by making the higher classes the instruments of all Government exactions, and thus throwing the odium upon them—whatever hatred the people might bear to the inferior officials of the State, there existed, upon the whole, little or no dissatisfaction with the Central Government. The Emperor was adored, and old Francis I seemed to be borne out by facts when, doubting of the durability of this system, he complacently added: "And yet it will hold while I live, and Metternich."

But there was a slow underground movement going on which baffled all Metternich's efforts. The wealth and influence of the manufacturing and trading middle class increased. The introduction of machinery and steam-power in manufactures upset in Austria, as it had done everywhere else, the old relations and vital conditions of whole classes of society; it changed serfs into free men, small farmers into manufacturing operatives; it undermined the old feudal trades corporations, and destroyed the means of existence of many of them. The new commercial and manufacturing population came everywhere into collision with the old feudal institutions. The middle classes, more and more induced by their business to travel abroad, introduced some mythical knowledge of the civilised countries situated beyond the Imperial line of customs; the introduction of railways finally accelerated both the industrial and intellectual movement. There was, too, a dangerous part in the Austrian State establishment, viz., the Hungarian feudal Constitution, with its parliamentary proceedings, and its struggles of the impoverished and oppositional mass of the nobility against the Government and its allies, the magnates. Presburg, the seat of the Diet, was at the very gates of Vienna. All the elements contributed to create among the middle classes of the towns a spirit, not exactly of opposition, for opposition was as yet impossible, but of discontent; a general wish for reforms, more of an administrative than of a constitutional nature. And in the same manner as in Prussia, a portion of the bureaucracy joined the bourgeoisie. Among this hereditary caste of officials the traditions of Joseph II were not forgotten; the more educated functionaries of the Government, who themselves sometimes meddled with imaginary possible reforms, by far preferred the progressive and intellectual despotism of that Emperor to the "paternal" despotism of Metternich. A portion of the poorer nobility equally sided with the middle class, and as to the lower classes of the population, who always had found plenty of grounds to complain of their superiors, if not of the Government, they in most cases could not but adhere to the reformatory wishes of the bourgeoisie.

It was about this time, say 1843 or 1844, that a particular branch of literature, agreeable to this change, was established in Germany. A few Austrian writers, novelists, literary critics, bad poets, the whole of them of very indifferent ability, but gifted with that peculiar industrialism proper to the Jewish race, established themselves in Leipsic and other German towns out of Austria, and there out of the reach of Metternich, published a number of books and pamphlets on Austrian affairs. They and their publishers made "a roaring trade" of it. All Germany was eager to become initiated into the secrets of the policy of European China; and the Austrians themselves, who obtained these publications by the wholesale smuggling carried on upon the Bohemian frontier, were still more curious. Of course the secrets let out in these publications were of no great importance, and the reform plans schemed out by their well-wishing authors bore the stamp of an innocuousness almost amounting to political virginity. A Constitution and a free press for Austria were things considered unattainable; administrative reforms, extension of the rights of the Provincial Diets, admission of foreign books and newspapers, and a less severe censorship—the loyal and humble desires of these good Austrians did hardly go any farther.

At all events the growing impossibility of preventing the literary intercourse of Austria with the rest of Germany, and through Germany with the rest of the world, contributed much toward the formation of an anti-Governmental public opinion, and brought at least some little political information within the reach of part of the Austrian population. Thus, by the end of

1847, Austria was seized, although in an inferior degree, by that political and politico-religious agitation which then prevailed in all Germany; and if its progress in Austria was more silent, it did, nevertheless, find revolutionary elements enough to work upon. There was the peasant, serf, or feudal tenant, ground down into the dust by lordly or Government exactions; then the factory operative, forced by the stick of the policeman to work upon any terms the manufacturer chose to grant; then the journeyman, debarred by the corporative laws from any chance of gaining an independence in his trade; then the merchant, stumbling at every step in business over absurd regulations; then the manufacturer, in uninterrupted conflict with trade guilds, jealous of their privileges, or with greedy and meddling officials; then the schoolmaster, the savant, the better educated functionary, vainly struggling against an ignorant and presumptuous clergy, or a stupid and dictating superior. In short, there was not a single class satisfied, for the small concessions Government was obliged now and then to make were not made at its own expense, for the Treasury could not afford that, but at the expense of the high aristocracy and clergy; and as to the great bankers, and fundholders, the late events in Italy, the increasing opposition of the Hungarian Diet, and the unwonted spirit of discontent and cry for reform, manifesting themselves all over the Empire, were not of a nature to strengthen their faith in the solidity and solvency of the Austrian Empire.

Thus Austria, too, was marching slowly but surely toward a mighty change, when, of a sudden, an event broke out in France, which at once brought down the impending storm, and gave the lie to old Francis's assertion, that the building would hold out both during his and Metternich's lifetime.

New York Daily Tribune, November 7th, 1851

V

On February 24th, 1848, Louis Philippe was driven out of Paris, and the French Republic was proclaimed. On March 13th following, the people of Vienna broke the power of Prince Metternich, and made him flee shamefully out of the country. On March 18th the people of Berlin rose in arms, and, after an obstinate struggle of eighteen hours, had the satisfaction of seeing the King surrender himself into their hands. Simultaneous outbreaks of a more or less violent nature, but all with the same success, occurred in the capitals of the smaller States of Germany. The German people, if they had not accomplished their first revolution, were at least fairly launched into the revolutionary career.

As to the incidents of these various insurrections, we cannot enter here into the details of them: what we have to explain is their character, and the position which the different classes of the population took up with regard to them.

The Revolution of Vienna may be said to have been made by an almost unanimous population. The bourgeoisie (with the exception of the bankers and stock-jobbers), the petty trading class, the working people, one and all arose at once against a Government detested by all, a Government so universally hated, that the small minority of nobles and money lords which had supported it made itself invisible on the very first attack. The middle classes had been kept in such a degree of political ignorance by Metternich that to them the news from Paris about the reign of Anarchy, Socialism, and terror, and about impending struggles between the class of capitalists and the class of labourers, proved quite unintelligible. They, in their political innocence, either could attach no meaning to these news, or they believed them to be fiendish inventions of Metternich, to frighten them into obedience. They, besides, had never seen working men acting as a class, or stand up for their own distinct class interests. They had, from their past experience, no idea of the possibility of any differences springing up between classes that now were so heartily united in upsetting a Government hated by all. They saw the working people agree with themselves upon all points: a Constitution, Trial by Jury, Liberty of the Press, etc. Thus they were, in March 1848, at least, heart and soul with the movement, and the movement, on the other hand, at once constituted them the (at least in theory) predominant class of the State.

But it is the fate of all revolutions that this union of different classes, which in some degree is always the necessary condition of any revolution, cannot subsist long. No sooner is the victory gained against the common enemy than the victors become divided among themselves into different camps, and turn their weapons against each other. It is this rapid and passionate development of class antagonism which, in old and complicated social organisms, makes a revolution such a powerful agent of social and political progress; it is this incessantly quick upshooting of new parties succeeding each other in power, which, during those violent commotions, makes a nation pass in five years over more ground than it would have done in a century under ordinary circumstances.

The Revolution in Vienna made the middle class the theoretically predominant class; that is to say, the concessions wrung from the Government were such as, once carried out practically and adhered to for a time, would inevitably have secured the supremacy of the middle class. But practically the supremacy of that class was far from being established. It is true that by the establishment of a national guard, which gave arms to the bourgeoisie and petty tradesmen, that class obtained both force

and importance; it is true that by the installation of a "Committee of Safety," a sort of revolutionary, irresponsible Government
in which the bourgeoisie predominated, it was placed at the
head of power. But, at the same time, the working classes were
partially armed too; they and the students had borne the brunt
of the fight, as far as fight there had been; and the students,
about 4,000 strong, well armed, and far better disciplined than
the national guard, formed the nucleus, the real strength of the
revolutionary force, and were no ways willing to act as a mere
instrument in the hands of the Committee of Safety. Though
they recognised it, and were even its most enthusiastic supporters, they yet formed a sort of independent and rather turbulent
body, deliberating for themselves in the "Aula," keeping an
intermediate position between the bourgeoisie and the working
classes, preventing by constant agitation things from settling
down to the old everyday tranquillity, and very often forcing
their resolutions upon the Committee of Safety. The working
men, on the other hand, almost entirely thrown out of employment, had to be employed in public works at the expense of the
State, and the money for this purpose had, of course, to be
taken out of the purse of the taxpayers or out of the chest of the
city of Vienna. All this could not but become very unpleasant to
the tradesmen of Vienna. The manufactures of the city, calcu-
lated for the consumption of the rich and aristocratic courts of a
large country, were as a matter of course entirely stopped by
the Revolution, by the flight of the aristocracy and Court; trade
was at a standstill, and the continuous agitation and excitement
kept up by the students and working people was certainly not
the means to "restore confidence," as the phrase went. Thus a
certain coolness very soon sprung up between the middle
classes on the one side and the turbulent students and working
people on the other; and if for a long time this coolness was not
ripened into open hostility, it was because the Ministry, and
particularly the Court, in their impatience to restore the old
order of things, constantly justified the suspicions and the turbulent activity of the more revolutionary parties, and constantly
made arise, even before the eyes of the middle classes, the

spectre of old Metternichian despotism. Thus on May 15th, and again on the 26th, there were fresh risings of all classes in Vienna, on account of the Government having tried to attack, or to undermine, some of the newly-conquered liberties, and on each occasion the alliance between the national guard or armed middle class, the students, and the working men, was again cemented for a time.

As to the other classes of the population, the aristocracy and the money lords had disappeared, and the peasantry were busily engaged everywhere in removing, down to the very last vestiges of feudalism. Thanks to the war in Italy, and the occupation which Vienna and Hungary gave to the Court, they were left at full liberty, and succeeded in their work of liberation in Austria, better than in any other part of Germany. The Austrian Diet had very shortly after only to confirm the steps already practically taken by the peasantry, and whatever else the Government of Prince Schwartzenberg may be enabled to restore, it will never have the power of re-establishing the feudal servitude of the peasantry. And if Austria at the present moment is again comparatively tranquil, and even strong, it is principally because the great majority of the people, the peasants, have been real gainers by the Revolution, and because whatever else has been attacked by the restored Government, those palpable, substantial advantages, conquered by the peasantry, are as yet untouched.

New York Daily Tribune, November 12th, 1851

VI

THE second centre of revolutionary action was Berlin, and from what has been stated in the foregoing papers, it may be guessed that there this action was far from having that unanimous support of almost all classes by which it was accompanied in Vienna. In Prussia, the bourgeoisie had been already involved in actual struggles with the Government; a rupture had been the result of the "United Diet"; a bourgeois revolution was impending, and that revolution might have been, in its first outbreak, quite as unanimous as that of Vienna, had it not been for the Paris Revolution of February. That event precipitated everything, while at the same time it was carried out under a banner totally different from that under which the Prussian bourgeoisie was preparing to defy its Government. The Revolution of February upset, in France, the very same sort of Government which the Prussian bourgeoisie was going to set up in their own country. The Revolution of February announced itself as a revolution of the working classes against the middle classes; it proclaimed the downfall of middle-class government and the emancipation of the working man. Now the Prussian bourgeoisie had, of late, had quite enough of working-class agitation in their own country. After the first terror of the Silesian riots had passed away, they had even tried to give this agitation a turn in their own favour; but they always had retained a salutary horror of revolutionary Socialism and Communism; and, therefore, when they saw men at the head of the

161

Government in Paris whom they considered as the most dangerous enemies of property, order, religion, family, and of the other
Penates of the modern bourgeois, they at once experienced a
considerable cooling down of their own revolutionary ardour.
They knew that the moment must be seized, and that, without
the aid of the working masses, they would be defeated; and yet
their courage failed them. Thus they sided with the Government in the first partial and provincial outbreaks, tried to keep
the people quiet in Berlin, who, during five days, met in crowds
before the royal palace to discuss the news and ask for changes
in the Government; and when at last, after the news of the
downfall of Metternich, the King made some slight concessions,
the bourgeoisie considered the Revolution as completed, and
went to thank His Majesty for having fulfilled all the wishes of
his people. But then followed the attack of the military on the
crowd, the barricades, the struggle, and the defeat of royalty.
Then everything was changed; the very working classes, which
it had been the tendency of the bourgeoisie to keep in the
background, had been pushed forward, had fought and conquered, and all at once were conscious of their strength. Restrictions of suffrage, of the Liberty of the Press, of the right to sit on
juries, of the right of meeting—restrictions that would have
been very agreeable to the bourgeoisie because they would
have touched upon such classes as were beneath them—now
were no longer possible. The danger of a repetition of the
Parisian scenes of "anarchy" was imminent. Before this danger
all former differences disappeared. Against the victorious working man, although he had not yet uttered any specific demands
for himself, the friends and the foes of many years united, and
the alliance between the bourgeoisie and the supporters of the
overturned system was concluded upon the very barricades of
Berlin. The necessary concessions, but no more than was unavoidable, were to be made; a ministry of the opposition leaders
of the United Diet was to be formed, and in return for its
services in saving the Crown, it was to have the support of all
the props of the old Government, the feudal aristocracy, the
bureaucracy, the army. These were the conditions upon which

Messrs. Camphausen and Hansemann undertook the formation of a cabinet.

Such was the dread evinced by the new ministers of the aroused masses, that in their eyes every means was good if it only tended to strengthen the shaken foundations of authority. They, poor deluded wretches, thought every danger of a restoration of the old system had passed away; and thus they made use of the whole of the old State machinery for the purpose of restoring "order." Not a single bureaucrat or military officer was dismissed; not the slightest change was made in the old bureaucratic system of administration. These precious constitutional and responsible ministers even restored to their posts those functionaries whom the people, in the first heat of revolutionary ardour, had driven away on account of their former acts of bureaucratic overbearing. There was nothing altered in Prussia but the persons of the ministers; even the ministerial staffs in the different departments were not touched upon, and all the constitutional place-hunters, who had formed the chorus of the newly-elevated rulers, and who had expected their share of power and office, were told to wait until restored stability allowed changes to be operated in the bureaucratic personnel which now were not without danger.

The King, chap-fallen in the highest degree after the insurrection of March 18th, very soon found out that he was quite as necessary to these "Liberal" ministers as they were to him. The throne had been spared by the insurrection; the throne was the last existing obstacle to "anarchy"; the Liberal middle class and its leaders, now in the ministry, had therefore every interest to keep on excellent terms with the Crown. The King, and the reactionary *camarilla* that surrounded him, were not slow in discovering this, and profited by the circumstance in order to fetter the march of the ministry even in those petty reforms that were from time to time intended.

The first care of the ministry was to give a sort of legal appearance to the recent violent changes. The United Diet was convoked in spite of all popular opposition, in order to vote as the legal and constitutional organ of the people a new electoral law for the election of an Assembly, which was to agree with the Crown upon a new Constitution. The elections were to be indirect, the mass of voters electing a number of electors, who then were to choose the representative. In spite of all opposition this system of double elections passed. The United Diet was then asked for a loan of twenty-five millions of dollars, opposed by the popular party, but equally agreed to.

These acts of the ministry gave a most rapid development to the popular, or as it now called itself, the Democratic Party. This party, headed by the petty trading and shopkeeping class, and uniting under its banner, in the beginning of the Revolution, the large majority of the working people, demanded direct and universal suffrage, the same as established in France, a single Legislative Assembly, and full and open recognition of the Revolution of March 18th, as the base of the new governmental system. The more moderate faction would be satisfied with a thus "democratised" monarchy, the more advanced demanded the ultimate establishment of the Republic. Both factions agreed in recognising the German National Assembly at Frankfort as the supreme authority of the country, while the Constitutionalists and Reactionists affected a great horror of the sovereignty of this body, which they professed to consider as utterly revolutionary.

The independent movement of the working classes had, by the Revolution, been broken up for a time. The immediate wants and circumstances of the movement were such as not to allow any of the specific demands of the Proletarian party to be put in the foreground. In fact, as long as the ground was not cleared for the independent action of the working men, as long as direct and universal suffrage was not yet established, as long as the thirty-six larger and smaller States continued to cut up Germany into numberless morsels, what else could the Proletarian party do but watch the—for them all-important—movement of Paris, and struggle in common with the petty shopkeepers for the attainment of those rights, which would allow them to fight afterwards their own battle?

There were only three points, then, by which the Proletarian party in its political action essentially distinguished itself from the petty trading class, or properly so-called Democratic party; firstly, in judging differently the French movement, with regard to which the Democrats attacked, and the Proletarian Revolutionists defended, the extreme party in Paris; secondly, in proclaiming the necessity of establishing a German Republic, one and indivisible, while the very extremest ultras among the Democrats only dared to sigh for a Federative Republic; and thirdly, in showing upon every occasion, that revolutionary boldness and readiness for action, in which any party headed by, and composed principally of petty tradesmen, will always be deficient.

The Proletarian, or really Revolutionary party, succeeded only very gradually in withdrawing the mass of the working people from the influence of the Democrats, whose tail they formed in the beginning of the Revolution. But in due time the indecision, weakness, and cowardice of the Democratic leaders did the rest, and it may now be said to be one of the principal results of the last years' convulsions, that wherever the working class is concerned in anything like considerable masses, they are entirely freed from that Democratic influence which led them into an endless series of blunders and misfortunes during 1848 and 1849. But we had better not anticipate; the events of these two years will give us plenty of opportunities to show the Democratic gentlemen at work.

The peasantry in Prussia, the same as in Austria, but with less energy, feudalism pressing, upon the whole, not quite so hardly upon them here, had profited by the Revolution to free themselves at once from all feudal shackles. But here, from the reasons stated before, the middle classes at once turned against them, their oldest, their most indispensable allies; the Democrats, equally frightened with the bourgeoisie, by what was called attacks upon private property, failed equally to support them; and thus, after three months' emancipation, after bloody struggles and military executions, particularly in Silesia, feudalism was restored by the hands of the, until yesterday, antifeudal bourgeoisie. There is not a more damning fact to be brought against them than this. Similar treason against its best allies, against itself, never was committed by any party in history, and whatever humiliation and chastisement may be in store for this middle-class party, it has deserved by this one act every morsel of it.

New York Daily Tribune, November 28th, 1851

VII

London, January 1852

IT will perhaps be in the recollection of our readers that in the
six preceding papers we followed up the revolutionary movement of Germany to the two great popular victories of March
13th in Vienna, and March 18th in Berlin. We saw, both in
Austria and Prussia, the establishment of Constitutional Governments and the proclamation, as leading rules for all future
policy, of Liberal, or middle-class principles; and the only
difference observable between the two great centres of action
was this, that in Prussia the Liberal bourgeoisie, in the persons
of two wealthy merchants, Messrs. Camphausen and Hansemann, directly seized upon the reins of power; while in Austria,
where the bourgeoisie was, politically, far less educated, the
Liberal bureaucracy walked into office, and professed to hold
power in trust for them. We have further seen, how the parties
and classes of society, that were heretofore all united in opposition to the old Government, got divided among themselves after
the victory, or even during the struggle; and how that same
Liberal bourgeoisie that alone profited from the victory turned
round immediately upon its allies of yesterday, assumed a hostile attitude against every class or party of a more advanced
character, and concluded an alliance with the conquered feudal
and bureaucratic interests. It was, in fact, evident, even from
the beginning of the revolutionary drama, that the Liberal
bourgeoisie could not hold its ground against the vanquished,
but not destroyed, feudal and bureaucratic parties except by

167

relying upon the assistance of the popular and more advanced parties; and that it equally required, against the torrent of these more advanced masses, the assistance of the feudal nobility and of the bureaucracy. Thus, it was clear enough that the bourgeoisie in Austria and Prussia did not possess sufficient strength to maintain their power, and to adapt the institutions of the country to their own wants and ideas. The Liberal bourgeois ministry was only a halting-place from which, according to the turn circumstances might take, the country would either have to go on to the more advanced stage of Unitarian Republicanism, or to relapse into the old clerico-feudal and bureaucratic regime. At all events, the real, decisive struggle was yet to come; the events of March had only engaged the combat.

Austria and Prussia being the two ruling States of Germany, every decisive revolutionary victory in Vienna or Berlin would have been decisive for all Germany. And as far as they went, the events of March 1848, in these two cities, decided the turn of German affairs. It would, then, be superfluous to recur to the movements that occurred in the minor States; and we might, indeed, confine ourselves to the consideration of Austrian and Prussian affairs exclusively, if the existence of these minor States had not given rise to a body which was, by its very existence, a most striking proof of the abnormal situation of Germany and of the incompleteness of the late Revolution; a body so abnormal, so ludicrous by its very position, and yet so full of its own importance, that history will, most likely, never afford a pendant to it. This body was the so-called *German National Assembly* at Frankfort-on-Main.

After the popular victories of Vienna and Berlin, it was a matter of course that there should be a Representative Assembly for all Germany. This body was consequently elected, and met at Frankfort, by the side of the old Federative Diet. The German National Assembly was expected, by the people, to settle every matter in dispute, and to act as the highest legislative authority for the whole of the German Confederation. But, at the same time, the Diet which had convoked it had in no way fixed its attributions. No one knew whether its decrees were to have force of law, or whether they were to be subject to the sanction of the Diet, or of the individual Governments. In this perplexity, if the Assembly had been possessed of the least energy, it would have immediately dissolved and sent home the Diet—than which no corporate body was more unpopular in Germany—and replaced it by a Federal Government, chosen from among its own members. It would have declared itself the only legal expression of the sovereign will of the German people, and thus have attached legal validity to every one of its decrees. It would, above all, have secured to itself an organised and armed force in the country sufficient to put down any opposition on the part of the Governments. And all this was easy, very easy, at that early period of the Revolution. But that would have been expecting a great deal too much from an Assembly composed in its majority of Liberal attorneys and doctrinaire professors, an Assembly which, while it pretended to embody the very essence of German intellect and science, was in reality nothing but a stage where old and worn-out political characters exhibited their involuntary ludicrousness and their impotence of thought, as well as action, before the eyes of all Germany. This Assembly of old women was, from the first day of its existence, more frightened of the least popular movement than of all the reactionary plots of all the German Governments put together. It deliberated under the eyes of the Diet, nay, it almost craved the Diet's sanction to its decrees, for its first resolutions had to be promulgated by that odious body. Instead of asserting its own sovereignty, it studiously avoided the discussion of any such dangerous question. Instead of surrounding itself by a popular force, it passed to the order of the day over all the violent encroachments of the Governments; Mayence, under its very eyes, was placed in a state of siege, and the people there disarmed, and the National Assembly did not stir. Later on it elected Archduke John of Austria Regent of Germany, and declared that all its resolutions were to have the force of law; but then Archduke John was only instituted in his new dignity after the consent of all the Governments had been obtained, and he was instituted not by the Assembly, but by the

Diet; and as to the legal force of the decrees of the Assembly, that point was never recognised by the larger Governments, nor enforced by the Assembly itself; it therefore remained in suspense. Thus we had the strange spectacle of an Assembly pretending to be the only legal representative of a great and sovereign nation, and yet never possessing either the will or the force to make its claims recognised. The debates of this body, without any practical result, were not even of any theoretical value, reproducing, as they did, nothing but the most hackneyed commonplace themes of superannuated philosophical and juridical schools; every sentence that was said, or rather stammered forth, in that Assembly having been printed a thousand times over, and a thousand times better, long before.

Thus the pretended new central authority of Germany left everything as it had found it. So far from realising the long-demanded unity of Germany, it did not dispossess the most insignificant of the princes who ruled her; it did not draw closer the bonds of union between her separated provinces; it never moved a single step to break down the custom-house barriers that separated Hanover from Prussia, and Prussia from Austria; it did not even make the slightest attempt to remove the obnoxious dues that everywhere obstruct river navigation in Prussia. But the less this Assembly did the more it blustered. It created a German Fleet—upon paper; it annexed Poland and Schleswig; it allowed German-Austria to carry on war against Italy, and yet prohibited the Italians from following up the Austrians into their safe retreat in Germany; it gave three cheers and one cheer more for the French Republic, and it received Hungarian embassies, which certainly went home with far more confused ideas about Germany than they had come with.

This Assembly had been, in the beginning of the Revolution, the bugbear of all German Governments. They had counted upon a very dictatorial and revolutionary action on its part—on account of the very want of definiteness in which it had been found necessary to leave its competency. These Governments, therefore, got up a most comprehensive system of intrigues in order to weaken the influence of this dreaded body; but they

170

proved to have more luck than wits, for this Assembly did the work of the Governments better than they themselves could have done. The chief feature among these intrigues was the convocation of local Legislative Assemblies, and in consequence, not only the lesser States convoked their Legislatures, but Prussia and Austria also called Constituent Assemblies. In these, as in the Frankfort House of Representatives, the Liberal middle class, or its allies, Liberal lawyers, and bureaucrats had the majority, and the turn affairs took in each of them was nearly the same. The only difference is this, that the German National Assembly was the Parliament of an imaginary country, as it had declined the task of forming what nevertheless was its own first condition of existence, viz., a United Germany; that it discussed the imaginary and never-to-be-carried-out measures of an imaginary Government of its own creation, and that it passed imaginary resolutions for which nobody cared; while in Austria and Prussia the constituent bodies were at least real parliaments, upsetting and creating real ministries, and forcing, for a time at least, their resolutions upon the princes with whom they had to contend. They, too, were cowardly, and lacked enlarged views of revolutionary resolutions; they, too, betrayed the people, and restored power to the hands of feudal, bureaucratic, and military despotism. But then they were at least obliged to discuss practical questions of immediate interest, and to live upon earth with other people, while the Frankfort humbugs were never happier than when they could roam in "the airy realms of dream," *im Luftreich des Traums*. Thus the proceedings of the Berlin and Vienna Constituents form an important part of German revolutionary history, while the lucubrations of the Frankfort collective tomfoolery merely interest the collector of literary and antiquarian curiosities.

The people of Germany, deeply feeling the necessity of doing away with the obnoxious territorial division that scattered and annihilated the collective force of the nation, for some time expected to find, in the Frankfort National Assembly at least, the beginning of a new era. But the childish conduct of that set of wiseacres soon disenchanted the national enthusiasm. The

171

disgraceful proceedings occasioned by the armistice of Malmoe (September 1848) made the popular indignation burst out against a body which, it had been hoped, would give the nation a fair field for action, and which, instead, carried away by unequalled cowardice, only restored to their former solidity the foundations upon which the present counter-revolutionary system is built.

New York Daily Tribune, February 27th, 1852

VIII

London, February 1852

FROM what has been stated in the foregoing articles, it is already evident that unless a fresh revolution was to follow that of March 1848, things would inevitably return, in Germany, to what they were before this event. But such is the complicated nature of the historical theme upon which we are trying to throw some light, that subsequent events cannot be clearly understood without taking into account what may be called the foreign relations of the German Revolution. And these foreign relations were of the same intricate nature as the home affairs.

The whole of the eastern half of Germany, as far as the Elbe, Saale, and Bohemian Forest, has, it is well known, been reconquered during the last thousand years, from invaders of Slavonic origin. The greater part of these territories have been Germanised, to the perfect extinction of all Slavonic nationality and language for several centuries past; and if we except a few totally isolated remnants, amounting in the aggregate to less than a hundred thousand souls (Kassubians in Pomerania, Wends or Sorbians in Lusatia), their inhabitants are, to all intents and purposes, Germans. But the case is different along the whole of the frontier of ancient Poland, and in the countries of the Tschechian tongue, in Bohemia and Moravia. Here the two nationalities are mixed up in every district, the towns being generally more or less German, while the Slavonic element prevails in the rural villages, where, however, it is also gradual-

173

ly disintegrated and forced back by the steady advance of German influence.

The reason of this state of things is this: ever since the time of Charlemagne, the Germans have directed their most constant and persevering efforts to the conquest, colonisation, or, at least, civilisation of the east of Europe. The conquests of the feudal nobility between the Elbe and the Oder, and the feudal colonies of the military orders of knights in Prussia and Livonia, only laid the ground for a far more extensive and effective system of Germanisation by the trading and manufacturing middle classes, which in Germany, as in the rest of Western Europe, rose into social and political importance since the fifteenth century. The Slavonians, and particularly the Western Slavonians (Poles and Tschechs), are essentially an agricultural race; trade and manufactures never were in great favour with them. The consequence was that, with the increase of population and the origin of cities in these regions, the production of all articles of manufacture fell into the hands of German immigrants, and the exchange of these commodities against agricultural produce became the exclusive monopoly of the Jews, who, if they belong to any nationality, are in these countries certainly rather Germans than Slavonians. This has been, though in a less degree, the case in all the east of Europe. The handicraftsman, the small shopkeeper, the petty manufacturer, is a German up to this day in Petersburg, Pesth, Jassy, and even Constantinople; while the money-lender, the publican, the hawker—a very important man in these thinly populated countries—is very generally a Jew, whose native tongue is a horribly corrupted German. The importance of the German element in the Slavonic frontier localities, thus rising with the growth of towns, trade, and manufactures, was still increased when it was found necessary to import almost every element of mental culture from Germany; after the German merchant and handicraftsman, the German clergyman, the German schoolmaster, the German savant came to establish himself upon Slavonic soil. And lastly, the iron tread of conquering armies, or the cautious, well-premeditated grasp of diplomacy, not only followed, but many times went ahead of the slow but sure advance of denationalisation by social developments. Thus, great parts of Western Prussia and Posen have been Germanised since the first partition of Poland, by sales and grants of public domains to German colonists, by encouragements given to German capitalists for the establishment of manufactories, etc., in those neighbourhoods, and very often, too, by excessively despotic measures against the Polish inhabitants of the country.

In this manner the last seventy years had entirely changed the line of demarcation between the German and Polish nationalities. The Revolution of 1848 calling forth at once the claim of all oppressed nations to an independent existence, and to the right of settling their own affairs for themselves, it was quite natural that the Poles should at once demand the restoration of their country within the frontiers of the old Polish Republic before 1772. It is true, this frontier, even at that time, had become obsolete, if taken as the delimitation of German and Polish nationality; it had become more so every year since by the progress of Germanisation; but then, the Germans had proclaimed such an enthusiasm for the restoration of Poland, that they must expect to be asked, as a first proof of the reality of their sympathies, to give up *their* share of the plunder. On the other hand, should whole tracts of land, inhabited chiefly by Germans, should large towns, entirely German, be given up to a people that as yet had never given any proofs of its capability of progressing beyond a state of feudalism based upon agricultural serfdom? The question was intricate enough. The only possible solution was in a war with Russia. The question of delimitation between the different revolutionised nations would have been made a secondary one to that of first establishing a safe frontier against the common enemy. The Poles, by receiving extended territories in the east, would have become more tractable and reasonable in the west; and Riga and Memel would have been deemed, after all, quite as important to them as Danzig and Elbing. Thus the advanced party in Germany, deeming a war with Russia necessary to keep up the Continental movement, and considering that the national re-establishment even of a part of Poland would inevitably lead to such a war, supported the Poles; while the reigning middle-class party clearly foresaw its downfall from any national war against Russia, which would have called more active and energetic men to the helm, and, therefore, with a feigned enthusiasm for the extension of German nationality, they declared Prussian Poland, the chief seat of Polish revolutionary agitation, to be part and parcel of the German Empire that was to be. The promises given to the Poles in the first days of excitement were shamefully broken. Polish armaments got up with the sanction of the Government were dispersed and massacred by Prussian artillery; and as soon as the month of April 1848, within six weeks of the Berlin Revolution, the Polish movement was crushed, and the old national hostility revived between Poles and Germans. This immense and incalculable service to the Russian autocrat was performed by the Liberal merchant-ministers, Camphausen and Hansemann. It must be added that this Polish campaign was the first means of reorganising and reassuring that same Prussian army, which afterward turned out the Liberal party, and crushed the movement which Messrs. Camphausen and Hansemann had taken such pains to bring about. "Whereby they sinned, thereby are they punished." Such has been the fate of all the upstarts of 1848 and 1849, from Ledru Rollin to Changarnier, and from Camphausen down to Haynau.

The question of nationality gave rise to another struggle in Bohemia. This country, inhabited by two millions of Germans, and three millions of Slavonians of the Tschechian tongue, had great historical recollections, almost all connected with the former supremacy of the Tschechs. But then the force of this branch of the Slavonic family had been broken ever since the wars of the Hussites in the fifteenth century. The province speaking the Tschechian tongue was divided, one part forming the kingdom of Bohemia, another the principality of Moravia, a third the Carpathian hill-country of the Slovaks, being part of Hungary. The Moravians and Slovaks had long since lost every vestige of national feeling and vitality, although mostly preserving their language. Bohemia was surrounded by thoroughly

176

German countries on three sides out of four. The German element had made great progress on her own territory; even in the capital, in Prague, the two nationalities were pretty equally matched; and everywhere capital, trade, industry, and mental culture were in the hands of the Germans. The chief champion of the Tschechian nationality, Professor Palacky, is himself nothing but a learned German run mad, who even now cannot speak the Tschechian language correctly and without foreign accent. But as it often happens, dying Tschechian nationality, dying according to every fact known in history for the last four hundred years, made in 1848 a last effort to regain its former vitality—an effort whose failure, independently of all revolutionary considerations, was to prove that Bohemia could only exist henceforth, as a portion of Germany, although part of her inhabitants might yet, for some centuries, continue to speak a non-German language.

New York Daily Tribune, March 5th, 1852

IX

BOHEMIA and Croatia (another disjected member of the Slavonic family, acted upon by the Hungarian, as Bohemia by the German) were the homes of what is called on the European continent "Panslavism." Neither Bohemia nor Croatia was strong enough to exist as a nation by herself. Their respective nationalities, gradually undermined by the action of historical causes that inevitably absorbs into a more energetic stock, could only hope to be restored to anything like independence by an alliance with other Slavonic nations. There were twenty-two millions of Poles, forty-five millions of Russians, eight millions of Serbians and Bulgarians; why not form a mighty confederation of the whole eighty millions of Slavonians, and drive back or exterminate the intruder upon the holy Slavonic soil, the Turk, the Hungarian, and above all the hated, but indispensable *Niemetz*, the German? Thus in the studies of a few Slavonian *dilettanti* of historical science was this ludicrous, this anti-historical movement got up, a movement which intended nothing less than to subjugate the civilised West under the barbarian East, the town under the country, trade, manufactures, intelligence, under the primitive agriculture of Slavonian serfs. But behind this ludicrous theory stood the terrible reality of the *Russian Empire;* that empire which by every movement proclaims the pretension of considering all Europe as the domain of the Slavonic race, and especially of the only energetic part of this race, of the Russians; that empire which, with two capitals such as St. Petersburg and Moscow, has not yet found its centre of gravity, as long as the "City of the Czar" (Constantinople, called in Russian Tzarigrad, the Czar's city), considered by every Russian peasant as the true metropolis of his religion and his nation, is not actually the residence of its Emperor; that empire which, for the last one hundred and fifty years, has never lost, but always gained territory by every war it has commenced. And well known in Central Europe are the intrigues by which Russian policy supported the new-fangled system of Panslavism, a system than which none better could be invented to suit its purposes. Thus, the Bohemian and Croatian Panslavists, some intentionally, some without knowing it, worked in the direct interest of Russia; they betrayed the revolutionary cause for the shadow of a nationality which, in the best of cases, would have shared the fate of the Polish nationality under Russian sway. It must, however, be said for the honour of the Poles, that they never get to be seriously entangled in these Panslavist traps, and if a few of the aristocracy turned furious Panslavists, they knew that by Russian subjugation they had less to lose than by a revolt of their own peasant serfs.

The Bohemians and Croatians called, then, a general Slavonic Congress at Prague, for the preparation of the universal Slavonian Alliance. This Congress would have proved a decided failure even without the interference of the Austrian military. The several Slavonic languages differ quite as much as the English, the German, and the Swedish, and when the proceedings opened, there was no common Slavonic tongue by which the speakers could make themselves understood. French was tried, but was equally unintelligible to the majority, and the poor Slavonic enthusiasts, whose only common feeling was a common hatred against the Germans, were at last obliged to express themselves in the hated German language, as the only one that was generally understood! But just then another Slavonic Congress was assembling in Prague, in the shape of Galician lancers, Croatian and Slovak grenadiers, and Bohemian gunners and cuirassiers; and this real, armed Slavonic Congress, under the command of Windischgrätz, in less than twenty-four hours drove the founders of an imaginary Slavonic supremacy out of the town, and dispersed them to the winds.

The Bohemian, Moravian, Dalmatian, and part of the Polish deputies (the aristocracy) to the Austrian Constituent Diet, made in that Assembly a systematic war upon the German element. The Germans, and part of the Poles (the impoverished nobility), were in this Assembly the chief supporters of revolutionary progress; the mass of the Slavonic deputies, in opposing them, were not satisfied with thus showing clearly the reactionary tendencies of their entire movement, but they were degraded enough to tamper and conspire with the very same Austrian Government which had dispersed their meeting at Prague. They, too, were paid for this infamous conduct; after supporting the Government during the insurrection of October 1848, an event which finally secured to them a majority in the Diet, this now almost exclusively Slavonic Diet was dispersed by Austrian soldiers, the same as the Prague Congress, and the Panslavists threatened with imprisonment if they should stir again. And they have only obtained this, that Slavonic nationality is now being everywhere undermined by Austrian centralisation, a result for which they may thank their own fanaticism and blindness.

If the frontiers of Hungary and Germany had admitted of any doubt, there would certainly have been another quarrel there. But, fortunately, there was no pretext, and the interests of both nations being intimately related, they struggled against the same enemies, viz., the Austrian Government and the Panslavistic fanaticism. The good understanding was not for a moment disturbed. But the Italian Revolution entangled at least a part of Germany in an internecine war, and it must be stated here, as a proof how far the Metternichian system had succeeded in keeping back the development of the public mind, that during the first six months of 1848, the same men that had in Vienna mounted the barricades, went, full of enthusiasm, to join the army that fought against the Italian patriots. This deplorable confusion of ideas did not, however, last long.

Lastly, there was the war with Denmark about Schleswig and Holstein. These countries, unquestionably German by nationality, language and predilection, are also from military, naval and commercial grounds necessary to Germany. Their inhabitants have, for the last three years, struggled hard against Danish intrusion. The right of treaties, besides, was for them. The Revolution of March brought them into open collision with the Danes, and Germany supported them. But while in Poland, in Italy, in Bohemia, and later on, in Hungary, military operations were pushed with the utmost vigour, in this the only popular, the only, at least partially, revolutionary war, a system of resultless marches and counter-marches was adopted, and an interference of foreign diplomacy was submitted to, which led, after many an heroic engagement, to a most miserable end. The German Government betrayed, during the war, the Schleswig-Holstein revolutionary army on every occasion, and allowed it purposely to be cut up, when dispersed or divided, by the Danes. The German corps of volunteers were treated the same.

But while thus the German name earned nothing but hatred on every side, the German Constitutional and Liberal Governments rubbed their hands for joy. They had succeeded in crushing the Polish and Bohemian movements. They had everywhere revived the old national animosities, which heretofore had prevented any common understanding and action between the German, the Pole, the Italian. They had accustomed the people to scenes of civil war and repression by the military. The Prussian army had regained its confidence in Poland, the Austrian army in Prague; and while the superabundant patriotism (*"die Patriotische Ueberkraft,"* as Heine has it) of revolutionary but short-sighted youth was led in Schleswig and Lombardy, to be crushed by the grape-shot of the enemy, the regular army, the real instrument of action, both of Prussia and Austria, was placed in a position to regain public favour by victories over the foreigner. But we repeat: these armies, strengthened by the Liberals as a means of action against the more advanced party, no sooner had recovered their self-confidence and their discipline in some degree, than they turned themselves against the

181

Liberals, and restored to power the men of the old system. When Radetzky, in his camp beyond the Adige, received the first orders from the "responsible ministers" at Vienna, he exclaimed: "Who are these ministers? They are not the Government of Austria! Austria is now nowhere but in my camp; I and my army, we are Austria; and when we shall have beaten the Italians we shall reconquer the Empire for the Emperor!" And old Radetzky was right—but the imbecile "responsible" ministers at Vienna heeded him not.

New York Daily Tribune, March 15th, 1852

X

As early as the beginning of April 1848, the revolutionary torrent had found itself stemmed all over the Continent of Europe by the league which those classes of society that had profited by the first victory immediately formed with the vanquished. In France, the petty trading class and the Republican faction of the bourgeoisie had combined with the Monarchist bourgeoisie against the proletarians; in Germany and Italy, the victorious bourgeoisie had eagerly courted the support of the feudal nobility, the official bureaucracy, and the army, against the mass of the people and the petty traders. Very soon the united Conservative and Counter-Revolutionary parties again regained the ascendant. In England, an untimely and ill-prepared popular demonstration (April 10th) turned out a complete and decisive defeat of the popular party. In France, two similar movements (April 16th and May 15th) were equally defeated. In Italy, King Bomba regained his authority by a single stroke on May 15th. In Germany, the different new bourgeois Governments and their respective constituent Assemblies consolidated themselves, and if the eventful May 15th gave rise, in Vienna, to a popular victory, this was an event of merely secondary importance, and may be considered the last successful flash of popular energy. In Hungary the movement appeared to turn into the quiet channel of perfect legality, and the Polish movement, as we have seen in our last, was stifled in the bud by Prussian bayonets. But as yet nothing was decided as to the eventual turn

183

which things would take, and every inch of ground lost by the Revolutionary parties in the different countries only tended to close their ranks more and more for the decisive action.

The decisive action drew near. It could be fought in France only; for France, as long as England took no part in the revolutionary strife, or as Germany remained divided, was, by its national independence, civilisation, and centralisation, the only country to impart the impulse of a mighty convulsion to the surrounding countries. Accordingly, when, on June 23rd, 1848, the bloody struggle began in Paris, when every succeeding telegraph or mail more clearly exposed the fact to the eyes of Europe, that this struggle was carried on between the mass of the working people on the one hand, and all the other classes of the Parisian population, supported by the army, on the other; when the fighting went on for several days with an exasperation unequalled in the history of modern civil warfare, but without any apparent advantage for either side—then it became evident to every one that this was the great decisive battle which would, if the insurrection were victorious, deluge the whole continent with renewed revolutions, or, if it was suppressed, bring about an at least momentary restoration of counter-revolutionary rule.

The proletarians of Paris were defeated, decimated, crushed with such an effect that even now they have not yet recovered from the blow. And immediately, all over Europe, the new and old Conservatives and Counter-Revolutionists raised their heads with an effrontery that showed how well they understood the importance of the event. The Press was everywhere attacked, the rights of meeting and association were interfered with, every little event in every small provincial town was taken profit of to disarm the people to declare a state of siege, to drill the troops in the new manoeuvres and artifices that Cavaignac had taught them. Besides, for the first time since February, the invincibility of a popular insurrection in a large town had been proved to be a delusion; the honour of the armies had been restored; the troops hitherto always defeated in street battles of importance regained confidence in their efficiency even in this kind of struggle.

From this defeat of the *ouvriers* of Paris may be dated the first positive steps and definite plans of the old feudal bureau-cratic party in Germany, to get rid even of their momentary allies, the middle classes, and to restore Germany to the state she was in before the events of March. The army again was the decisive power in the State, and the army belonged not to the middle classes but to themselves. Even in Prussia, where before 1848 a considerable leaning of part of the lower grades of officers towards a Constitutional Government had been ob-served, the disorder introduced into the army by the Revolution had brought back those reasoning young men to their alle-giance; as soon as the private soldier took a few liberties with regard to the officers, the necessity of discipline and passive obedience became at once strikingly evident to them. The van-quished nobles and bureaucrats now began to see their way before them; the army, more united than ever, flushed with victory in minor insurrections and in foreign warfare, jealous of the great success the French soldiers had just attained—this army had only to be kept in constant petty conflicts with the people, and the decisive moment once at hand, it could with one great blow crush the Revolutionists, and set aside the presumptions of the middle-class Parliamentarians. And the proper moment for such a decisive blow arrived soon enough.

We pass over the sometimes curious, but mostly tedious, parliamentary proceedings and local struggles that occupied, in Germany, the different parties during the summer. Suffice it to say that the supporters of the middle-class interest in spite of numerous parliamentary triumphs, not one of which led to any practical result, very generally felt that their position between the extreme parties became daily more untenable, and that, therefore, they were obliged now to seek the alliance of the reactionists, and the next day to court the favour of the more popular factions. This constant vacillation gave the finishing stroke to their character in public opinion, and according to the turn events were taking, the contempt into which they had sunk, profited for the movement principally to the bureaucrats and feudalists.

By the beginning of autumn the relative position of the different parties had become exasperated and critical enough to make a decisive battle inevitable. The first engagements in this war between the democratic and revolutionary masses and the army took place at Frankfort. Though a mere secondary engagement, it was the first advantage of any note the troops acquired over the insurrection, and had a great moral effect. The fancy Government established by the Frankfort National Assembly had been allowed by Prussia, for very obvious reasons, to conclude an armistice with Denmark, which not only surrendered to Danish vengeance the Germans of Schleswig, but which also entirely disclaimed the more or less revolutionary principles which were generally supposed in the Danish war. This armistice was, by a majority of two or three, rejected in the Frankfort Assembly. A sham ministerial crisis followed this vote, but three days later the Assembly reconsidered their vote, and were actually induced to cancel it and acknowledge the armistice. This disgraceful proceeding roused the indignation of the people. Barricades were erected, but already sufficient troops had been drawn to Frankfort, and after six hours' fighting, the insurrection was suppressed. Similar, but less important, movements connected with this event took place in other parts of Germany (Baden, Cologne), but were equally defeated.

This preliminary engagement gave to the Counter-Revolutionary party the one great advantage, that now the only Government which had entirely—at least in semblance— originated with popular election, the Imperial Government of Frankfort, as well as the National Assembly, was ruined in the eyes of the people. This Government and this Assembly had been obliged to appeal to the bayonets of the troops against the manifestation of the popular will. They were compromised, and what little regard they might have been hitherto enabled to claim, this repudiation of their origin, the dependency upon the anti-popular Governments and their troops, made both the Lieutenant of the Empire, his ministers and his deputies, henceforth to be complete nullities. We shall soon see how first Austria, then Prussia, and later on the smaller States too, treated with contempt every order, every request, every deputation they received from this body of impotent dreamers.

We now come to the great counter-stroke in Germany, of the French battle of June, to that event which was as decisive for Germany as the proletarian struggle of Paris had been for France; we mean the revolution and subsequent storming of Vienna, October 1848. But the importance of this battle is such, and the explanation of the different circumstances that more immediately contributed to its issue will take up such a portion of the *Tribune's* columns, as to necessitate its being treated in a separate letter.

New York Daily Tribune, March 18th, 1852

XI

London, March 1852

WE now come to the decisive events which formed the counter-revolutionary part in Germany to the Parisian insurrection of June, and which, by a single blow, turned the scale in favour of the Counter-Revolutionary party,—the insurrection of October 1848, in Vienna.

We have seen what the position of the different classes was, in Vienna, after the victory of March 12th. We have also seen how the movement of German-Austria was entangled with and impeded by the events in the non-German provinces of Austria. It only remains for us, then, briefly to survey the causes which led to the last and most formidable rising of German-Austria.

The high aristocracy and the stock-jobbing bourgeoisie, which had formed the principal non-official supports of the Metternichian Government, were enabled, even after the events of March, to maintain a predominating influence with the Government, not only by the Court, the army and the bureaucracy, but still more by the horror of "anarchy," which rapidly spread among the middle classes. They very soon ventured a few feelers in the shape of a Press Law, a nondescript Aristocratic Constitution, and an Electoral Law based upon the old division of "estates." The so-called Constitutional ministry, consisting of half Liberal, timid, incapable bureaucrats, on May 14th, even ventured a direct attack upon the revolutionary organisations of the masses by dissolving the Central Committee of Delegates of the National Guard and Academic Legion, a body formed for the express purpose of controlling the Government, and calling out against it, in case of need, the popular forces. But this act only provoked the insurrection of May 15th, by which the Government was forced to acknowledge the Committee, to repeal the Constitution and the Electoral Law, and to grant the power of framing a new Fundamental Law to a Constitutional Diet, elected by universal suffrage. All this was confirmed on the following day by an Imperial proclamation. But the reactionary party, which also had its representatives in the ministry, soon got their "Liberal" colleagues to undertake a new attack upon the popular conquests. The Academic Legion, the stronghold of the movement party, the centre of continuous agitation, had, on this very account, become obnoxious to the more moderate burghers of Vienna; on the 26th a ministerial decree dissolved it. Perhaps this blow might have succeeded, if it had been carried out by a part of the National Guard only, but the Government, not trusting them either, brought the military forward, and at once the National Guard turned round, united with the Academic Legion, and thus frustrated the ministerial project.

In the meantime, however, the Emperor and his Court had, on May 16th, left Vienna, and fled to Innsbruck. Here, surrounded by the bigoted Tyroleans, whose loyalty was roused again by the danger of an invasion of their country by the Sardo-Lombardian army, supported by the vicinity of Radetzky's troops, with shell-range of whom Innsbruck lay, here the Counter-Revolutionary party found an asylum, from whence, uncontrolled, unobserved and safe, it might rally its scattered forces, repair and spread again all over the country the network of its plots. Communications were reopened with Radetzky, with Jellachich, and with Windischgrätz, as well as with the reliable men in the administrative hierarchy of the different provinces; intrigues were set on foot with the Slavonic chiefs, and thus a real force at the disposal of the Counter-Revolutionary *camarilla* was formed, while the impotent ministers in Vienna were allowed to wear their short and feeble popularity out in continual bickerings with the revolutionary masses, and in the debates of the forthcoming Constituent Assembly. Thus the policy of leaving the movement of the capital to itself for a time; a policy which must have led to the omnipotence of the movement party in a centralised and homogeneous country like France, here in Austria, in heterogeneous political conglomerate, was one of the safest means of reorganising the strength of the reactionists.

In Vienna the middle class, persuaded that after three successive defeats, and in the face of a Constituent Assembly based upon universal suffrage, the Court was no longer an opponent to be dreaded, fell more and more into that weariness and apathy, and that eternal outcry for order and tranquillity, which has everywhere seized this class after violent commotions and consequent derangement of trade. The manufactures of the Austrian capital are almost exclusively limited to articles of luxury, for which, since the Revolution and the flight of the Court, there had necessarily been little demand. The shout for a return to a regular system of government, and for a return of the Court, both of which were expected to bring about a revival of commercial prosperity—this shout became now general among the middle classes. The meeting of the Constituent Assembly in July was hailed with delight as the end of the revolutionary era; so was the return of the Court, which, after the victories of Radetzky in Italy, and after the advent of the reactionary ministry of Doblhoff, considered itself strong enough to brave the popular torrent, and which, at the same time, was wanted in Vienna in order to complete its intrigues with the Slavonic majority of the Diet. While the Constituent Diet discussed the laws on the emancipation of the peasantry from feudal bondage and forced labour for the nobility, the Court completed a master stroke. On August 19th the Emperor was made to review the National Guard; the Imperial family, the courtiers, the general officers, outbade each other in flatteries to the armed burghers who were already intoxicated with pride at thus seeing themselves publicly acknowledged as one of the important bodies of the State; and immediately afterwards a decree, signed by Herr Schwarzer, the only popular minister in the Cabinet, was published, withdrawing the Government aid, given hitherto to the workmen out of employ. The trick succeeded; the working classes got up a demonstration; the middle-class National Guards declared for the decree of their minister; they were launched upon the "Anarchists," fell like tigers on the unarmed and unresisting workpeople, and massacred a great number of them on August 23rd. Thus the unity and strength of the revolutionary force was broken; the class-struggle between bourgeois and proletarian had come in Vienna, too, to a bloody outbreak, and the counter-revolutionary *camarilla* saw the day approaching on which it might strike its grand blow.

The Hungarian affairs very soon offered an opportunity to proclaim openly the principles upon which it intended to act. On October 5th an Imperial decree in the *Vienna Gazette*—a decree countersigned by none of the responsible ministers for Hungary—declared the Hungarian Diet dissolved, and named the Ban Jellachich, of Croatia, Civil and Military Governor of that country—Jellachich, the leader of South Slavonian reaction, a man who was actually at war with the lawful authorities of Hungary. At the same time orders were given to the troops in Vienna to march out and form part of the army which was to enforce Jellachich's authority. This, however, was showing the cloven foot too openly; every man in Vienna felt that war upon Hungary was war upon the principle of Constitutional Government, which principle was in the very decree trampled upon by the attempt of the Emperor to make decrees with legal force, without the countersign of a responsible minister. The people, the Academic Legion, the National Guard of Vienna, on October 6th rose in mass, and resisted the departure of the troops; some grenadiers passed over to the people, a short struggle took place between the popular forces and the troops; the Minister of War, Latour, was massacred by the people, and in the evening the latter were victors. In the meantime, Ban Jellachich, beaten at Stuhlweissenburg by Perczel, had taken refuge near Vienna on German-Austrian territory; the Viennese troops that were to march to his support now took up an ostensibly hostile and defensive position against him; and the Emperor and Court had again fled to Olmütz, on semi-Slavonic territory.

But at Olmütz the Court found itself in very different circumstances from what it had been at Innsbruck. It was now in a position to open immediately the campaign against the Revolution. It was surrounded by the Slavonian deputies of the Constituent, who flocked in masses to Olmütz, and by the Slavonian enthusiasts from all parts of the monarchy. The campaign, in their eyes, was to be a war of Slavonian restoration and of extermination, against the two intruders, upon what was considered Slavonian soil, against the German and the Magyar. Windischgrätz, the conqueror of Prague, now commander of the army that was concentrated around Vienna, became at once the hero of Slavonian nationality. And his army concentrated rapidly from all sides. From Bohemia, Moravia, Styria, Upper Austria, and Italy, marched regiment after regiment on routes that converged at Vienna, to join the troops of Jellachich and the ex-garrison of the capital. Above sixty thousand men were thus united towards the end of October, and soon they commenced hemming in the Imperial city on all sides, until, on October 30th, they were far enough advanced to venture upon the decisive attack.

In Vienna, in the meantime, confusion and helplessness was prevalent. The middle class, as soon as the victory was gained, became again possessed of their old distrust against the "anarchic" working classes; the working men, mindful of the treatment they had received, six weeks before, at the hands of the armed tradesmen, and of the unsteady, wavering policy of the middle class at large, would not trust to them defence of the city, and demanded arms and military organisation for themselves. The Academic Legion, full of zeal for the struggle against Imperial despotism, were entirely incapable of understanding the nature of the estrangement of the two classes, or of otherwise comprehending the necessities of the situation. There was confusion in the public mind, confusion in the ruling councils. The remnant of the German Diet deputies, and a few Slavonians, acting the part of spies for their friends at Olmütz, besides a few of the more revolutionary Polish deputies, sat in permanency; but instead of taking part resolutely, they lost all their time in idle debates upon the possibility of resisting the Imperial army without overstepping the bounds of constitutional conventionalities. The Committee of Safety, composed of deputies from almost all the popular bodies of Vienna, although resolved to resist, was yet dominated by a majority of burghers and petty tradesmen, who never allowed it to follow up any determined, energetic line of action. The Council of the Academic Legion passed heroic resolutions, but was no ways able to take the lead. The working classes, distrusted, disarmed, disorganised, hardly emerging from the intellectual bondage of the old regime, hardly awaking, not to a knowledge, but to a mere instinct of their social position and proper political line of action, could only make themselves heard by loud demonstrations, and could not be expected to be up to the difficulties of the moment. But they were ready—as they ever were in Germany during the Revolution—to fight to the last, as soon as they obtained arms.

That was the state of things in Vienna. Outside, the reorganised Austrian army flushed with the victories of Radetzky in Italy; sixty or seventy thousand men well armed, well organised, and if not well commanded at least possessing commanders. Inside, confusion, class division, disorganisation; a National Guard, part of which was resolved not to fight at all, part irresolute, and only the smallest part ready to act; a proletarian mass, powerful by numbers but without leaders, without any political education, subject to panic as well as to fits of fury almost without cause, a prey to every false rumour spread about, quite ready to fight, but unarmed, at least in the beginning, and incompletely armed, and barely organised when at last they were led to battle; a helpless Diet, discussing theoretical quibbles while the roof over their heads was almost burning; a leading Committee without impulse or energy. Everything was changed from the days of March and May, when, in the Counter-Revolutionary camp, all was confusion, and when the only organised force was that created by the Revolution. There could hardly be a doubt about the issue of such a struggle, and whatever doubt there might be, was settled by the events of October 30th and 31st, and November 1st.

New York Daily Tribune, March 19th, 1852

XII

London, March 1852

WHEN at last the concentrated army of Windischgrätz commenced the attack upon Vienna, the forces that could be brought forward in defence were exceedingly insufficient for the purpose. Of the National Guard only a portion was to be brought to the entrenchments. A Proletarian Guard, it is true, had at last been hastily formed, but owing to the lateness of the attempt to thus make available the most numerous, most daring, and most energetic part of the population, it was too little inured to the use of arms and to the very first rudiments of discipline to offer a successful resistance. Thus the Academic Legion, three to four thousand strong, well exercised and disciplined to a certain degree, brave and enthusiastic, was, militarily speaking, the only force which was in a state to do its work successfully. But what were they, together with the few reliable National Guards, and with the confused mass of the armed proletarians, in opposition to the far more numerous regulars of Windischgrätz, not counting even the brigand hordes of Jellachich, hordes that were, by the very nature of their habits, very useful in a war from house to house, from lane to lane? And what but a few old, out-worn, ill-mounted, and ill-served pieces of ordnance had the insurgents to oppose to that numerous and well-appointed artillery, of which Windischgrätz made such an unscrupulous use?

The nearer the danger drew, the more grew the confusion in Vienna. The Diet, up to the last moment, could not collect sufficient energy to call in for aid the Hungarian army of Perc-zel, encamped a few leagues below the capital. The Committee passed contradictory resolutions, they themselves being, like the popular armed masses, floated up and down with the alternate-ly rising and receding tide of rumours and counter-rumours. There was only one thing upon which all agreed—to respect property; and this was done in a degree almost ludicrous for such times. As to the final arrangement of a plan of defence, very little was done. Bem, the only man present who could have saved Vienna, if any could then in Vienna, an almost unknown foreigner, a Slavonian by birth, gave up the task, overwhelmed as he was by universal distrust. Had he persevered, he might have been lynched as a traitor. Messenhauser, the commander of the insurgent forces, more of a novel-writer than even of a subaltern officer, was totally inadequate to the task; and yet, after eight months of revolutionary struggles, the popular party had not produced or acquired a military man of more ability than he. Thus the contest began. The Viennese, considering their utterly inadequate means of defence, considering their utter absence of military skill and organisation in the ranks, offered a most heroic resistance. In many places the order given by Bem, when he was in command, "to defend that post to the last man," was carried out to the letter. But force prevailed. Barricade after barricade was swept away by the Imperial artillery in the long and wide avenues which form the main streets of the suburbs; and on the evening of the second day's fighting the Croats occupied the range of houses facing the glacis of the Old Town. A feeble and disorderly attack of the Hungarian army had been utterly defeated; and during an armistice, while some parties in the Old Town capitulated, while others hesitated and spread confusion, while the rem-nants of the Academic Legion prepared fresh entrenchments, and entrance was made by the Imperialists, and in the midst of the general disorder the Old Town was carried.

The immediate consequences of this victory, the brutalities and executions by martial law, the unheard-of cruelties and infamies committed by the Slavonian hordes let loose upon

Vienna, are too well known to be detailed here. The ulterior consequences, the entirely new turn given to German affairs by the defeat of the Revolution in Vienna, we shall have reason to notice hereafter. There remain two points to be considered in connection with the storming of Vienna. The people of that capital had two allies—the Hungarians and the German people. Where were they in the hour of trial?

We have seen that the Viennese, with all the generosity of a newly freed people, had risen for a cause which, though ultimately their own, was, in the first instance, and above all, that of the Hungarians. Rather than suffer the Austrian troops to march upon Hungary, they would draw their first and most terrific onslaught upon themselves. And while they thus nobly came forward for the support of their allies, the Hungarians, successful against Jellachich, drove him upon Vienna, and by their victory strengthened the force that was to attack that town. Under these circumstances it was the clear duty of Hungary to support, without delay, and with all disposable forces, not the Diet of Vienna, not the Committee of Safety or any other official body at Vienna, but the *Viennese Revolution*. And if Hungary should even have forgotten that Vienna had fought the first battle of Hungary, she owed it to her own safety not to forget that Vienna was the only outpost of Hungarian independence, and that after the fall of Vienna nothing could meet the advance of the Imperial troops against herself. Now, we know very well all the Hungarians can say and have said in defence of their inactivity during the blockade and storming of Vienna: the insufficient state of their own force, the refusal of the Diet or any other official body in Vienna to call them in, the necessity to keep on constitutional ground, and to avoid complications with the German Central power. But the fact is, as to the insufficient state of the Hungarian army, that in the first days after the Viennese Revolution and the arrival of Jellachich, nothing was wanted in the shape of regular troops, as the Austrian regulars were very far from being concentrated; and that a courageous, unrelenting following up of the first advantage over Jellachich, even with nothing but the *Land Sturm* that had fought at Stuhlweissenburg, would have sufficed to effect a junction with the Viennese, and to adjourn to that day six months every concentration of an Austrian army. In war, and particularly in revolutionary warfare, rapidity of action until some decided advantage is gained is the first rule, and we have no hesitation in saying that upon *merely military grounds*, Perczel ought not to have stopped until his junction with the Viennese was effected. There was certainly some risk, but who ever won a battle without risking something? And did the people of Vienna risk nothing when they drew upon themselves—they, a population of four hundred thousand—the forces that were to march to the conquest of twelve millions of Hungarians? The military fault committed by waiting until the Austrians had united, and by making the feeble demonstration at Schwechat which ended, as it deserved to do, in an inglorious defeat—this military fault certainly incurred more risks than a resolute march upon Vienna against the disbanded brigands of Jellachich would have done.

But, it is said, such an advance of the Hungarians, unless authorised by some official body, would have been a violation of the German territory, would have brought on complications with the Central Power at Frankfort, and would have been, above all, an abandonment of the legal and constitutional policy which formed the strength of the Hungarian cause. Why, the official bodies in Vienna were nonentities! Was it the Diet, was it the popular Committees, who had risen for Hungary, or was it the people of Vienna, and they alone, who had taken to the musket to stand the brunt of the first battle for Hungary's independence? It was not this nor that official body in Vienna which it was important to uphold; all these bodies might, and would have been, upset very soon in the progress of the revolutionary development; but it was the ascendancy of the revolutionary movement, the unbroken progress of popular action itself, which alone was in question, and which alone could save Hungary from invasion. What forms this revolutionary movement afterwards might take, was the business of the Viennese, not of the Hungarians, so long as Vienna and German Austria at large continued their allies against the common enemy. But the question is, whether in this stickling of the Hungarian Government for some quasi-legal authorisation, we are not to see the first clear symptom of that pretence to a rather doubtful legality of proceeding, which, if it did not save Hungary, at least told very well, at a later period, before the English middle-class audiences.

As to the pretext of possible conflicts with the Central Power of Germany at Frankfort, it is quite futile. The Frankfort authorities were *de facto* upset by the victory of the Counter-Revolution at Vienna; they would have been equally upset had the Revolution there found the support necessary to defeat its enemies. And lastly, the great argument that Hungary could not leave legal and constitutional ground, may do very well for British free-traders, but it will never be deemed sufficient in the eyes of history. Suppose the people of Vienna had stuck to "legal and constitutional means" on March 13th, and on October 6th, what then of the "legal and constitutional" movement, and of all the glorious battles which, for the first time, brought Hungary to the notice of the civilised world? The very legal and constitutional ground upon which it is asserted the Hungarians moved in 1848 and 1849 was conquered for them by the exceedingly illegal and unconstitutional rising of the people of Vienna on March 13th. It is not to our purpose here to discuss the revolutionary history of Hungary, but it may be deemed proper if we observe that it is utterly useless to professedly use merely legal means of resistance against an enemy who scorns such scruples; and if we add, that had it not been for this eternal pretence of legality which Görgey seized upon and turned against the Government, the devotion of Görgey's army to its general, and the disgraceful catastrophe of Villagos, would have been impossible. And when, at last, to save their honour, the Hungarians came across the Leitha, in the latter end of October 1848, was not this quite as illegal as any immediate and resolute attack would have been?

We are known to harbour no unfriendly feeling toward Hungary. We stood by her during the struggles; we may be allowed to say that our paper, the *Neue Rheinische Zeitung,* has done more than any other to render the Hungarian cause popular in Germany, by explaining the nature of the struggle between the Magyar and Slavonian races, and by following up the Hungarian war in a series of articles which have had paid them the compliment of being plagiarised in almost every subsequent book upon the subject, the works of native Hungarians and "eye-witnesses" not excepted. We even now, in any future continental convulsion, consider Hungary as the necessary and natural ally of Germany. But we have been severe enough upon our own countrymen, to have a right to speak out upon our neighbours; and then we have here to record facts with historical impartiality, and we must say that in this particular instance, the generous bravery of the people of Vienna was not only far more noble, but also more far-sighted than the cautious circumspection of the Hungarian Government. And, as a German, we may further be allowed to say, that not for all the showy victories and glorious battles of the Hungarian campaign, would we exchange that spontaneous, single-handed rising, and heroic resistance of the people of Vienna, our countrymen, which gave Hungary the time to organise the army that could do such great things.

The second ally of Vienna was the German people. But they were everywhere engaged in the same struggle as the Viennese. Frankfort, Baden, Cologne, had just been defeated and disarmed. In Berlin and Breslau the people were at daggers drawn with the army, and daily expected to come to blows. Thus it was in every local centre of action. Everywhere questions were pending that could only be settled by the force of arms; and now it was that for the first time were severely felt the disastrous consequences of the continuation of the old dismemberment and decentralisation of Germany. The different questions in every State, every province, every town, were fundamentally the same; but they were brought forward everywhere under different shapes and pretexts, and had everywhere attained different degrees of maturity. Thus it happened that while in every locality the decisive gravity of the events at Vienna was felt, yet nowhere could an important blow be struck with any hope of bringing the Viennese succour, or making a diversion in their favour; and there remained nothing to aid them but the Parliament and Central Power of Frankfort; they were appealed to on all hands; but what did they do?

The Frankfort Parliament and the bastard child it had brought to light by incestuous intercourse with the old German Diet, the so-called Central Power, profited by the Viennese movement to show forth their utter nullity. This contemptible Assembly, as we have seen, had long since sacrificed its virginity, and young as it was, it was already turning grey-headed and experienced in all the artifices of prating and pseudo-diplomatic prostitution. Of the dreams and illusions of power, of German regeneration and unity, that in the beginning had pervaded it, nothing remained but a set of Teutonic claptrap phraseology, that was repeated on every occasion, and a firm belief of each individual member in his own importance, as well as in the credulity of the public. The original naïveté was discarded; the representatives of the German people had turned practical men, that is to say, they had made it out that the less they did, and the more they prated, the safer would be their position as the umpires of the fate of Germany. Not that they considered their proceedings superfluous; quite the contrary. But they had found out that all really great questions, being to them forbidden ground, had better be let alone, and there, like a set of Byzantine doctors of the Lower Empire, they discussed with an importance and assiduity worthy of the fate that at last overtook them, theoretical dogmas long ago settled in every part of the civilised world, or microscopical practical questions which never led to any practical result. Thus, the Assembly being a sort of Lancastrian School for the mutual instruction of members, and being, therefore, very important to themselves, they were persuaded it was doing even more than the German people had a right to expect, and looked upon everyone as a traitor to the country who had the impudence to ask them to come to any result.

When the Viennese insurrection broke out, there was a host

of interpellations, debates, motions, and amendments upon it, which, of course, led to nothing. The Central Power was to interfere. It sent two commissioners, Welcker; the ex-Liberal, and Mosle, to Vienna. The travels of Don Quixote and Sancho Panza form matter for an Odyssey in comparison with the heroic feats and wonderful adventures of those two knight-errants of German Unity. Not daring to go to Vienna, they were bullied by Windischgrätz, wondered at by the idiot Emperor, and impudently hoaxed by the Minister Stadion. Their des-patches and reports are perhaps the only portion of the Frank-fort transactions that will retain a place in German literature; they are a perfect satirical romance, ready cut and dried, and an eternal monument of disgrace for the Frankfort Assembly and its Government.

The left side of the Assembly had also sent two commission-ers to Vienna, in order to uphold its authority there—Froebel and Robert Blum. Blum, when danger drew near, judged right-ly that here the great battle of the German Revolution was to be fought, and unhesitatingly resolved to stake his head on the issue. Froebel, on the contrary, was of opinion that it was his duty to preserve himself for the important duties of his post at Frankfort. Blum was considered one of the most eloquent men of the Frankfort Assembly; he certainly was the most popular. His eloquence would not have stood the test of any experienced Parliamentary Assembly; he was too fond of the shallow dec-lamations of a German dissenting preacher, and his arguments wanted both philosophical acumen and acquaintance with prac-tical matters of fact. In politics he belonged to "Moderate Democracy," a rather indefinite sort of thing, cherished on account of this very want of definiteness in its principles. But with all this Robert Blum was by nature a thorough, though somewhat polished, plebeian, and in decisive moments his plebeian instinct and plebeian energy got the better of his indefiniteness, and, therefore, indecisive political persuasion and knowledge. In such moments he raised himself far above the usual standard of his capacities.

Thus, in Vienna, he saw at a glance that here, not in the midst of the would-be elegant debates of Frankfort, the fate of his country would have to be decided. He at once made up his mind, gave up all idea of retreat, took a command in the revolutionary force, and behaved with extraordinary coolness and decision. It was he who retarded for a considerable time the taking of the town, and covered one of its sides from attack by burning the Tabor Bridge over the Danube. Everybody knows how, after the storming, he was arrested, tried by court-martial, and shot. He died like a hero. And the Frankfort Assembly, horror-struck as it was, yet took the bloody insult with a seeming good grace. A resolution was carried, which, by the softness and diplomatic decency of its language, was more an insult to the grave of the murdered martyr than a damning stain upon Austria. But it was not to be expected that this contemptible Assembly should resent the assassination of one of its members, particularly of the leader of the Left.

New York Daily Tribune, April 9th, 1852

XIII

London, March 1852

ON November 1st Vienna fell, and on the 9th of the same month the dissolution of the Constituent Assembly in Berlin showed how much this event had at once raised the spirit and the strength of the Counter-Revolutionary party all over Germany.

The events of the summer of 1848 in Prussia are soon told. The Constituent Assembly, or rather "the Assembly elected for the purpose of agreeing upon a Constitution with the Crown," and its majority of representatives of the middle-class interest, had long since forfeited all public esteem by lending itself to the intrigues of the Court, from fear of the more energetic elements of the population. They had confirmed, or rather restored, the obnoxious privileges of feudalism, and thus betrayed the liberty and the interests of the peasantry. They had neither been able to draw up a Constitution, nor to amend in any way the general legislation. They had occupied themselves almost exclusively with nice theoretical distinctions, mere formalities, and questions of constitutional etiquette. The Assembly, in fact, was more a school of Parliamentary *savoir vivre* for its members, than a body in which the people could take any interest. The majorities were, besides, very nicely balanced, and almost always decided by the wavering centres whose oscillations from right to left, and vice versa, upset, first the ministry of Camphausen, then that of Auerswald and Hansemann. But while thus the Liberals, here as everywhere else, let the occasion slip out of their hands, the Court reorganised its elements of

204

strength among the nobility, and the most uncultivated portion of the rural population, as well as in the army and the bureaucracy. After Hansemann's downfall, a ministry of bureaucrats and military officers, all staunch reactionists, was formed, which, however, seemingly gave way to the demand of the Parliament; and the Assembly acting upon the commodious principle of "measures, not men," were actually duped into applauding this ministry, while they, of course, had no eyes for the concentration and organisation of Counter-Revolutionary forces, which that same ministry carried on pretty openly. At last, the signal being given by the fall of Vienna, the King dismissed its ministers, and replaced them by "men of action," under the leadership of the present premier, Manteufel. Then the dreaming Assembly at once awoke to the danger; it passed a vote of no confidence in the Cabinet, which was at once replied to by a decree removing the Assembly from Berlin, where it might, in case of a conflict, count upon the support of the masses, to Brandenburg, a petty provincial town dependent entirely upon the Government. The Assembly, however, declared that it could not be adjourned, removed, or dissolved, except with its own consent. In the meantime, General Wrangel entered Berlin at the head of some forty thousand troops. In a meeting of the municipal magistrates and the officers of the National Guard, it was resolved not to offer any resistance. And now, after the Assembly and its Constituents, the Liberal bourgeoisie, had allowed the combined reactionary party to occupy every important position, and to wrest from their hands almost every means of defence, began that grand comedy of "passive and legal resistance" which they intended to be a glorious imitation of the example of Hampden, and of the first efforts of the Americans of the War of Independence. Berlin was declared in a state of siege, and Berlin remained tranquil; the National Guard was dissolved by the Government, and its arms were delivered up with the greatest punctuality. The Assembly was hunted down during a fortnight, from one place of meeting to another, and everywhere dispersed by the military, and the members of the Assembly begged of the citizens to remain tranquil. At last the Government having declared the Assembly dissolved, it passed a resolution to declare the levying of taxes illegal, and then its members dispersed themselves over the country to organise the refusal of taxes. But they found that they had been woefully mistaken in the choice of their means. After a few agitated weeks followed by severe measures of the Government against the Opposition, everyone gave up the idea of refusing the taxes in order to please a defunct Assembly that had not even had the courage to defend itself.

Whether it was in the beginning of November 1848, already too late to try armed resistance, or whether a part of the army, on finding serious opposition, would have turned over to the side of the Assembly, and thus decided the matter in its favour, is a question which may never be solved. But in revolution as in war, it is always necessary to show a strong front, and he who attacks is in the advantage; and in revolution as in war, it is of the highest necessity to stake everything on the decisive moment, whatever the odds may be. There is not a single successful revolution in history that does not prove the truth of these axioms. Now, for the Prussian Revolution, the decisive moment had come in November 1848; the Assembly, at the head, officially, of the whole revolutionary interest, did neither show a strong front, for it receded at every advance of the enemy; much less did it attack, for it chose even not to defend itself; and when the decisive moment came, when Wrangel, at the head of forty thousand men, knocked at the gates of Berlin, instead of finding as he and all his officers fully expected, every street studded with barricades, every window turned into a loop-hole, he found the gates open, and the streets obstructed only by peaceful Berliner burghers, enjoying the joke they had played upon him, by delivering themselves up, hands and feet tied, unto the astonished soldiers. It is true, the Assembly and the people, if they had resisted, might have been beaten; Berlin might have been bombarded, and many hundreds might have been killed, without preventing the ultimate victory of the Royalist party. But that was no reason why they should surrender their arms at once. A well-contested defeat is a fact of as much revolutionary importance as an easily-won victory. The defeats of Paris in June 1848 and of Vienna in October, certainly did far more in revolutionising the minds of the people of these two cities than the victories of February and March. The Assembly and the people of Berlin would, probably, have shared the fate of the two towns above-named; but they would have fallen gloriously, and would have left behind themselves, in the minds of the survivors, a wish of revenge, which in revolutionary times is one of the highest incentives to energetic and passionate action. It is a matter of course that, in every struggle, he who takes up the gauntlet risks being beaten; but is that a reason why he should confess himself beaten, and submit to the yoke without drawing the sword?

In a revolution he who commands a decisive position and surrenders it, instead of forcing the enemy to try his hand at an assault, invariably deserves to be treated as a traitor.

The same decree of the King of Prussia which dissolved the Constituent Assembly also proclaimed a new Constitution, founded upon the draft which had been made by a Committee of that Assembly, but enlarging in some points the powers of the Crown, and rendering doubtful in others those of the Parliament. This Constitution established two Chambers, which were to meet soon for the purpose of confirming and revising it.

We need hardly ask where the German National Assembly was during the "legal and peaceful" struggle of the Prussian Constitutionalists. It was, as usual, at Frankfort, occupied with passing very tame resolutions against the proceedings of the Prussian Government, and admiring the "imposing spectacle of the passive, legal, and unanimous resistance of a whole people against brutal force." The Central Government sent commissioners to Berlin to intercede between the Ministry and the Assembly; but they met the same fate as their predecessors at Olmütz, and were politely shown out. The Left of the National Assembly, i.e., the so-called Radical party, sent also their commissioners; but after having duly convinced themselves of the utter helplessness of the Berlin Assembly, and confessed their own equal helplessness, they returned to Frankfort to report progress, and to testify to the admirably peaceful conduct of the population of Berlin. Nay, more; when Herr Bassermann, one of the Central Government's commissioners, reported that the late stringent measures of the Prussian ministers were not without foundation, inasmuch as there had of late been seen loitering about the streets of Berlin sundry savage-looking characters, such as always appear previous to anarchical movements (and which ever since have been named "Bassermannic characters"), these worthy deputies of the Left and energetic representatives of the revolutionary interest actually arose to make oath, and testify that such was not the case! Thus within two months the total impotency of the Frankfort Assembly was signally proved. There could be no more glaring proofs that this body was totally inadequate to its task; nay, that it had not even the remotest idea of what its task really was. The fact that both in Vienna and in Berlin the fate of the Revolution was settled, that in both these capitals the most important and vital questions were disposed of, without the existence of the Frankfort Assembly ever being taken the slightest notice of—this fact alone is sufficient to establish that the body in question was a mere debating-club, composed of a set of dupes, who allowed the Governments to use them as a Parliamentary puppet, shown to amuse the shopkeepers and petty tradesmen of petty States and petty towns, as long as it was considered convenient to divert the attention of these parties. How long this was considered convenient we shall soon see. But it is a fact worthy of attention that among all the "eminent" men of this Assembly there was not one who had the slightest apprehension of the part they were made to perform, and that even up to the present day exmembers of the Frankfort club have invariably organs of historical perception quite peculiar to themselves.

New York Daily Tribune, April 17th, 1852

XIV

THE first months of the year 1849 were employed by the Austrian and Prussian Governments in following up the advantages obtained in October and November 1848. The Austrian Diet, ever since the taking of Vienna, had carried on a merely nominal existence in a small Moravian country town, named Kremsir. Here the Slavonian deputies, who, with their constituents, had been mainly instrumental in raising the Austrian Government from its prostration, were singularly punished for their treachery against the European Revolution. As soon as the Government had recovered its strength, it treated the Diet and its Slavonian majority with the utmost contempt, and when the first successes of the Imperial arms foreboded a speedy termination of the Hungarian War, the Diet, on March 4th, was dissolved, and the deputies dispersed by military force. Then at last the Slavonians saw that they were duped, and then they shouted: "Let us go to Frankfort and carry on there the opposition which we cannot pursue here!" But it was then too late, and the very fact that they had no other alternative than either to remain quiet or to join the impotent Frankfort Assembly, this fact alone was sufficient to show their utter helplessmess.

Thus ended for the present, and most likely for ever, the attempts of the Slavonians of Germany to recover an independent national existence. Scattered remnants of numerous nations, whose nationality and political vitality had long been extinguished, and who in consequence had been obliged, for almost a thousand years, to follow in the wake of a mightier nation, their conqueror, the same as the Welsh in England, the Basques in Spain, the Bas-Bretons in France, and at a more recent period the Spanish and French Creoles in those portions of North America occupied of late by the Anglo-American race—these dying nationalities, the Bohemians, Carinthians, Dalmatians, etc., had tried to profit by the universal confusion of 1848, in order to restore their political *status quo* of A.D. 800. The history of a thousand years ought to have shown them that such a retrogression was impossible; that if all the territory east of the Elbe and Saale had at one time been occupied by kindred Slavonians, this fact merely proved the historical tendency, and at the same time physical and intellectual power of the German nation to subdue, absorb, and assimilate its ancient eastern neighbours; that this tendency of absorption on the part of the Germans had always been, and still was, one of the mightiest means by which the civilisation of Western Europe had been spread in the east of that continent; that it could only cease whenever the process of Germanisation had reached the frontier of large, compact, unbroken nations, capable of an independent national life, such as the Hungarians, and in some degree the Poles; and that, therefore, the natural and inevitable fate of these dying nations was to allow this process of dissolution and absorption by their stronger neighbours to complete itself. Certainly this is no very flattering prospect for the national ambition of the Panslavistic dreamers who succeeded in agitating a portion of the Bohemian and South Slavonian people; but can they expect that history would retrograde a thousand years in order to please a few phthisical bodies of men, who in every part of the territory they occupy are interspersed with and surrounded by Germans, who from time almost immemorial have had for all purposes of civilisation no other language but the German, and who lack the very first conditions of national existence, numbers and compactness of territory? Thus, the Panslavistic rising, which everywhere in the German and Hungarian Slavonic territories was the cloak for the restoration to independence of all these numberless petty nations, everywhere clashed with the European revolutionary movements, and the Slavonians, although pretending to fight for liberty, were invariably (the Democratic portion of the Poles excepted) found on the side of despotism and reaction. Thus it was in Germany, thus in Hungary, thus even here and there in Turkey. Traitors to the popular cause, supporters and chief props to the Austrian Government's cabal, they placed themselves in the position of outlaws in the eyes of all revolutionary nations. And although nowhere the mass of the people had a part in the petty squabbles about nationality raised by the Panslavistic leaders, for the very reason that they were too ignorant, yet it will never be forgotten that in Prague, in a half-German town, crowds of Slavonian fanatics cheered and repeated the cry: "Rather the Russian knout than German Liberty!" After their first evaporated effort in 1848, and after the lesson the Austrian Government gave them, it is not likely that another attempt at a later opportunity will be made. But if they should try again under similar pretexts to ally themselves to the counter-revolutionary force, the duty of Germany is clear. No country in a state of revolution and involved in external war can tolerate a Vendée in its very heart.

As to the Constitution proclaimed by the Emperor at the same time with the dissolution of the Diet, there is no need to revert to it, as it never had a practical existence, and is now done away with altogether. Absolutism had been restored in Austria to all intents and purposes ever since March 4th, 1849.

In Prussia, the Chambers met in February for the ratification and revision of the new Charter proclaimed by the King. They sat for about six weeks, humble and meek enough in their behaviour toward the Government, yet not quite prepared to go the lengths the King and his ministers wished them to go. Therefore, as soon as a suitable occasion presented itself, they were dissolved.

Thus both Austria and Prussia had for the moment got rid of the shackles of parliamentary control. The Governments now concentrated all power in themselves, and could bring that power to bear wherever it was wanted: Austria upon Hungary and Italy, Prussia upon Germany. For Prussia, too, was preparing for a campaign by which "order" was to be restored in the smaller States.

Counter-revolution being now paramount in the two great centres of action in Germany,—in Vienna and Berlin,—there remained only the lesser States in which the struggle was still undecided, although the balance there, too, was leaning more and more against the revolutionary interest. These smaller States, we have said, found a common centre in the National Assembly at Frankfort. Now, this so-called National Assembly, although its reactionist spirit had long been evident, so much so that the very people of Frankfort had risen in arms against it, yet its origin was of a more or less revolutionary nature; it occupied an abnormal, revolutionary position in January; its competence had never been defined, and it had at last come to the decision—which, however, was never recognised by the larger States—that its resolutions had the force of law. Under these circumstances, and when the Constitutionalist-Monarchical party saw their positions turned by the recovering Absolutists, it is not to be wondered that the Liberal, monarchical bourgeoisie of almost the whole of Germany should place their last hopes upon the majority of this Assembly, just as the petty shopkeepers in the rest, the nucleus of the Democratic party, gathered in their growing distress around the minority of that same body, which indeed formed the last compact Parliamentary phalanx of Democracy. On the other hand, the larger Governments, and particularly the Prussian Ministry, saw more and more the incompatibility of such an irregular elective body with the restored monarchical system of Germany, and if they did not at once force its dissolution, it was only because the time had not yet come, and because Prussia hoped first to use it for the furthering of its own ambitious purposes.

In the meantime, that poor Assembly itself fell into a greater and greater confusion. Its deputations and commissaries had been treated with the utmost contempt, both in Vienna and

Berlin; one of its members, in spite of his parliamentary inviolability, had been executed in Vienna as a common rebel. Its decrees were nowhere heeded; if they were noticed at all by the larger powers, it was merely by protesting notes which disputed the authority of the Assembly to pass laws and resolutions binding upon their Governments. The Representative of the Assembly, the Central Executive power, was involved in diplomatic squabbles with almost all the Cabinets of Germany, and, in spite of all their efforts, neither Assembly nor Central Government could bring Austria and Prussia to state their ultimate views, plans and demands. The Assembly, at last, commenced to see clearly, at least so far, that it had allowed all power to slip out of its hands, that it was at the mercy of Austria and Prussia, and that if it intended making a Federal Constitution for Germany at all, it must set about the thing at once and in good earnest. And many of the vacillating members also saw clearly that they had been egregiously duped by the Governments. But what were they, in their impotent position, able to do now? The only thing that could have saved them would have been promptly and decidedly to pass over into the popular camp; but the success, even of that step, was more than doubtful; and then, where in this helpless crowd of undecided, short-sighted, self-conceited beings, who, when the eternal noise of contradictory rumours and diplomatic notes completely stunned them, sought their only consolation and support in the everlastingly repeated assurance that they were the best, the greatest, the wisest men of the country, and that they alone could save Germany—where, we say, among these poor creatures, whom a single year of Parliamentary life had turned into complete idiots, where were the men for a prompt and decisive resolution, much less for energetic and consistent action?

At last the Austrian Government threw off the mask. In its Constitution of March 4th, it proclaimed Austria an indivisible monarchy, with common finances, system of customs-duties, of military establishments, thereby effacing every barrier and distinction between the German and non-German provinces. This declaration was made in the face of resolutions and articles of the intended Federal Constitution which had been already passed by the Frankfort Assembly. It was the gauntlet of war thrown down to it by Austria, and the poor Assembly had no other choice but to take it up. This it did with a deal of blustering, which Austria, in the consciousness of her power, and of the utter nothingness of the Assembly, could well afford to allow to pass. And this precious representation, as it styled itself, of the German people, in order to revenge itself for this insult on the part of Austria, saw nothing better before it than to throw itself, hands and feet tied, at the feet of the Prussian Government. Incredible as it would seem, it bent its knees before the very ministers whom it had condemned as unconstitutional and anti-popular, and whose dismissal it had in vain insisted upon. The details of this disgraceful transaction, and the tragi-comical events that followed, will form the subject of our next.

New York Daily Tribune, April 24th, 1852

XV

WE now come to the last chapter in the history of the German
Revolution; the conflict of the National Assembly with the
Governments of the different States, especially of Prussia; the
insurrection of Southern and Western Germany, and its final
overthrow by Prussia.

We have already seen the Frankfort National Assembly at
work. We have seen it kicked by Austria, insulted by Prussia,
disobeyed by the lesser States, duped by its own impotent
Central "Government," which again was the dupe of all and
every prince in the country. But at last things began to look
threatening for this weak, vacillating, insipid legislative body. It
was forced to come to the conclusion that "the sublime idea of
German unity was threatened in its realisation," which meant
neither more nor less than that the Frankfort Assembly and all
it had done, and was about to do, were very likely to end in
smoke. Thus it set to work in good earnest in order to bring
forth, as soon as possible, its grand production, the "Imperial
Constitution." There was, however, one difficulty. What Executive Government was there to be? An Executive Council? No;
that would have been, they thought in their wisdom, making
Germany a Republic. A "president"? That would come to the
same. Thus they must revive the old Imperial dignity. But—as
of course, a prince was to be emperor—who should it be?
Certainly none of the *Dei minorum gentium*, from Reuss-
Schleitz-Greitz-Lobenstein-Ebersdorf up to Bavaria; neither

Austria nor Prussia would have borne that. It could only be Austria or Prussia. But which of the two? There is no doubt that, under otherwise favourable circumstances, this august Assembly would be sitting up to the present day, discussing this important dilemma without being able to come to a conclusion, if the Austrian Government had not cut the Gordian knot, and saved them the trouble.

Austria knew very well that from the moment in which she could again appear before Europe with all her provinces subdued, as a strong and great European power, the very law of political gravitation would draw the remainder of Germany into her orbit, without the help of any authority which an Imperial crown, conferred by the Frankfort Assembly, could give her. Austria had been far stronger, far freer in her movements, since she shook off the powerless crown of the German Empire—a crown which clogged her own independent policy, while it added not one iota to her strength, either within or without Germany. And supposing the case that Austria could not maintain her footing in Italy and Hungary, why, then she was dissolved, annihilated in Germany too, and could never pretend to re-seize a crown which had slipped from her hands while she was in the full possession of her strength. Thus Austria at once declared against all imperialist resurrections, and plainly demanded the restoration of the German Diet, the only Central Government of Germany known and recognised by the treaties of 1815; and on March 4th, 1849, issued that Constitution which had no other meaning than to declare Austria an indivisible, centralised, and independent monarchy, distinct even from that Germany which the Frankfort Assembly was to reorganise.

This open declaration of war left, indeed, the Frankfort wise-acres no other choice but to exclude Austria from Germany, and to create out of the remainder of that country a sort of lower empire, a "little Germany," the rather shabby Imperial mantle of which was to fall on the shoulders of His Majesty of Prussia. This, it will be recollected, was the renewal of an old project fostered some six or eight years ago by a party of South and Middle German Liberal doctrinaires, who considered as a god-send the degrading circumstances by which their old crotchet was now again brought forward as the latest "new move" for the salvation of the country.

They accordingly finished, in February and March 1849, the debate on the Imperial Constitution, together with the Declaration of Rights and the Imperial Electoral Law; not, however, without being obliged to make, in a great many points, the most contradictory concessions—now to the Conservative or rather Reactionary party—now to the more advanced factions of the Assembly. In fact, it was evident that the leadership of the Assembly, which had formerly belonged to the Right and Right Centre (the Conservatives and Reactionists), was gradually, although slowly, passing toward the Left or Democratic side of that body. The rather dubious position of the Austrian deputies in an Assembly which had excluded their country from Germany, and in which they yet were called upon to sit and vote, favoured the derangement of its equipoise; and thus, as early as the end of February, the Left Centre and Left found themselves, by the help of the Austrian votes, very generally in a majority, while on other days the Conservative faction of the Austrians, all of a sudden, and for the fun of the thing, voting with the Right, threw the balance again on the other side. They intended, by these sudden *soubresauts,* to bring the Assembly into contempt, which, however, was quite unnecessary, the mass of the people being long since convinced of the utter hollowness and futility of anything coming from Frankfort. What a specimen of a Constitution, in the meantime, was framed under such jumping and counter-jumping, may easily be imagined.

The Left of the Assembly—this *élite* and pride of revolutionary Germany, as it believed itself to be—was entirely intoxicated with the few paltry successes it obtained by the goodwill, or rather the ill will, of a set of Austrian politicians, acting under the instigation and for the interest of Austrian despotism. Whenever the slightest approximation to their own not very well-defined principles had, in a homoeopathically diluted shape, obtained a sort of sanction by the Frankfort Assembly, these Democrats proclaimed that they had saved the country and the people. These poor, weak-minded men, during the course of their generally very obscure lives, had been so little accustomed to anything like success, that they actually believed their paltry amendments, passed with two or three votes majority, would change the face of Europe. They had, from the beginning of their legislative career, been more imbued than any other faction of the Assembly with that incurable malady *Parliamentary crétinism,* a disorder which penetrates its unfortunate victims with the solemn conviction that the whole world, its history and future, are governed and determined by a majority of votes in that particular representative body which has the honour to count them among its members, and that all and everything going on outside the walls of their house—wars, revolutions, railway-constructing, colonising of whole new continents, California gold discoveries, Central American canals, Russian armies, and whatever else may have some little claim to influence upon the destinies of mankind—is nothing compared with the incommensurable events hinging upon the important question, whatever it may be, just at that moment occupying the attention of their honourable house. Thus it was the Democratic party of the Assembly, by effectually smuggling a few of their nostrums into the "imperial Constitution," first became bound to support it, although in every essential point it flatly contradicted their own oft-proclaimed principles, and at last, when this mongrel work was abandoned, and bequeathed to them by its main authors, accepted the inheritance, and held out for this *Monarchical* Constitution, even in opposition to everybody who *then* proclaimed their own *Republican* principles.

But it must be confessed that in this the contradiction was merely apparent. The indeterminate, self-contradictory, immature character of the Imperial Constitution was the very image of the immature, confused, conflicting political ideas of these Democratic gentlemen. And if their own sayings and writings—as far as they could write—were not sufficient proof of this, their action would furnish such proof; for among sensible people it is a matter of course to judge of a man, not by his professions, but by his actions; not by what he pretends to be, but by what he does, and what he really is; and the deeds of these heroes of German Democracy speak loud enough for themselves, as we shall learn by and by. However, the Imperial Constitution, with all its appendages and paraphernalia, was definitely passed, and on March 28th, the King of Prussia was, by 290 votes against 248 who abstained, and 200 who were absent, elected Emperor of Germany *minus* Austria. The historical irony was complete; the Imperial farce executed in the streets of astonished Berlin, three days after the Revolution of March 18th, 1848, by Frederick William IV, while in a state which elsewhere would come under the Maine Liquor Law—this disgusting farce, just one year afterwards, had been sanctioned by the pretended Representative Assembly of all Germany. That, then, was the result of the German Revolution!

New York Daily Tribune, July 27th, 1852

XVI

THE National Assembly of Frankfort, after having elected the King of Prussia Emperor of Germany (*minus* Austria), sent a deputation to Berlin to offer him the crown, and then adjourned. On April 3rd, Frederick William received the deputies. He told them that, although he accepted the right of precedence over all the other princes of Germany, which this vote of the people's representatives had given him, yet he could not accept the Imperial crown as long as he was not sure that the remaining princes acknowledged his supremacy, and the Imperial Constitution conferring those rights upon him. It would be, he added, for the Governments of Germany to see whether this Constitution was such as could be ratified by them. At all events, Emperor or not, he always would be found ready, he concluded, to draw the sword against either the external or the internal foe. We shall see how he kept his promise in a manner rather startling for the National Assembly.

The Frankfort wiseacres, after profound diplomatic inquiry, at last came to the conclusion that this answer amounted to a refusal of the crown. They then (April 12th) resolved: That the Imperial Constitution was the law of the land, and must be maintained; and not seeing their way at all before them, elected a Committee of thirty, to make proposals as to the means how this Constitution could be carried out.

This resolution was the signal for the conflict between the Frankfort Assembly and the German Governments which now

broke out. The middle classes, and especially the smaller trading class, had all at once declared for the new Frankfort Constitution. They could not await any longer the moment which was
"to close the Revolution." In Austria and Prussia the Revolution
had, for the moment, been closed by the interference of the
armed power. The classes in question would have preferred a
less forcible mode of performing that operation, but they had
not had a chance; the thing was done, and they had to make
the best of it, a resolution which they at once took and carried
out most heroically. In the smaller States, where things had
been going on comparatively smoothly, the middle classes had
long since been thrown back into that showy, but resultless,
because powerless, parliamentary agitation, which was most
congenial to themselves. The different States of Germany, as
regarded each of them separately, appeared thus to have attained that new and definite form which was supposed to
enable them to enter henceforth the path of peaceful constitutional development. There only remained one open question,
that of the new political organisation of the German Confederacy. And this question, the only one which still appeared fraught
with danger, it was considered a necessity to resolve at once.
Hence the pressure exerted upon the Frankfort Assembly by the
middle classes, in order to induce it to get the Constitution
ready as soon as possible; hence the resolution among the
higher and lower bourgeoisie to accept and support this Constitution, whatever it might be, in order to create a settled state of
things without delay. Thus from the very beginning the agitation for the Imperial Constitution arose out of a reactionary
feeling, and sprang up among these classes which were long
since tired of the Revolution.

But there was another feature in it. The first and fundamental
principles of the future German Constitution had been voted
during the first months of spring and summer, 1848, a time
when popular agitation was still rife. The resolutions then
passed, though completely reactionary *then*, now, after the arbitrary acts of the Austrian and Prussian Governments, appeared
exceedingly Liberal, and even Democratic. The standard of

comparison had changed. The Frankfort Assembly could not, without moral suicide, strike out these once-voted provisions, and model the Imperial Constitution upon those which the Austrian and Prussian Governments had dictated, sword in hand. Besides, as we have seen, the majority in that Assembly had changed sides, and the Liberal and Democratic party were rising in influence. Thus the Imperial Constitution not only was distinguished by its apparently exclusive popular origin, but at the same time, full of contradiction as it was, it yet was the most Liberal Constitution in all Germany. Its greatest fault was, that it was a mere sheet of paper, with no power to back its provisions.

Under these circumstances it was natural that the so-called Democratic party, that is, the mass of the petty trading class, should cling to the Imperial Constitution. This class had always been more forward in its demands than the Liberal-Monarchico-Constitutional bourgeoisie; it had shown a bolder front, it had very often threatened armed resistance, it was lavish in its promises to sacrifice its blood and its existence in the struggle for freedom; but it had already given plenty of proofs that on the day of danger it was nowhere, and that it never felt more comfortable than the day after a decisive defeat, when everything being lost, it had at least the consolation to know that somehow or other the matter *was* settled. While, therefore, the adhesion of the large bankers, manufacturers, and merchants was of a more reserved character, more like a simple demonstration in favour of the Frankfort Constitution, the class just beneath them, our valiant Democratic shopkeepers, came forward in grand style, and, as usual, proclaimed they would rather spill their last drop of blood than let the Imperial Constitution fall to the ground.

Supported by these two parties, the bourgeois adherents of the Constitutional Royalty, and the more or less Democratic shopkeepers, the agitation for the immediate establishment of the Imperial Constitution gained ground rapidly, and found its most powerful expression in the Parliaments of the several States. The Chambers of Prussia, of Hanover, of Saxony, of

Baden, of Würtemburg, declared in its favour. The struggle between the Governments and the Frankfort Assembly assumed a threatening aspect.

The Governments, however, acted rapidly. The Prussian Chambers were dissolved, anti-constitutionally, as they had to revise and confirm the Constitution; riots broke out at Berlin, provoked intentionally by the Government, and the next day, April 28th, the Prussian Ministry issued a circular note, in which the Imperial Constitution was held up as a most anarchical and revolutionary document, which it was for the Governments of Germany to remodel and purify. Thus Prussia denied, point-blank, that sovereign constituent power which the wise men at Frankfort had always boasted of, but never established. Thus a Congress of Princes, a renewal of the old Federal Diet, was called upon to sit in judgment on that Constitution which had already been promulgated as law. And at the same time Prussia concentrated troops at Kreuznach, three days' march from Frankfort, and called upon the smaller States to follow its example, by also dissolving their Chambers as soon as they should give their adhesion to the Frankfort Assembly. This example was speedily followed by Hanover and Saxony.

It was evident that a decision of the struggle by force of arms could not be avoided. The hostility of the Governments, the agitation among the people, were daily showing themselves in stronger colours. The military were everywhere worked upon by the Democratic citizens, and in the south of Germany with great success. Large mass meetings were everywhere held, passing resolutions to support the Imperial Constitution and the National Assembly, if need should be, with force of arms. At Cologne, a meeting of deputies of all the municipal councils of Rhenish Prussia took place for the same purpose. In the Palatinate, at Bergen, Fulda, Nuremberg, in the Odenwald, the peasantry met by myriads and worked themselves up into enthusiasm. At the same time the Constituent Assembly of France dissolved, and the new elections were prepared amid violent agitation, while on the eastern frontier of Germany, the Hungarians had within a month, by a succession of brilliant victories, rolled back the tide of Austrian invasion from the Theiss to the Leitha, and were every day expected to take Vienna by storm. Thus, popular imagination being on all hands worked up to the highest pitch, and the aggressive policy of the Governments defining itself more clearly every day, a violent collision could not be avoided, and cowardly imbecility only could persuade itself that the struggle was to come off peaceably. But this cowardly imbecility was most extensively represented in the Frankfort Assembly.

New York Daily Tribune, August 19th, 1852

XVII

THE inevitable conflict between the National Assembly of Frankfort and the States Governments of Germany at last broke out in open hostilities during the first days of May 1849. The Austrian deputies, recalled by their Government, had already left the Assembly and returned home, with the exception of a few members of the Left or Democratic party. The great body of the Conservative members, aware of the turn things were about to take, withdrew even before they were called upon to do so by their respective Governments. Thus, even independently of the causes which in the foregoing letters have been shown to strengthen the influence of the Left, the mere desertion of their posts by the members of the Right, sufficed to turn the old minority into a majority of the Assembly. The new majority, which, at no former time, had dreamt of ever obtaining that good fortune, had profited by their places on the opposition benches to spout against the weakness, the indecision, the indolence of the old majority, and of its Imperial Lieutenancy. Now all at once, *they* were called on to replace the old majority. *They* were now to show what they could perform. Of course, *their* career was to be one of energy, determination, activity. *They*, the *élite* of Germany, would soon be able to drive onwards the senile Lieutenant of the Empire, and his vacillating ministers, and in case that was impossible they would—there could be no doubt about it—by force of the sovereign right of the people, depose that impotent Government, and replace it by an energetic, indefatigable Executive, who would assure the salvation of Germany. Poor fellows! *Their* rule—if rule it can be named, where no one obeyed—was a still more ridiculous affair than even the rule of their predecessors.

The new majority declared that, in spite of all obstacles, the Imperial Constitution must be carried out, and *at once;* that on July 15th ensuing, the people were to elect the deputies of the new House of Representatives, and that this House was to meet at Frankfort on August 15th following. Now, this was an open declaration of war against those Governments that had not recognised the Imperial Constitution, the foremost among which were Prussia, Austria, Bavaria, comprising more than three-fourths of the German population; a declaration of war which was speedily accepted by them. Prussia and Bavaria, too, recalled the deputies sent from their territories to Frankfort, and hastened their military preparations against the National Assembly, while, on the other hand, the demonstrations of the Democratic party (out of Parliament) in favour of the Imperial Constitution and of the National Assembly, acquired a more turbulent and violent character, and the mass of the working people, led by the men of the most extreme party, were ready to take up arms in a cause which, if it was not their own, at least gave them a chance of somewhat approaching their aims by clearing Germany of its old monarchical encumbrances. Thus everywhere the people and the Governments were at daggers drawn upon this subject; the outbreak was inevitable; the mine was charged, and it only wanted a spark to make it explode. The dissolution of the Chambers in Saxony, the calling in of the Landwehr (military reserve) in Prussia, the open resistance of the Government to the Imperial Constitution, were such sparks; they fell, and all at once the country was in a blaze. In Dresden, on May 4th, the people victoriously took possession of the town, and drove out the King, while all the surrounding districts sent reinforcements to the insurgents. In Rhenish Prussia and West-phalia the Landwehr refused to march, took possession of the arsenals, and armed itself in defence of the Imperial Constitution. In the Palatinate the people seized the Bavarian Government officials, and the public moneys, and instituted a Committee of Defence, which placed the province under the protection of the National Assembly. In Würtemberg the people forced the King to acknowledge the Imperial Constitution, and in Baden the army, united with the people, forced the Grand Duke to flight, and erected a Provincial Government. In other parts of Germany the people only awaited a decisive signal from the National Assembly to rise in arms and place themselves at its disposal.

The position of the National Assembly was far more favourable than could have been expected after its ignoble career. The western half of Germany had taken up arms in its behalf; the military everywhere were vacillating; in the lesser States they were undoubtedly favourable to the movement. Austria was prostrated by the victorious advance of the Hungarians, and Russia, that reserve force of the German Governments, was straining all its powers in order to support Austria against the Magyar armies. There was only Prussia to subdue, and with the revolutionary sympathies existing in that country, a chance certainly existed of attaining that end. Everything then depended upon the conduct of the Assembly.

Now, insurrection is an art quite as much as war or any other, and subject to certain rules of proceeding, which, when neglected, will produce the ruin of the party neglecting them. Those rules, logical deductions from the nature of the parties and the circumstances one has to deal with in such a case, are so plain and simple that the short experience of 1848 had made the Germans pretty well acquainted with them. Firstly, never play with insurrection unless you are fully prepared to face the consequences of your play. Insurrection is a calculus with very indefinite magnitudes the value of which may change every day; the forces opposed to you have all the advantage of organisation, discipline, and habitual authority; unless you bring strong odds against them you are defeated and ruined. Secondly, the insurrectionary career once entered upon, act with the greatest determination, and on the offensive. The defensive is the death of every armed rising; it is lost before it measures itself with its enemies. Surprise your antagonists while their forces are scattering, prepare new successes, however small, but daily; keep up the moral ascendancy which the first successful rising has given to you; rally those vacillating elements to your side which always follow the strongest impulse, and which always look out for the safer side; force your enemies to a retreat before they can collect their strength against you; in the words of Danton, the greatest master of revolutionary policy yet known, *de l'audace, de l'audace, encore de l'audace!*

What, then, was the National Assembly of Frankfort to do if it would escape the certain ruin which it was threatened with? First of all, to see clearly through the situation, and to convince itself that there was now no other choice than either to submit to the Governments unconditionally, or take up the cause of the armed insurrection without reserve or hesitation. Secondly, to publicly recognise all the insurrections that had already broken out, and to call the people to take up arms everywhere in defence of the national representation, outlawing all princes, ministers and others who should dare to oppose the sovereign people represented by its mandatories. Thirdly, to at once depose the German Imperial Lieutenant, to create a strong, active, unscrupulous Executive, to call insurgent troops to Frankfort for its immediate protection, thus offering at the same time a legal pretext for the spread of the insurrection, to organise into a compact body all the forces at its disposal, and, in short, to profit quickly and unhesitatingly by every available means for strengthening its position and impairing that of its opponents.

Of all this the virtuous Democrats in the Frankfort Assembly did just the contrary. Not content with letting things take the course they liked, these worthies went so far as to suppress by their opposition all insurrectionary movements which were preparing. Thus, for instance, did Herr Karl Vogt at Nuremberg. They allowed the insurrections of Saxony, of Rhenish Prussia, of Westphalia to be suppressed without any other help than a posthumous, sentimental protest against the unfeeling violence of the Prussian Government. They kept up an underhand diplomatic intercourse with the South German insurrections but never gave them the support of their open acknowledgment. They knew that the Lieutenant of the Empire sided with the Governments, and yet they called upon *him*, who never stirred, to oppose the intrigues of these Governments. The ministers of the Empire, old Conservatives, ridiculed this impotent Assembly in every sitting, and they suffered it. And when William Wolff, a Silesian deputy, and one of the editors of the *New Rhenish Gazette*, called upon them to outlaw the Lieutenant of the Empire—who was, he justly said, nothing but the first and greatest traitor to the Empire, he was hooted down by the unanimous and virtuous indignation of those Democratic Revolutionists! In short, they went on talking, protesting, proclaiming, pronouncing, but never had the courage or the sense to act; while the hostile troops of the Governments drew nearer and nearer, and their own Executive, the Lieutenant of the Empire, was busily plotting with the German princes their speedy destruction. Thus even the last vestige of consideration was lost to this contemptible Assembly; the insurgents who had risen to defend it ceased to care any more for it, and when at last it came to a shameful end, as we shallsee, it died without anybody taking any notice of its unhonoured exit.

New York Daily Tribune, September 18th, 1852

XVIII

IN our last we showed that the struggle between the German Governments on the one side, and the Frankfort Parliament on the other, had ultimately acquired such a degree of violence that in the first days of May, a great portion of Germany broke out in open insurrection; first Dresden, then the Bavarian Palatinate, parts of Rhenish Prussia, and at last Baden.

In all cases, the *real fighting* body of the insurgents, that body which first took up arms and gave battle to the troops, consisted of the *working classes of the towns.* A portion of the poorer country population, labourers and petty farmers, generally joined them after the outbreak of the conflict. The greater number of the young men of all classes, below the capitalist class, were to be found, for a time at least, in the ranks of the insurgent armies, but this rather indiscriminate aggregate of young men very soon thinned as the aspect of affairs took a somewhat serious turn. The students particularly, those "representatives of intellect," as they liked to call themselves, were the first to quit their standards, unless they were retained by the bestowal of officer's rank, for which they, of course, had very seldom any qualifications.

The working class entered upon this insurrection as they would have done upon any other which promised either to remove some obstacles in their progress towards political dominion and social revolution, or, at least, to tie the more influential but less courageous classes of society to a more decided and

230

revolutionary course than they had followed hitherto. The working class took up arms with a full knowledge that this was, in the direct bearings of the case, no quarrel of its own; but it followed up its only true policy, to allow no class that has risen on its shoulders (as the bourgeoisie had done in 1848) to fortify its class-government, without opening, at least, a fair field to the working classes for the struggle for its own interests, and, in any case, to bring matters to a crisis, by which either the nation was fairly and irresistibly launched in the revolutionary career, or else the *status quo* before the Revolution restored as nearly as possible, and, thereby, a new revolution rendered unavoidable. In both cases the working classes represented the real and well-understood interest of the nation at large, in hastening as much as possible that revolutionary course which for the old societies of civilised Europe has now become a historical necessity, before any of them can again aspire to a more quiet and regular development of their resources.

As to country people that joined the insurrection, they were principally thrown into the arms of the Revolutionary party, partly by the relatively enormous load of taxation, and partly of feudal burdens pressing upon them.

Without any initiative of their own, they formed the tail of the other classes engaged in the insurrection, wavering between the working men on the one side, and the petty trading class on the other. Their own private social position, in almost every case decided which way they turned; the agricultural labourer generally supported the city artisan; the small farmer was apt to go hand in hand with the small shopkeeper.

This class of petty tradesmen, the great importance and influence of which we have already several times adverted to, may be considered as the leading class of the insurrection of May 1849. There being, this time, none of the large towns of Germany among the centre of the movement, the petty trading class, which in middling and lesser towns always predominates, found the means of getting the direction of the movement into its hands. We have, moreover, seen that, in this struggle for the Imperial Constitution, and for the rights of the German Parliament, there were the interests of this peculiar class at stake. The Provisional Governments formed in all the insurgent districts represented in the majority of each of them this section of the people, and the length they went to may therefore be fairly taken as the measure of what the German petty bourgeoisie is capable of—capable, as we shall see, of nothing but ruining any movement that entrusts itself to its hands.

The petty bourgeoisie, great in boasting, is very impotent for action, and very shy in risking anything. The *mesquin* character of its commercial transactions and its credit operations is eminently apt to stamp its character with a want of energy and enterprise; it is, then, to be expected that similar qualities will mark its political career. Accordingly the petty bourgeoisie encouraged insurrection by big words, and great boasting as to what it was going to do; it was eager to seize upon power as soon as the insurrection, much against its will, had broken out; it used this power to no other purpose but to destroy the effects of the insurrection. Wherever an armed conflict had brought matters to a serious crisis, there the shopkeepers stood aghast at the dangerous situation created for them; aghast at the people who had taken their boasting appeals to arms in earnest; aghast at the power thus thrust into their own hands; aghast, above all, at the consequences for themselves, for their social positions, for their fortunes, of the policy in which they were forced to engage themselves. Were they not expected to risk "life and property," as they used to say, for the cause of the insurrection? Were they not forced to take official positions in the insurrection, whereby, in the case of defeat, they risked the loss of their capital? And in case of victory, were they not sure to be immediately turned out of office, and to see their entire policy subverted by the victorious proletarians who formed the main body of their fighting army? Thus placed between opposing dangers which surrounded them on every side, the petty bourgeoisie knew not to turn its power to any other account than to let everything take its chance, whereby, of course, there was lost what little chance of success there might have been, and thus to ruin the insurrection altogether. Its policy, or rather want of policy, everywhere was the same, and, therefore, the insurrections of May 1849, in all parts of Germany, are all cut out to the same pattern.

In Dresden, the struggle was kept on for four days in the streets of the town. The shopkeepers of Dresden, the "communal guard," not only did not fight, but in many instances favoured the proceedings of the troops against the insurgents. These again consisted almost exclusively of working men from the surrounding manufacturing districts. They found an able and cool-headed commander in the Russian refugee Michael Bakunin, who afterwards was taken prisoner, and now is confined in the dungeons of Munkacs, Hungary. The intervention of numerous Prussian troops crushed this insurrection.

In Rhenish Prussia the actual fighting was of little importance. All the large towns being fortresses commanded by citadels, there could be only skirmishing on the part of the insurgents. As soon as a sufficient number of troops had been drawn together, there was an end to armed opposition.

In the Palatinate and Baden, on the contrary, a rich, fruitful province and an entire state fell into the hands of the insurrection. Money, arms, soldiers, warlike stores, everything was ready for use. The soldiers of the regular army themselves joined the insurgents; nay, in Baden, they were amongst the foremost of them. The insurrectionists in Saxony and Rhenish Prussia sacrificed themselves in order to gain time for the organisation of the South German movement. Never was there such a favourable position for a provincial and partial insurrection as this. A revolution was expected in Paris; the Hungarians were at the gates of Vienna; in all the central States of Germany, not only the people, but even the troops, were strongly in favour of the insurrection, and only wanted an opportunity to join it openly. And yet the movement, having once got into the hands of the petty bourgeoisie, was ruined from its very beginning. The petty-bourgeois rulers, particularly of Baden—Herr Brentano at the head of them—never forgot that by usurping the place and prerogatives of the "lawful" sovereign, the Grand Duke, they were committing high treason. They sat down in their ministerial arm-chairs with the consciousness of criminality in their hearts. What can you expect of such cowards? They not only abandoned the insurrection to its own uncentralised, and therefore ineffective, spontaneity, they actually did everything in their power to take the sting out of the movement, to unman, to destroy it. And they succeeded, thanks to the zealous support of that deep class of politicians, the "Democratic" heroes of the petty bourgeoisie, who actually thought they were "saving the country," while they allowed themselves to be led by their noses by a few men of a sharper cast, such as Brentano.

As to the fighting part of the business, never were military operations carried on in a more slovenly, more stolid way than under the Baden General-in-Chief Sigel, an ex-lieutenant of the regular army. Everything was got into confusion, every good opportunity was lost, every precious moment was loitered away with planning colossal, but impracticable projects, until, when at last the talented Pole Mieroslawski took up the command, the army was disorganised, beaten, dispirited, badly provided for, opposed to an enemy four times more numerous, and withal, he could do nothing more than fight, at Waghäusel, a glorious though unsuccessful battle, carry out a clever retreat, offer a last hopeless fight under the walls of Rastatt, and resign. As in every insurrectionary war where armies are mixed of well-drilled soldiers and raw levies, there was plenty of heroism, and plenty of unsoldierlike, often unconceivable panic, in the revolutionary army; but, imperfect as it could not but be, it had at least the satisfaction that four times its number were not considered sufficient to put it to the rout, and that a hundred thousand regular troops, in a campaign against twenty thousand insurgents, treated them, militarily, with as much respect as if they had had to fight the Old Guard of Napoleon.

In May the insurrection had broken out; by the middle of July 1849, it was entirely subdued, and the first German Revolution was closed.

New York Daily Tribune, October 2nd, 1852

XIX

London, September 24th, 1852

WHILE the south and west of Germany was in open insurrection, and while it took the Governments from the first opening of hostilities at Dresden to the capitulation of Rastatt, rather more than ten weeks, to stifle this final blazing up of the first German Revolution, the National Assembly disappeared from the political theatre without any notice being taken of its exit.

We left this august body at Frankfort, perplexed by the insolent attacks of the Governments upon its dignity, by the impotency and treacherous listlessness of the Central Power it had itself created, by the risings of the petty trading class for its defence, and of the working class for a more revolutionary ultimate end. Desolation and despair reigned supreme among its members; events had at once assumed such a definite and decisive shape that in a few days the illusions of these learned legislators as to their real power and influence were entirely broken down. The Conservatives, at the signal given by the Governments, had already retired from a body which, henceforth, could not exist any longer, except in defiance of the constituted authorities. The Liberals gave the matter up in utter discomfiture; they, too, threw up their commissions as representatives. Honourable gentlemen decamped by hundreds. From eight or nine hundred members the number had dwindled down so rapidly that now one hundred and fifty, and a few days after one hundred, were declared a quorum. And even these were difficult to muster, although the whole of the Democratic party remained.

The course to be followed by the remnants of a parliament was plain enough. They had only to take their stand openly and decidedly with the insurrection, to give it, thereby, whatever strength legality could confer upon it, while they themselves at once acquired an army for their own defence. They had to summon the Central Power to stop all hostilities at once; and if, as could be foreseen, this power neither could nor would do so, to depose it at once and put another more energetic Government in its place. If insurgent troops could not be brought to Frankfort (which, in the beginning when the State Governments were little prepared and still hesitating, might have been easily done), then the Assembly could have adjourned at once to the very centre of the insurgent district. All this done at once, and resolutely, not later than the middle or end of May, might have opened chances both for the insurrection and for the National Assembly.

But such a determined course was not to be expected from the representatives of German shopocracy. These aspiring statesmen were not at all freed from their illusions. Those members who had lost their fatal belief in the strength and inviolability of the Parliament had already taken to their heels; the Democrats who remained, were not so easily induced to give up dreams of power and greatness which they had cherished for a twelvemonth. True to the course they had hitherto pursued, they shrank back from decisive action until every chance of success, nay, every chance to succumb, with at least the honours of war, had passed away. In order, then, to develop a fictitious, busy-body sort of activity, the sheer impotency of which, coupled with its high pretension, could not but excite pity and ridicule, they continued insinuating resolutions, addressed, and requests to an Imperial Lieutenant, who not even noticed them; to ministers who were in open league with the enemy. And when at last William Wolff, member for Striegan, one of the editors of the *New Rhenish Gazette,* the only really revolutionary man in the whole Assembly, told them that if they meant what they said, they had better give over talking, and declare the Imperial Lieutenant, the chief traitor to the country, an outlaw at once; then the entire compressed virtuous indignation of these parliamentary gentlemen burst out with an energy which they never found when the Government heaped insult after insult upon them.

Of course, for Wolff's proposition was the first sensible word spoken within the walls of St. Paul's Church; of course, for it was the very thing that was to be done, and such plain language going so direct to the purpose, could not but insult a set of sentimentalists, who were resolute in nothing but irresolution, and who, too cowardly to act, had once for all made up their minds that in doing nothing, they were doing exactly what was to be done. Every word which cleared up, like lightning, the infatuated, but intentional nebulosity of their minds, every hint that was adapted to lead them out of the labyrinth where they obstinated themselves to take up as lasting an abode as possible, every clear conception of matters as they actually stood, was, of course, a crime against the majesty of this Sovereign Assembly.

Shortly after the position of the honourable gentlemen in Frankfort became untenable, in spite of resolutions, appeals, interpellations, and proclamations, they retreated, but not into the insurgent districts; that would have been too resolute a step. They went to Stuttgart, where the Würtemberg Government kept up a sort of expectative neutrality. There, at last, they declared the Lieutenant of the Empire to have forfeited his power, and elected from their own body a Regency of five. This Regency at once proceeded to pass a Militia law, which was actually in all due force sent to all the Governments of Germany.

They, the very enemies of the Assembly, were ordered to levy forces in its defence! Then there was created—on paper, of course—an army for the defence of the National Assembly. Divisions, brigades, regiments, batteries, everything was regulated and ordained. Nothing was wanted but reality, for that army, of course, was never called into existence.

One last scheme offered itself to the General Assembly. The Democratic population from all parts of the country sent deputations to place itself at the disposal of the Parliament, and to urge it on to a decisive action. The people, knowing what the intentions of the Würtemberg Government were, implored the National Assembly to force that Government into an open and active participation with their insurgent neighbours. But no. The National Assembly, in going to Stuttgart, had delivered itself up to the tender mercies of the Würtemberg Government. The members knew it, and repressed the agitation among the people. They thus lost the last remnant of influence which they might yet have retained. They earned the contempt they deserved, and the Würtemberg Government, pressed by Prussia and the Imperial Lieutenant, put a stop to the Democratic farce by shutting up, on June 18th, 1849, the room where the Parliament met, and by ordering the members of the Regency to leave the country.

Next they went to Baden, into the camp of the insurrection; but there they were now useless. Nobody noticed them. The Regency, however, in the name of the Sovereign German people, continued to save the country by its exertions. It made an attempt to get recognised by foreign powers, by delivering *passports* to anybody who would accept them. It issued proclamations, and sent commissioners to insurge those very districts of Würtemberg whose active assistance it had refused when it was yet time; of course, without effect. We have now under our eye an original report, sent to the Regency by one of these commissioners, Herr Roesler (member for Oels), the contents of which are rather characteristic. It is dated, Stuttgart, June 30th, 1849. After describing the adventures of half a dozen of these commissioners in a resultless search for cash, he gives a series of excuses for not having yet gone to his post, and then delivers himself of a most weighty argument respecting possible differences between Prussia, Austria, Bavaria, and Würtemberg, with their possible consequences. After having fully considered this, he comes, however, to the conclusion that there is no more chance. Next, he proposes to establish relays of trustworthy men for the conveyance of intelligence, and a system of espionage as to the intentions of the Würtemberg Ministry and the movements of the troops. This letter never reached its address, for when it was written the "Regency" had already passed entirely into the "foreign department," viz., Switzerland; and while poor Herr Roesler troubled his head about the intentions of the formidable ministry of a sixth-rate kingdom, a hundred thousand Prussian, Bavarian, and Hessian soldiers had already settled the whole affair in the last battle under the walls of Rastatt.

Thus vanished the German Parliament, and with it the first and last creation of the Revolution. Its convocation had been the first evidence that there actually *had been* a revolution in January; and it existed as long as this, the first modern German Revolution, was not yet brought to a close. Chosen under the influence of the capitalist class by a dismembered, scattered, rural population, for the most part only awakening from the dumbness of feudalism, this Parliament served to bring in one body upon the political arena all the great popular names of 1820–48, and then to utterly ruin them. All the celebrities of middle-class Liberalism were here collected. The bourgeoisie expected wonders; it earned shame for itself and its representatives. The industrial and commercial capitalist class were more severely defeated in Germany than in any other country; they were first worsted, broken, expelled from office in every individual State of Germany, and then put to rout, disgraced and hooted in the Central German Parliament. Political Liberalism, the rule of the bourgeoisie, be it under a Monarchical or Republican form of government, is forever impossible in Germany.

In the latter period of its existence, the German Parliament served to disgrace forever that section which had ever since March 1848 headed the official opposition, the Democrats representing the interest of the small trading, and partially of the farming class. That class was, in May and June 1849, given a chance to show its means of forming a stable Government in Germany. We have seen how it failed; not so much by adverse circumstances as by the actual and continued cowardice in all trying movements that had occurred since the outbreak of the revolution; by showing in politics the same short-sighted, pusillanimous, wavering spirit, which is characteristic of its commercial operations. In May 1849, it had, by this course, lost the confidence of the real fighting mass of all European insurrections, the working class. But yet, it had a fair chance. The German Parliament belonged to it, exclusively, after the Reactionists and Liberals had withdrawn. The rural population was in its favour. Two-thirds of the armies of the smaller States, one-third of the Prussian army, the majority of the Prussian Landwehr (reserve or militia), were ready to join it, if it only acted resolutely, and with that courage which is the result of a clear insight into the state of things. But the politicians who led on this class were not more clear-sighted than the host of petty tradesmen which followed them. They proved even to be more infatuated, more ardently attached to delusions voluntarily kept up, more credulous, more incapable of resolutely dealing with facts than the Liberals. Their political importance, too, is reduced below the freezing-point. But not having actually carried their commonplace principles into execution, they were, under *very* favourable circumstances, capable of a momentary resurrection, when this last hope was taken from them, just as it was taken from their colleagues of the "pure Democracy" in France by the *coup d'état* of Louis Bonaparte.

The defeat of the south-west German insurrection, and the dispersion of the German Parliament, bring the history of the first German insurrection to a close. We have now to cast a parting glance upon the victorious members of the counter-revolutionary alliance; we shall do this in our next letter.[1]

New York Daily Tribune, October 23rd, 1852

---

[1] Neither a subsequent article nor a relevant manuscript has been found. Presumably it was to have been the concluding chapter that Marx promised to write and never delivered. See above pp. xxxvii–xxxviii. Usually, an article written by Engels on "The Late Trial at Cologne," dated December 1, 1852, and published in the *Tribune* on December 22, has been printed with *Germany: Revolution and Counter-Revolution* as its conclusion. But the Marx/Engels correspondence shows clearly that both Marx and Engels thought of the piece on the Cologne trial as entirely independent of the historical series that had preceded it, and it will not be included here. See Engels to Marx, November 5–6, 1852, and Marx to Engels, November 16, 1852, in Marx/Engels, *Gesamtausgabe,* Part III, Vol. 1, pp. 429–30, 436.—Editor's Note.

Index

Engels provided no index to either work. In compiling the joint listing that follows, I have supplemented the text for three kinds of occasions. (1) When Engels identifies a figure only by his position (for example, "Archbishop of Trier"), the name is here provided and the reference entered under it as well as under the mentioned place. (2) When a name in the text varies from the accepted form, the entry is made under the latter, with the textual variant in parentheses. (3) When Engels does not specify given names, they are supplied in this index.

[EDITOR'S NOTE]

Index

Index